Children and Families "at Promise"

SUNY Series, The Social Context of Education
Christine E. Sleeter, Editor

Children and Families "at Promise"

Deconstructing the Discourse of Risk

Beth Blue Swadener
and
Sally Lubeck,
Editors

STATE UNIVERSITY OF NEW YORK PRESS

Published by
State University of New York Press, Albany

For information, address State University of New York
Press, State University Plaza, Albany, N.Y., 12246

Production by E. Moore
Marketing by Nancy Farrell

Library of Congress Cataloging-in-Publication Data

Children and families "at promise" : deconstructing the discourse of
    risk / Beth Blue Swadener and Sally Lubeck, editors.
        p.   cm. — (SUNY series, the social context of education)
    Includes bibliographical references and index.
        ISBN 0–7914–2291–7 (alk. paper). — ISBN 0–7914–2292–5 (pbk. :
    alk. paper)
        1. Socially handicapped children—United States. 2. Socially
handicapped children—Education—United States. 3. Socially
handicapped—United States. 4. United States—Ethnic relations.
5. United States—Race relations.   I. Swadener, Beth Blue.
II. Lubeck, Sally.   III. Series: SUNY series, social context of
education.
HV741.C536125   1995
362.7—dc20.   94–7750
                                                                 CIP

10 9 8 7 6 5 4 3 2 1

*This book is dedicated to our
"children of promise,"
Rachel, Julie, and Aaron*

Contents

Foreword   ix
   Christine E. Sleeter

The Social Construction of Children and Families   1
"at Risk": An Introduction
   Beth Blue Swadener and Sally Lubeck

I
Deconstructing the "at Risk" Label

1. Children and Families "at Promise": Deconstructing   17
   the Discourse of Risk
   Beth Blue Swadener

2. Mothers at Risk   50
   Sally Lubeck

3. The Politics of Who's "at Risk"   76
   Michelle Fine

II
Children and Families at Promise

4. Voice Unaltered: Marginalized Young Writers Speak   97
   Elizabeth Quintero and Mary Kay Rummel

5. "Motherwit": Childrearing Lessons from African   118
   American Mothers of Low Income
   Donelda A. Cook and Michelle Fine

6. Exploding the Myths: African American Families   143
   at Promise
   Mary Smith Arnold

7. Native Americans at Promise: Travel in Borderlands   163
   Carolyne J. White

III
Reconstructing Classrooms and Community Contexts

8. Learning in and out of School: Critical Perspectives   187
   on the Theory of Cultural Compatibility
   B. Robert Tabachnick and Marianne N. Bloch

9. Creating a Classroom Culture of Promise: 210
   Lessons from a First Grade
   Mary E. Hauser and Cynthia Thompson

10. Student Success: A Matter of Compatibility   224
    and Expectations
    Joyce S. Waldoch

11. Advocating for Aric: Strategies for Full Inclusion   238
    Lisa Leifield and Tina Murray

Epilogue
   Naming and Blaming: Beyond a Pedagogy of the Poor   263
   Valerie Polakow

Contributors   271

Index   275

CHRISTINE E. SLEETER

Foreword

The discourse over "children at risk" can be understood as a struggle for power over how to define children, families, and communities who are poor, of color, and/or native speakers of languages other than English. The dominant discourse attempts to frame such children and their families as lacking the cultural and moral resources for success in a presumed fair and open society and as in need of compensatory help from the dominant society. During the early 1960s, White professionals referred to children from oppressed groups as "disadvantaged" and "culturally deprived," believing that their families provide "few of the experiences which produce readiness for academic learning either intellectually or attitudinally" (Goldberg, 1963, p. 87).

In the struggles of the Civil Rights movement of the 1960s and early 1970s, oppressed groups attempted to redefine both their political and economic positions relative to the dominant society, as well as the language and metaphors used to describe themselves. Educators and other activists of color reframed home and community as sources of strength and the dominant society as a source of barriers to advancement. For example, hooks (1990) discusses "homeplace" as a site of strength and resistance to the colonizing power of the dominant society, advocating that "We can make homeplace that space where we return for renewal and self-recovery, where we can heal our wounds and become whole" (p. 49).

In the 1980s, as conservative attacks against oppressed groups mounted, the dominant society resurrected the earlier metaphor of "cultural deprivation" but gave it a different term: "children at risk." Since the terminology appeared to be new and was linked with what seemed to be a new crisis of a "nation at risk," many educators disassociated the "at risk" discourse from any context of historic political struggle. Thus, teachers occasionally tell me that children today are put at risk by the recent introduction of crack, the cycle of welfare dependency, or even bilingual education, which many monolinguals assume retards acquisition of English language skills.

Like the discourse of "cultural deprivation" and "disadvantage" of the 1960s, however, the discourse of "children at risk" deflects attention away from injustices perpetrated and institutionalized by the dominant society and again frames oppressed communities and homes as lacking in the cultural and moral resources for advancement. This is part of a broader political strategy to consolidate the power of White male capital domestically as well as internationally, at a time when most Americans feel uncertain about their own position and future. In attacking the home, hooks (1990) argues that the dominant society attacks the very center of resistance of those who are most disenfranchised:

> For those who dominate and oppress us benefit most when we have nothing to give our own, when they have so taken from us our dignity, our humanness that we have nothing left, no "homeplace" where we can recover ourselves. (p. 43)

Children and Families "at Promise": Deconstructing the Discourse of Risk challenges the metaphor of the "at risk" discourse, situating it in a context of struggle over the power to define language and policy and the right of all groups to material and psychological well-being. Swadener and Lubeck offer both a critique and a re-visioning of possibility. Several chapters in this book critique the construction of the "at risk" discourse and the policy responses that flow from that discourse. Chapters also reframe oppressed groups in terms of "promise," presenting portraits of children, parents, and teachers who refused to accept definitions based on deficiency and mobilized local cultural and personal resources to achieve with excellence.

This book should serve as an inspiration to educators and parents, as well as offering the metaphor of "promise" as a counter to that of "risk." As such, it should invite collaboration and power-sharing rather than patronizing assistance, respect rather than pity, and belief in potential rather than failure. In so doing, the book challenges us to critique ourselves and our framing of "Others."

REFERENCES

Goldberg, M. L. (1963). Factors affecting educational attainment in depressed urban areas. In A. H. Passow (Ed.), *Education in depressed areas* (pp. 63–100). New York: Teachers College Press.

hooks, b. (1990). *Yearning: Race, gender, and cultural politics.* Boston: South End Press.

BETH BLUE SWADENER
SALLY LUBECK

The Social Construction
of Children and
Families "at Risk":
An Introduction

The pervasiveness of the construct "children and families at risk" hardly needs an introduction. Since 1989, over 2,500 articles and conference papers have focused on this topic, and a growing number of state and national reports continue to address the "at risk" theme. Countless task forces and school district and state committees have made recommendations for addressing this "crisis" in American education and have received widespread media attention (Swadener, 1990). Partly in response to the implementation of Public Law 99/457, which mandates states to serve preschool-age children with developmental disabilities or "at risk" status, many states have begun programs for "at risk" children. The term "at risk" has thus become a buzzword much like "diversity," "choice," or "privatization," and, like these terms, the assumptions that underlie its usage have gone largely unexamined.

This book suggests that the term obfuscates as much as it informs and advocates both a deconstruction of this construct and a reconceptualization of how families are viewed. Instead of seeing children and families as "at risk," *all* children and families might be viewed as "at promise."

Currently, one of the most striking images of "children and families at risk" is that of families of low income. This volume offers an analysis and interrogation of the rhetoric of risk as it relates to the persistent social stratification in U.S. society and the ways in which it uses a medical *language of pathology* to label persons based on their race, first language, class, family structure, geographic location, and gender as "at risk for failure" (Swadener, 1990). Historically, the language of maladjustment evolved to a discourse of cultural deprivation, with families labeled as pathological, broken, non-intact and dysfunctional; "from the pauper child as potential criminal to the at-risk student delinquent" (Polakow, 1993, p. 103).

This deficit model discourse typically gets framed as private and personal, often taking the form of blaming the victim—particularly in a nation whose dominant culture perpetuates the myth of meritocracy (McIntosh, 1988, 1992), in which all privileges are assumed to be earned or deserved, a nation which systematically denies or attempts to ignore the pervasive exclusionary and oppressive practices in society. This, in turn, reflects the much-noted popular ideology of private, competitive individualism, as reflected in child and family policy in the United States. Strikingly absent from discussions of risk factors and poverty is an interrogation of privilege and the possibility that a more equitable distribution of materials, resources, education, power, and self-sufficiency may put the stark discrepancies of privilege at risk. Valerie Polakow (1993) has recently discussed how underlying the public discourse of a nation at risk, children at risk, and families at risk is the corollary, *privilege at risk*. It is also interesting to note the tacit assumptions which many children of privilege receive and internalize concerning both their right to such privileges and the limitations of those who do not enjoy their standard of living and quality of schools (Arnold & Swadener, 1993).

How have pervasive images of "the underclass" and assumptions about children and families "at risk" become "deeply entrenched common sense" (Reed, 1992) in the United States? The racism and sexism inherent in much of the current popular discourse on "the urban underclass" or the "culture of poverty" is evident. Reed (1992), Fine (1990, 1993), and others have attributed the popularity of such concepts to the shift to the right during the late 1970s and 1980s in terms of policies and public debate about social welfare and education policy. Reed (1992) asserts that right-wing beliefs about poverty have pervaded the discourse and policies of even "self-consciously liberal friends of the poor," who have come to "assume the need to correct, or at least take into account, poor people's defective tendencies as an essential limit on social policy" (p. 22). This strong attribution of behavioral characteristics, personal (versus income) deficiencies, and marginal or even "deviant" lifestyles to those living in poverty is another persistent theme. Mead (1986), for example, suggests that "unstable family life marked by absent fathers, erratic parents, and low self-esteem and aspiration" (p. 22) can be used to identify underclass families.

There is a long history of such "othering" and of class stratification which operates painfully in the lives of poor children and parents in the United States (Swadener, 1993). Unlike many nations which have made a strong commitment to families and have viewed children as a public responsibility and resource, U.S. government policies do not yet consider the care and welfare of children a basic social right (Lubeck, 1991, p. 236). As Polakow (1993) states:

> Still, in the late twentieth century, it is the poor who have only themselves to blame. The Pygmalion predictions persist, implicating poor young children as the "dangerous classes." Early education becomes another form of cost-effective crime prevention. . . . But a different question hovers about this instrumental discourse—Do poor children's lives matter? . . . are poor children cheap? (p. 102)

A basic premise of this book is that the generalized use of the "at risk" label is highly problematic and implicitly racist, classist, sexist, and ableist, a 1990s version of the cultural deficit model which locates problems or "pathologies" in individuals, families, and communities rather than in institutional structures that create and maintain inequality (Lubeck & Garrett, 1990). The critique of this pervasive construct has been relatively limited, particularly as it applies to young children and their families (Castell, 1991; Fine, 1990; Ford & Harris, 1990; Lubeck & Garrett, 1990; Polakow,

1992, 1993; Popkewitz, in press; Soto, 1992; Swadener, 1990; Swadener & Niles, 1991). Thus, this edited volume has two foci:

1. to deconstruct the "at risk" label through an analysis of historical and contextual issues, and discussions of contemporary critiques and to include voices and perspectives which have been largely absent from the discussion, and
2. to suggest that we begin to utilize the construct "children and families at promise" to convey the potential *all* children hold (Ford & Harris, 1991; Shaklee & Biedler, 1992; Swadener & Niles, 1991; Arnold & Swadener, 1993).

The chapters in this book move from historical, demographic, and critical analyses of the literature and popular perceptions of "children and families at risk" to success stories, drawn from multiple cultures in the United States, and collaboratively written chapters describing partnerships and initiatives between teachers and students and between families and schools. The voices in the chapters comprising this book move the discourse of children "at risk" from a discussion of "them" or "the other" to a discussion of "us" and "our children" and offer a number of recommendations for policy, research, pedagogy, teacher preparation, and parent and community empowerment.

Our intent is that this volume provide a needed interrogation of the ways in which poor and racial and ethnic "minority" children and families are perceived within American society. Chapter authors share a concern about issues of race, class, gender, linguistic diversity, and developmental differences. Chapters draw from critical theory, feminist theory, life history and teacher-as-researcher studies, and other perspectives that both illuminate and begin to reconstruct several dimensions of the "at risk" rhetoric and assumptions. Contributors include a parent fighting for full inclusion for her son who has cerebral palsy; life history interviews with African American mothers; academically successful Native American students; the powerful poetry of young Latino, Southeast Asian and African American writers; and the voices of Hmong, Latino, and African American children and families and the teachers who work with them.

Throughout this volume, we will raise questions, many of which a growing number of parents, educators, researchers, and child advocates have been discussing for the past several years:

1. Who is at risk?
2. At risk for what?
3. Who defines risk? How have the criteria for or definitions of risk changed?
4. What is the "etiology" of this term and its related discourse? How is this discourse one of instrumental crisis, pathology, and blame? Is "at risk" merely a cultural deprivation/deficit model retooled for the 90s? In what ways is it socially constructed and to what ends?
5. What myths and folklore have been generated about risk and risk factors? In what ways is our "common sense" about children and families "at risk" racist, classist, sexist, ableist, and paternalistic?
6. How can the discourse transcend mere stereotypes and debates of semantics and contribute to real gains for children who are poor and children of color?
7. How are those of us who engage in child advocacy, work with families, grant writing, or related policy research reinforcing it? Who are the stakeholders in the use of the "at risk" label, and what roles do each of us play—personally and professionally—in maintaining its use and abuse?
8. In what ways is the discourse of risk essentialist, reductionistic, and dogmatic? What are some of the complexities and contradictions in the dominant discourse of risk—and what are their costs to children?
9. How might "success stories," culturally sensitive and inclusive pedagogy, family literacy, and community empowerment interrupt the hegemony of the risk rhetoric and ideology—and get needed programs funded and oppressive policies and practices changed?
10. How are people to whom this label is applied resisting, questioning, or contradicting it? How can those who exist at the margins of power gain more power and more control of their discourses and practices?

Finally, we are curious about what interest the powerful have in correcting the problems described in much of the pervasive literature of risk—the apartheid of U.S. public schools as described by Kozol (1991), life in the "projects" as described by Kotlowitz (1991), and other "texts of despair," as Michelle Fine describes them (1993). How are the economically privileged and powerful affected, directly and indirectly, by the "savage inequalities" described by Kozol and others (Arnold & Swadener, 1993)? Our questions are underscored by the following issues raised by Adolph Reed Jr. in an article entitled "The Underclass as Myth and Symbol: The Poverty of Discourse About Poverty" (1992).

> In recent years the image of an urban "underclass" has become the central representation of poverty in American society. It has come also to shape much of public discussion—both academic and popular—and policymakers' agendas concerning racial democratization, cities, and social welfare. In less than a decade the notion has taken hold of the public imagination and has gone, across the ideological spectrum, from novel, sensational expression to deeply entrenched common sense. But what does it all mean? What is so compelling about the underclass image? What is its significance in American political life? And, finally, how should we talk, instead, about those who are stigmatized as the "underclass"? (p. 21)

Similar to the questions being asked by feminists and postmodernists (e.g., Ellsworth, 1989; Greene, 1986; Lather, 1991; Polakow, 1993), many of the contributors to this volume would join us in asking the questions, "How can educators and parents gain control of their discourses and practices, instead of being controlled by them?" and "How can we better listen to, rather than always talk about or speak for, those who are at the margins of the culture of power?" (Arnold & Swadener, 1993). Thus, we have tried, in this collection of essays and research reports, to promote inclusion and to avoid some of the problems of researcher as "ventriloquist" (Fine & Weis, 1993), speaking for the "other" in a discourse of risk, rather than from a perspective of promise.

We share with Cameron McCarthy (1993) a concern about the various forms of essentialism, reductionism, and dogmatism found in much of the discourse about children and families "at risk." This discourse tends to reduce the complexities and contradictions of children's lives. Though the prevailing literature does not typically attribute a single cause for children "at risk," explicit, in fact ever-expanding, categories which generalize across individual situations and complex dynamics are employed in the identification of such children.

ORGANIZATION OF THE BOOK

This book is organized into three sections. The first section provides historical, political, and theoretical contexts for deconstructing the discourse on children and families "at risk." In the first chapter, Beth Blue Swadener provides an "etiology" of the terminology and social constructions of risk, analyzing the many disciplines and theories which have contributed to the construct "at risk." A systematic deconstruction of this term is presented, including an analysis of ways in which several disciplines (e.g., child welfare, medicine, early education/special education, and sociology) have formulated models of risk and an analysis of the implicit deficit model in these discourses. The metaphor "children and families at promise" is further developed, and questions raised in the introduction are used to engage a number of "what if?" questions and to explore directions for addressing these problems.

In chapter 2, Sally Lubeck maintains that it is mothers who are at risk, because increasing numbers are in extreme economic and social circumstances that make it unlikely that they will be able to care for children in ways mythologized to be normal and optimal. The chapter has four sections. The first and second examine and critique how women are blamed, overtly and covertly, for children's "at risk" status and detail how risk status is defined. The third explores how national statistics have been used in interpretive contexts—conservative and progressive/liberal—which define the nature of problems and their likely resolution in very different ways. The final section argues that much political rhetoric continues to translate social and economic inequity into tales of individual recalcitrance and deficiency. Thus, women come to be implicated in the reproduction not just of children, but of poverty itself.

In her chapter on "The Politics of Who's at Risk," Michelle Fine peels through the layers of debate that give ideological shape to the current "dropout problem." She analyzes ways in which the language of risk pervades our daily consciousness, educational practices, and bureaucratic policy-making. Fine contends that we have all been quick to name, identify, and ossify those who presumably suffer at the mercy of "risk factors," satisfying the desire both of the Right to isolate such people and the Left to display them. This chapter waves a reminder: The cultural construction of a group defined through a discourse of "risk" represents a "shaved and partial image." It is an image that typically strengthens those institutions and groups which have denied connection to and then promised to "save" those who will undoubtedly remain "at risk." Most fundamentally, "the rhetoric of risk keeps us from being broadly, radically, and structurally creative about transforming schools and social conditions for today's and tomorrow's youth."

It strikes us as particularly ironic that the voices typically most absent from, or at best at the margins of, the discourse of risk are those that have been assigned the label of children and families "at risk." Just as narratives, success stories, and other forms of "heteroglossia" (Bakhtin, 1981) or multiple discourses and voices are increasingly evident in educational theory, research, and related disciplines (e.g., Carter, 1993; Paley, 1990; Rosenwald & Ochberg, 1992; Soto, 1992; Weis & Fine, 1993; Witherell & Noddings, 1991), we feel such stories and their critical framing are necessary to a deconstruction of risk. We share with Jameson (1984), however, the view that all narratives must generate an "imaginary resolution of real contradictions" (Levi-Strauss, quoted in Jameson, 1984). We do not seek to create another "master narrative" but to engage a dialogue which includes perspectives of those whose narratives have been absent in much of the "masterscript" on risk.

The second section of the book is a collection of "success stories," beginning with two chapters that look at issues of empowerment, family literacy, resistance, and resilience in children and families of color and in poor families. In "Voice Unaltered: Marginalized Young Writers Speak," Elizabeth Quintero and Mary Kay Rummel analyze the writing of young girls and children from culturally and linguistically diverse families, using a methodology that combines reflections of unique detail and metaphor as strong indication of voice. The voices in this chapter—primarily Latino, African American, and Southeast Asian kindergarten and primary students who had participated in family literacy projects—provide dramatic evidence of voice in children before this voice has been "socialized away." The authors contend that this evidence supports a classroom context that encourages and enhances voice "in a generative transformative way," while, at the same time, helping to deconstruct the myth that children are "at risk" by virtue of their racial or ethnic status.

In chapter 5, Donelda Cook and Michelle Fine analyze ways in which low-income African American families are being blamed for the nation's social problems, while the dominant discourse fails to acknowledge political, social, and economic conditions and the abandonment of urban communities. In order to reframe the conversation about urban families "at risk," they utilize narratives drawn from interviews with twelve African American mothers who participated in a program designed to activate and involve parents.

Mary Smith Arnold, in chapter 6, furthers the discussion of family strengths and maternal struggles and stances in the African American community, emphasizing the long-standing tradition of commitment to education and literacy. Drawing on interview data from sixty low-income African American mothers in a large mid-western city regarding their attitudes concerning the education of preadolescent children, this chapter provides strong evidence that such families value educational success and are troubled by the current liberal use of the "at risk" label for children of color. This essay also clarifies many of the family strengths, as well as needed supports, of successful low-income families.

In chapter 7, Carolyne White presents a critical feminist interrogation of the cultural construction of the "at risk" student by focusing upon "contingencies of studenthood" experienced by academically successful Native American students and interrogates her position as a European American crossing borders. White draws from continuing research with former participants in Upward Bound, calling attention to students' perceptions of the consequences of their participation in this program. Eight of the narrators of this chapter are Navajo, three are Hopi, and one is European American. Together, the authors of this collaborative chapter seek political intervention against discourse that portrays families as failures and children "at risk" within professional and popular literatures.

The third and final section of the book focuses on specific case studies of successful home-school partnerships, "at promise" classrooms, full inclusion initiatives, and other collaborations. It raises further issues drawing from "insider" perspectives on the construction and interruption of "risk." Theoretical frameworks for better reconstructing children, families, and programs "at promise" are explored primarily through personal and collaborative narratives from settings across the United States.

In their chapter, Robert Tabachnick and Marianne Bloch discuss related themes and lessons from a three-year qualitative study of home-school relations in two desegregated elementary schools, including the perspectives of Hmong, Latino, and African American families and their children's teachers. Going beyond a cultural continuity/discontinuity model, this chapter raises a number of methodological issues and argues in support of viewing such families as at promise, rather than at risk for failure, in the schools studied. Some of the challenges and dilemmas of encouraging teachers to hold such a view of children and families are also discussed.

Continuing the focus on the importance of strengthening home-school relations and understandings in culturally pluralistic classrooms, Mary Hauser and Cynthia Thompson explore the concept of risk at the level of the classroom by providing an example of a classroom culture in which students are "at promise." This chapter draws from a three-year collaborative ethnography conducted by an exemplary educator and a university researcher. According to any checklist, all of Thompson's students would be considered "at risk." None of her students were native English speakers, all qualified for Chapter 1 services, all families received Aid to Families with Dependent Children (AFDC) and all belonged to cultural groups that many consider to compare "unfavorably" to the mainstream. Yet, her students demonstrate behaviors that do not allow the observer to be aware of conditions of risk.

In chapter 10, Joyce Waldoch, an elementary special educator, describes a project that merged a special education class with an "at risk" regular education class. The program built on students' strengths, required no extra funding, and was created within the existing school structure. A portion of the school day was restructured to provide unmotivated learners with a variety of teaching styles/learning opportunities, hands-on activities, and opportunities to develop more positive views of themselves in relation to their peers. Through the voice of a confident "teacher reformer," this chapter encourages so-called "students at risk" to become active learners and confident risk-takers in the school environment.

The final chapter provides a narrative account of a mother's experiences in advocating for and attempting to maintain a regular education classroom placement for her son, Aric, who has cerebral palsy and is labeled "multiply handicapped." This chapter is coauthored by a researcher, friend, and ally who interviews Tina Murray about her many challenges, disappointments, and successes. The authors share the perspective that full inclusion is not restricted to the school setting but extends into other community settings as well. Murray and Lisa Leifield's dialogue regarding full inclusion provides a basis for their discussion of barriers, teacher strategies for promoting full classroom membership, advocacy strategies utilized by this family, implications for teacher preparation, and the benefits of full inclusion in several community contexts.

The epilogue, written by Valerie Polakow, draws from her extensive work with single mothers of low income and their children, both of whom remain in the "shadows of democracy" (Polakow, 1992) and reside in the "other" America. In her critique of the "privatization of poverty" in western policy discourse, Polakow (1993, October) speaks plainly—"poor children are cheap; they matter instrumentally, not existentially" (p.1). She also demonstrates how the risk industry rests heavily on the poverty industry (Funiciello, 1993) and further deconstructs the politics and priorities of savage distributions in the United States. A reconstruction of risk, which would effectively address poverty and redistribution, quickly yields the notion of "privilege at risk."

In rendering the "at risk" metaphor problematic, this book interrogates the ways constructions of "the other" perpetuate the pervasive, often damaging, discourse of risk. In deconstructing risk, we honor the many storytellers whose work is included in this volume, both for their contradictions to common sense assumptions about children and families "at risk" and their vision of children and families "at promise."

REFERENCES

Arnold, M. S., & Swadener, B. B (1993). *Savage Inequalities* and the discourse of risk: What of the white children who have so much green grass? *Educational Review*, *15*, 261–272.

Bakhtin, M. M. (1981). *The dialogic imagination: Four essays*. Trans. C. Emerson. Ed. M. Holquist. Austin: University of Texas Press.

Carter, K. (1993). The place of the story in the study of teaching and teacher education. *Educational Researcher*, *22*(1), 5–12, 18.

Castell, R. (1991). From dangerousness to risk. In G. Burchell, C. Gordon, & P. Miller, (Eds.). *The Foucault effect: Studies in governmentality.* (pp. 281–298). Chicago: University of Chicago Press.

Ellsworth, E. (1989). Why doesn't this feel empowering? Working through the repressive myths of critical pedagogy. *Harvard Educational Review*, *59*, 297–298.

Fine, M. (1990). Making controversy: Who's "at risk"? *Journal of Cultural Studies*, 1(1), 55–68.

Fine, M. (1993). A diary on privatization and on public possibilities. *Educational Theory*, 43(1).

Fine, M. & Weis, L. (1993). Introduction. In L. Weis & M. Fine *Beyond silenced voices: Class, race and gender in United States schools*, (pp. 1–6) Albany, NY: State University of New York Press.

Ford, D. Y. & Harris, J. J., III. (1991). Black students: "At promise" not "at Risk" for giftedness. *Journal of Human Behavior and Learning*, 7(2), 21–29.

Funiciello, T. (1993). *The tyranny of kindness*. New York: Atlantic Monthly Press.

Greene, M. (1986). In search of a critical pedagogy. *Harvard Educational Review*, 56, 427–441.

Greene, M. (1991). Foreword. In C. Witherell & N. Noddings (Eds.) *Stories lives tell: Narrative and dialogue in education*. (pp. ix–xi) New York: Teachers College Press.

Jameson, F. (1984). Foreword. In J. F. Lyotard (Ed.) *The postmodern condition: A report on knowledge* (pp. vii–xcxi). Minneapolis: University of Minnesota Press.

Kotlowitz, A. (1991). *There are no children here: The story of two boys growing up in the other America*. New York: Doubleday.

Kozol, J. (1991). *Savage inequalities: Children in America's schools*. New York: Crown Publishers.

Lather, P. (1991). *Getting smart: Feminist research and pedagogy with/in the post modern*. New York: Routledge.

Lubeck, S. (1991). A world of difference: American child care policy in cross-national perspective. In L. Weis, P. Altbach, G. Kelly, & H. Petrie (Eds.). *Critical perspectives on early childhood education*. Albany, NY: State University of New York Press.

Lubeck, S., & Garrett, P. (1990). The social construction of the "at-risk" child. *British Journal of Sociology of Education*, 11(3), 327–340.

McCarthy, C. (1993). Beyond the poverty of theory in race relations: Non-synchrony an social difference in education. In L. Weis & M. Fine (Eds.). *Beyond silenced voices: Class, race, and gender in United States Schools*, (pp. 325–346). Albany, NY: State University of New York Press.

McIntosh, P. (1988). *White privilege and male privilege: A personal account of coming to see correspondences through work in*

Women's Studies. Working paper No. 189. Wellesley, MA: Wellesley College Center for Research on Women.

McIntosh, P. (1992, January-February). White privilege: Unpacking the invisible knapsack. *Creation Spirituality,* 33–35 & 53.

Mead, L. M. (1986). *Beyond entitlement: The social obligations of citizenship.* New York: Free Press.

Paley, V. G. (1990). *The boy who would be a helicopter: The uses of storytelling in the classroom.* Cambridge, MA: Harvard University Press.

Polakow, V. (1992). Deconstructing the discourse of care: Young children in the shadows of democracy. In S. A. Kessler & B. B. Swadener (Eds.), 123–148. *Reconceptualizing the early childhood curriculum: Beginning the dialogue.* New York: Teachers College Press.

Polakow, V. (1993). *Lives on the edge: Single mothers and their children in the other America.* Chicago: University of Chicago Press.

Polakow, V. (1993, October). *Welfare reform and the assault on daily life: Targeting single mothers and their children.* Testimony given to the U.S. Congress, Women and Welfare Reform: Women's Poverty, Women's Welfare: A Policy Conference to Break Myths and Create Solutions (Chairs: Congresswomen Patsy Min, Lynn Waters, Lynn Woolsey, and Congressman Ed Pastor) Washington, D.C.

Popkewitz, T. S. (in press). Policy, knowledge, and power: Some issues for the study of educational reform. In P. Cookson & B. Schneider (Eds.). *Transforming schools: Trends, dilemmas and prospects.* NY: Garland Press.

Reed, A., Jr. (1992). The underclass as myth and symbol: The poverty of discourse about poverty. *Radical America, 24*(1), 21–40.

Rosenwald, G. C., & Ochberg, R. L. (Eds.). (1992). *Storied lives: The cultural politics of self-understanding.* New Haven: Yale University Press.

Shaklee, B. D., & Biedler, F. M. (1992). Changing at-risk settings for at-promise students. *General Music Today, 5*(2), 5–7.

Soto, L. D. (1992). Success stories. In C. A. Grant (Ed.) *Research in multicultural education: From the margins to the mainstream.* (pp. 153–164). New York: Falmer Press.

Swadener, E. B. (1990). Children and families "at risk": Etiology, critique, and alternative paradigms. *Educational Foundations.* 4(4), 17–39.

Swadener, B. B., & Niles, K. (1991). Children and families "at promise": Making home-school-community connections. *Democracy in Education, 5*(3), 13–18.

Swadener, B. B. (1993, June). *Stratification in early childhood social policy and programs in the United States: Historical and contemporary manifestations.* Paper presented at Social Safety Nets in Child Care Policy in Eastern Europe During the Transition to a Market Economy invitational conference, University of Wisconsin-Madison.

Weis, L., & Fine, M. (Eds.) (1993). *Beyond silenced voices: Class, race, and gender in United States Schools.* Albany, NY: State University of New York Press.

Witherell, C., & Noddings, N. (1991). *Stories lives tell: Narrative and dialogue in education.* New York: Teachers College Press.

I. Deconstructing the "at Risk" Label

1

Children and Families "at Promise": Deconstructing the Discourse of Risk

To assess the damage is a dangerous act.
        —Cherrie Moraga, 1981
To the real question, How does it feel to be a problem? I answer seldom a word.
        —W. E. B. DuBois, 1903

How the term "at risk" is constructed and the definitions ascribed to this growing conceptualization of children and families are critical for researchers, educators, child advocates, and other stakeholders to address. Lubeck and Garrett (1990) discuss the importance of the definition of the "at risk" label and suggest that the definitions implicitly point to what should be done. Whether the construct "at risk" is framed as an individual attribute (e.g., non-normative development) or set of problems (e.g., a response to environmental and familial circumstances), a psychological and counseling issue, a pedagogical or learning problem, or is seen as an institutional and societal problem becomes critical to the discussion of what can be done or what "remedies" are "prescribed." The location of blame and responsibility also becomes a significant issue in the debate surrounding the various social constructions of the "at risk" child. Put another way, there is an emerging ideology of risk, which has embedded in it interpretations of children's deficiencies or likelihood of failure due to environmental, as well as individual, variables. The problem of locating pathology in the victim is the most objectionable tenet of much of the dominant rhetoric of risk.

For example, if risk factors are conceptualized primarily as individual attributes which may lead to learning difficulties, earlier and "more effective" screening tools are often advocated, as are inoculation style early intervention programs designed to minimize later educational problems. This type of definition often embodies a deficit model, which ascribes deficiencies to the individual and family. The emphasis within this framework, then, is upon getting the child "ready" for school, rather than getting the school "ready" to serve increasingly diverse children. In contrast, if risk factors are viewed as largely structural (e.g., environmental and societal), far different strategies are likely to be advocated for children and families.

Child advocacy organizations such as the Children's Defense Fund work to dispel myths about children and families in poverty (e.g., by providing evidence that the most rapid increase in poverty is not in inner cities but in suburbs, with large increases in poor White children) and advocate for governmental policies and programs that would begin to address the needs of such families, particularly through enhancing their self-sufficiency or "empowerment." Rather than blame individual families, such groups locate the responsibility for 14 million children living in poverty in the United States largely in the public domain and advocate access to affordable child care, parental leaves, more accessible housing, health care, full funding of Head Start and Women, Infants, and Children (WIC), and increased employment opportunities.

In terms of the number of children considered to be "at risk," Levin (1989) estimates that approximately one-third of all children in elementary and secondary schools should be considered "at risk for academic failure." Other reports frame this problem in virtually all-inclusive terms, as Lubeck and Garrett (1990) point out with a quote from a report of the Council of Chief State School Officers (1988), which recommends universal access to preschool programs based on "an emerging awareness that all children are at risk to some degree and therefore will require prevention or intervention services at one point or another" (p. 40).

The construct at risk has been referred to as a "wolf in sheep's clothing" (Tyack, 1989), in part because of the problem of definition, deficit model assumptions, and potential for racism and classism. Michelle Fine (1988) asserts that "the term 'students at risk' smells of kitsch. It suggests that a small group of students are educationally and economically vulnerable; they are able to be isolated and fixed" (p. 16). I have tended to refer to the construction of children and families "at risk" as the deficit/disadvantage model of the social meliorists, retooled for the 1990s, placing yet another repressive label on an ever widening group of young people and their families (Swadener, 1990). The inherent racism and classism in a label of anticipated failure is particularly problematic. Commenting on the fact that children labeled "at risk" frequently are children of color from low socioeconomic situations, Winborne (1991) states, "the distinctions must sharpen when one considers a term as detrimental as 'at risk.' . . . One cannot suppose that all those from a certain background run the risk of failure; often (thankfully) the failures do not occur. Many successes occur within traditional schools where students come from diverse cultural, ethnic, and racial backgrounds and are poor" (p. 253).

As discussed in our Introduction, the critique of this pervasive construct has been relatively limited—particularly as it applies to young children and their families, an area in which the idea of being "at risk" has widespread acceptance and identification (Lightfoot, 1993; Lubeck & Garrett, 1990; Polakow, 1992,1993; Soto, 1992; Swadener, 1990; Swadener & Niles, 1991; Wollons, 1993). In fact, more recent analyses have demonstrated an increase in cultural capital and funding potential for documentation of large numbers of "at risk" children and families (e.g., Placier, 1993). Thus, a major purpose of this chapter, as well as the larger book, is to deconstruct the "at risk" label through an analysis of historical and contextual issues and discussion of contemporary critiques and to suggest that we begin to utilize the construct "children at promise" to convey the potential for all children to succeed (Swadener & Niles, 1991; Arnold & Swadener, 1993).

Finally, I am curious about what stake the powerful have in correcting the problems described in much of the pervasive "at risk" literature (e.g., the apartheid of U.S. public schools as described by Kozol [1992] or life in the "projects" as described by Kotlowitz [1991]). How are those with the most power and unearned privilege affected—directly and indirectly—by the "savage inequalities" described by Kozol and others (Arnold & Swadener, 1993).

Recent historical analyses of the origins and complexities of meaning-making implicit in the discourse of risk also include the relationship of risk factors to educational reform movements, power relationships, and use as a powerful metaphor adapted from the *insurance* industry and its public discourse. Popkewitz (in press) describes "at risk" as part of the "double hermeneutics" of schooling which provides focus for school reform and is associated with programmatic activities and research "about instruction and children thought of as in special need" (p. 27). Popkewitz draws from several chapters in Burchell, et. al's (1991) volume *The Foucault Effect* in the following quote (Popkewitz, in press):

> In focusing on "risk," for example, recent scholarship has located the changing meaning of the concept of risk as it is formed through the financing of insurance for commerce and as it is reinscribed into social welfare policies as a state tactic to organize the welfare of citizens (see, for example, Ewald, 1991; Defert, 1991; Castell, 1991). . . . It is best to speak of risk as a social technology that involved moral, judicial and political dimensions. Risk is a moral technology used to master time and discipline the future. Risk is a technique to administer justice through its conceptions or reparation and indemnification of damages; conceptions very different from the legal system itself which is tied to particular people and events.

Similarly, in Valerie Polakow's analysis of the discourse of risk (1992), the notion of the distancing of the dominant class from the urban, homeless, single parent "other" is integrally related to the implicit assumptions of much of the "at risk" literature and policy practices. As she states, "Every at-risk child in our early childhood classrooms is a potential victim of such public indifference, of our disenfranchisement of the poor—a witness to our failure to provide entitlements for all children" (p. 140). She goes on to assert that "funding for early intervention programs for poor children is premised on cost-benefit accountability," using the segregated landscape of early childhood programs (e.g., pay-for-service preschools and day care centers versus Head Start) as a further example (p. 141).

When listening in on the "discourse of risk," I am increasingly concerned about who the implied or intended audience may be for many of the popular accounts of the underclass, mounting risk factors for the majority of urban children, and so on, and to what end? Related to this question is the issue of whether such treatments of the problems affecting children and families lock us into oppressor/oppressed, helper/helped, benefactor/beneficiary roles that function to preclude authentic collaborator relationships (Arnold & Swadener, 1993). In other words, do such accounts prevent the powerful and privileged from noticing the intrinsic value of those who have been abused by the system? Similarly, the agency of "the victims" of poverty and the efforts to correct the problem from within also get dismissed—or hidden—in order to make the powerful feel they must rescue the ones "at risk" of failure without their intervention.

HISTORICAL AND CONTEXTUAL BACKGROUND

It is the telling of our history that enables
political self-recovery.
                                   —bell hooks, 1992

Much as good, contextualized research should avoid presenting data or interpretations in an ahistorical or atheoretical manner, it is important to review some of the historical antecedents and "etiology" of the notion of children and families "at risk." It is also important to analyze the assumptions and contexts within which educational and societal problems are framed and socially constructed. As Cuban (1989) reminds us, with a George Bernanos quote, "There is no worse lie than a problem poorly stated" (p. 780).

Historical contexts or antecedents for the contemporary "at risk" discourse can be identified in many different disciplines, including medicine and public health, sociology, child welfare and social work, developmental psychology, early childhood education, special education, public policy, economics, and demography. This chapter will focus on three broad disciplines: (1) medical and public health, (2) child welfare and social policy, and (3) child psychology and early education, and their often parallel and interrelated contributions to the evolution of the construct of children "at risk."

Medical and Public Health

*If we say poor people are poor because of bad
values, we let government off the hook. . . . I do
not want to hear another word about drugs or
crime without hearing about decent jobs, adequate housing and egalitarian education in the
same breath.*
                                    —*Adolph Reed Jr.,1992*

The medical and public health model for children "at risk" is
perhaps most obvious and explicit. Terms such as "risk factors"
come largely from an epidemiological and public health perspective, which seeks to identify both internal (hereditary) and external
(environmental, nutritional) risk factors and minimize their
impact on the individual and family. One such medical intervention with children is immunization against later contagious disease. For example, the immunization metaphor can be applied to
Head Start and other antipoverty intervention programs which
have been considered instrumental in preventing (inoculating
against) later school failure (the anticipated "disease") through an
early academic and social "shot in the arm."

As Duvon Winborne (1991) asserts,

> The phrase "at risk," appearing frequently in education and
> social science literature, comes from medicine and alludes to
> the threat of disease or injury. During the past decade, practi-
> tioners and researchers in education adopted this conceptual
> paradigm for elucidating educational problems. They defined
> those conditions that tend to affect children in negative ways
> and reduce success in traditional school settings as producing
> "risks," and, gradually, educators developed a set of charac-
> teristics that place children "at risk" for school failure. (p.
> 252)

Other antecedent themes, more clearly linked to the current
discourse on children at risk, include prevention, early intervention, and developmental screening—areas which typically are
addressed across the disciplines of medicine, special education,
school psychology, and various specialized therapies. Of particular
relevance are the use of the Early Periodic Screening, Diagnosis,
and Treatment program and other screening and "child find" programs and approaches. While there is little doubt that appropriate

supports and other "interventions" for disabled and developmentally delayed children are optimized by early opportunities to benefit from needed and appropriate services, the point here is to better understand the other disciplines from which the underlying assumptions about "children at risk" have come—in this case, the fields of pediatric medicine and special education.

In recent years, however, "premature screening" might be an appropriate description for some of the research on, for example, early identification of learning disabilities or risk of later learning disabilities. How early? More infant assessments are being utilized, including assessing six-week-old infants and labeling them "learning disabled" based on such early screening procedures. This is a very different perspective than that of infant competence, as emphasized in the Brazelton and other infant screening approaches.

As mentioned in our Introduction, Public Law 99/457 provides yet another way to identify children at risk without labeling them per se, using the phrase "deferred diagnosis" as well as "at risk for developmental delays." Other screening instruments being used with increasing frequency by schools for kindergarten and first grade include the "Early Prevention of School Failure" assessment and the Gessell Developmental Readiness Screening Assessment. Though the topic of kindergarten screening and related "readiness" issues are beyond the scope of this chapter, the relation of the growing use of screenings and delayed school entry as well as rising rates of preschool, kindergarten, and first grade "red shirting" or retentions are certainly related to the growing acceptance of the "at risk" construct. All such approaches emphasize early identification of those children least likely to succeed, or most at risk to fail, in existing school programs (e.g., Graue, 1992).

One of the most powerful accounts of a child caught in the web of over-assessment and resulting mis-education is Denny Taylor's case study *Learning Denied* (1991). This book captures, in often painful detail, ways in which educational abuse is committed against children identified as "slow learners" or learning disabled. Such abuses include excessive and often inappropriate assessment, discontinuity of daily activities, and lack of opportunities to demonstrate abilities. Such examples provide powerful documentation of a sort of out-of-control self-fulfilling prophecy of failure, made even more ironic by the inaccurate "diagnosis" in the case of Patrick, the subject of this study.

Other medical, as well as special education, themes include the idea of early identification and treatment, public campaigns for inoculation or detection, family intervention, and parent training. The idea of optimal times for certain early identification and intervention procedures has many parallels between child health and both special education and early childhood education and care— particularly for low-income children. A medical regimen intended to minimize possible negative outcomes (e.g., illness, disability, or even death) has further parallels with an educational regimen, or prescription, aimed at preventing later school failure, crime, drug abuse, teenage parenthood, or dropping/stopping out of school.

Many medical model intervention programs for children have begun to concentrate more on the prescription than the diagnosis and even refer to children by their treatment regiment. Thus, children who have typically been labeled by some professionals according to their disability (e.g., "EMRs," "LD kids," or "ADD children") or particular coping or mental health problems (e.g., "ED kids"), for example, are more frequently being labeled according to their treatment plan or type of therapy (e.g., "the Ritalin kids in my class"). The traditional child-centered orientation, focusing on the "whole child" or even moving toward a more "normalized" or "regular education initiative" approach to working with children with a variety of "special needs" appears to have taken a back seat in recent years to a renewed, and often feverish, diagnostic and prescriptive approach. This shift has been fueled, in part, by the growth in acceptance and wider application of the "at risk" paradigm and related ideology.

One of the most pervasive medically-based constructions of children and families at risk comes from the highly publicized crisis in prenatally drug-exposed infants and their mothers. This area, particularly through popular media accounts, parallels many of the myths and assumptions, also fueled by media images of "the other," related to "crack babies," prenatally exposed infants and their mothers. Perhaps there is no better example of blaming the victim than that of criminalizing, rather than rehabilitating or effectively intervening with, mothers who are addicted to cocaine and other drugs. This criminalization movement does not consider the level of internalized oppression and malaise which leads to powerful addictions such as to crack cocaine. It also ignores the many White mothers who are drug users and abusers, and has, once again, given the perpetrators of risk Black faces and urban lives of "the other."

Some of the popular assumptions and myths about prenatally drug-exposed infants and children, as outlined by Leifield (1992), include: (1) Crack cocaine is primarily a drug of inner-city women of color; (2) utilization of cocaine during pregnancy is predictive of poor developmental outcome and aberrant behavior; and (3) a new set of curriculum strategies will need to be devised to work with infants, toddlers, and children prenatally exposed to drugs—or at risk for developmental delays and unpredictable negative behavior. With cover stories and headlines about a "generation of crack babies," the popular media has played into the perpetuation of such assumptions and myths and contributed to the creation of a "bio-underclass" (Blackwell, Buell, & Burns, 1991).

In sum, the term and underlying assumptions of being "at risk" are anchored in a medical model which, if given sufficient time and financial resources, can find cures, or at least short- and long-term treatment regimens, for virtually any disease which can be detected through widespread screening mechanisms. Questions such as how problems are defined, under what circumstances particular "vulnerabilities" are problematic, and matters of "degree" to which potential or real problems put children "at risk" all deserve further reflection and critique. What is particularly troubling and problematic is the degree to which children's race, gender, class, first language, family makeup, and environment all target them for this "at risk" label and associated interventions.

Child Welfare and Social Policy

In the end, "underclass" assumptions serve to take the focus away from (costly) demands for responsible government policies, blaming poor people, not societal choices, for another pat phrase, "persistent poverty."
—Adolph Reed Jr., 1992

The second category of historical antecedents of the "at risk" construction includes the sociopolitical disciplines (e.g., sociology, social work, political science, economics, and demography). It is often in these disciplines that the deficit model, child-saving slogans, recurrent insinuations of cultural deprivation, and labeling and analysis of a growing number of family and community risk variables have been most thoroughly articulated, analyzed, promoted, and perpetuated. In a history of childsaving in America, Hamilton Cravens (1993) describes three distinct eras of childsaving, with the 1870s through 1920s emphasizing "subnormal" and "abnormal" children, and the 1920s through 1950s emphasizing the "endless variations of normal children among the nation's many religious, nativity, and economic groups" (p. 6), with all but the most difficult children considered able to assimilate or adapt to society's norms. In the 1950s, or beginning of the "contemporary era, child savers abandoned the group determinism of the earlier epochs. They stressed that the individual child, with his or her difficulties with the system, was a child at risk, either potentially or in reality" (p. 6). In the following quote from Cravens (1993), the assumptions of child-savers, particularly in the first era but persistent today (as chapters in this volume demonstrate), were described as follows:

> In the main for child savers, normal, middle-class, white children of Anglo-Saxon Protestant background as a group exemplified the highest standards of modern culture, to which the subnormal and abnormal groups should be compared. The child savers, then, focused on the types of subnormal and abnormal children. (p. 5)

Whether we are considering the impact of changing family demographics (e.g., more single-parent, female-headed families, or other "nontraditional" family groups), socioeconomic variables (e.g., the rise in numbers of children in poverty, the growth of the "underclass," growing unemployment and minimum wage poverty, or homelessness), or cultural variables (e.g., increasing number of bilingual and limited-English-proficient families, caste systems, cultural conflict models, and parental values regarding education), the systematizing of *risk factors* for children and families seems apparent.

Luis Laosa (1984) and others (Bremmer, 1974; Grotberg, 1976; Steiner, 1976) have argued that the identification of certain groups of children as "at risk" goes back well over two-hundred years in U.S. public policy. Laosa (1984) writes, "There is historical continuity in Anglo-American social welfare policies toward children; in every era over the past 400 or more years certain groups of children have been considered as being 'at risk,' and hence of social concern and responsibility" (p. 1). Included in these groups are children with handicaps and serious diseases, orphans, indigent children, and neglected, abused, and delinquent children. He adds, "Only very recently have the children belonging to specified ethnic, racial and language groups been added as major 'risk' categories and thus become a major focus of social concern and public responsibility" (p. 1). Laosa and others argue that the source of this social concern is the alleged inability of the family to cope with the problems implied by group membership, coupled with a fear of the public danger or societal impact of leaving these problems "untreated." This argument draws from the same material as instrumental or intervention-emphasizing cost-benefit analyses and "pay now to prevent or pay later" arguments discussed earlier (e.g., Polakow, 1992).

Another metaphor for "at risk" children, particularly children of color, has been the image of a "domestic third world" (Pellicano, 1987), in which children considered at risk are described as placing "society at risk of becoming a 'Third World' inhabited by individuals who are dependent, underdeveloped and noncompetitive" (p. 68). Assigning this neocolonial metaphor to groups—with emphasis on children—would seem to further marginalize and disempower oppressed groups and only add to the construction of a dominant culture "us" versus a so-called "underclass culture" of "them." I believe such a paradigm was evident in the plethora of reports such as the Governors' Task Force on Education report and goals, which placed heavy emphasis on preparation of a competitive workforce and meeting the needs of business and industry through lessening the risks of school failure. The contributions of sociopolitical disciplines to the cultural deficit model underlying prevailing assumptions about children and families are many.

To whom do such underclass constructions or depictions appeal and by whom are they most perpetuated? Reed (1992) asserts that "the underclass notion appeals to three distinct ideological dispositions. Most immediately, it resonates with the ahistorical individualism rampant in the Reagan/Bush era" (p. 32). He also feels that the underclass construct appeals to middle-class Blacks who use it as a comparison to their success, an assertion I find more problematic. Finally, Reed (1992) discusses the tendency to use "the idea of a behaviorally defined underclass" to affirm "an ensemble of racial and class prejudices that lurk beneath an apparently innocuous, certainly stupid tendency to reduce the social world to aggregates of good people and bad people. " This, in turn, reinforces the social construction of "good people" as similar to the dominant culture "us" and ensures that the same behavior will be "assessed differently depending on the category into which the perpetrator falls" (p. 32) or to what degree the perpetrator becomes the "other." Although a detailed deconstruction of the popular media's role in constructing images of urban children, families, and schools is beyond the scope of this chapter, it is critical to understanding the pervasiveness of many popular assumptions about those labeled "at risk."

I further agree with Reed's (1992) central point that "the behavioral tendencies supposedly characterizing the underclass exist generally throughout the society. Drug use, divorce, educational underattainment, laziness, and empty consumerism exist no less in upper status suburbs than in inner-city bantustans. The difference lies not in the behavior but in the social position of those exhibiting it" (p. 33). Not only is the social position an important variable in the social construction of the "underclass" and of "families at risk," but many of the variables said to best identify "risk factors" are gendered.

Similarly, Polakow (1992, 1993) provides an important historical context for the current "at risk" rhetoric, particularly as it pertains to poor families and assumptions about childhood and mother-child bonds. She reminds us that "childhood is not and never has been a timeless unchanging developmental essence; rather, it is an economic and cultural construction, rooted in prevailing historical and contemporary images of class, culture, and gender. Family, too, is a contingent social category . . . produced and reproduced . . . and the stable "natural order' from which all diversity of form and resultant pathology diverge" (Polakow, 1992, p. 125). Polakow and others discuss ways in which rising poverty, economic injustice, class stratification, racism, and sexism have contributed to a "social pathology of poverty," which is being increasingly redefined as an individual developmental disability or as being "at risk."

Laosa (1984) discusses the role of social and behavioral science in early childhood and family policies and the underlying ideologies and values related to the so-called "culture of poverty." He groups such definitions and explanations of disadvantaged groups into the following five paradigms: (1) cultural deficit or pathology, (2) genetic inheritance, (3) institutional deficiency, (4) structural characteristics, and (5) developmental, sociocultural, relativism. Space will not permit a thorough discussion of each paradigm, but the role of each in the genealogy of the contemporary "at risk" paradigm and discourse should be considered. In particular, I believe that the role of the cultural deficit model in child development and family research and policy for the past thirty years, much of it aimed at the home environment and maternal behaviors of African American and Latino/Latina families, is clearly linked to present assumptions about "at risk" children. As with any metaphor, we must ask "What is illuminated?" and "What is obscured?"

Child Psychology and Early Education

*The struggle for liberation must begin with
each of us. It is because our parents are the
first, and therefore, most important teachers,
that we must reevaluate current practices and
teaching that we have readily accepted from
the dominant culture.*
　　　　　　　　—Richard Simmons, 1988

　　　The roots of child psychology and early childhood education's conceptualizations of "at risk" children and families can be traced through Puritan ideology in the early colonization of North America, missionary movements with indigenous Americans, and later social meliorist activities in which specific groups of mothers and children have been targeted for special interventions (e.g., boarding schools, adoption policies, mothers' schools, social welfare related day care settings for poor working mothers, and emergent "scientific" child development and psychology theories and programs). It should be noted, as well, that this is a Eurocentric history of early education and care, based on the interpretations of Western, predominantly European and Euro-American middle-class experiences and assumptions.

　　　Puritan child rearing and education literature of the early colonizers of North America reflected the assumption of a basically evil child for whom adult discipline and Christian guidance were the "optimal interventions." These themes have been recurrent in U.S. education and continue to be present in contemporary education settings. From images of urban principals with baseball bats, skill and drill teaching approaches, pull-out programs, and "tough love" approaches to young people with a variety of problems, the theme may just have changed to "spare the special program and spoil the child."

　　　Cuban (1989) and others have spoken to the threat "poor children—often nonwhite and from 'other' cultures—have been seen to pose to the larger society because neither parents nor existing community institutions could control their unacceptable behavior" (p. 781). Some of the programs discussed earlier can be seen as directly related to Cuban's further claim that "fear of having to spend more for welfare payments and prisons drove public officials to compel attendance in schools as a solution to the problem of children we would today label 'at risk'" (p. 781).

For over one hundred years, this use of compulsory schooling, with increasingly "sophisticated" (i.e., positivist/empiricist-based) identification, sifting, and sorting technology, has been the dominant model for U.S. policy-makers and schools. Yet, for African Americans during the eighteenth and much of the nineteenth century, education, including basic literacy instruction, was *against the law*. To push the metaphor further, where African American children were concerned, one of the first applications of the "at risk" notion was paradoxically "children at risk of literacy." African American children were not "legally" educated until the late nineteenth century. Later in this chapter, parallels between the "freedom" and "citizenship" schools and some of the contemporary alternative schools, including Afrocentric and progressive schools, will be discussed.

Yet, even given the multiple oppressions of slavery, often only knowing one's mother by a lock of her hair and having to acquire literacy secretly, African American families and children have persisted and shown much "promise." As Tony Martin (1993) puts it in an essay titled "From Slavery to Rodney King: Continuity and Change":

> Crucial to the survival of Africans in this hostile environment have been two factors—fearless leadership and unrelenting struggle. These factors will have to be wedded to economic and political power before freedom, justice and equality are achieved. But they have been sufficient to ensure survival, no mean feat in the circumstances. Despite enforced illiteracy during slavery and enforced inferior education thereafter, African Americans have managed to maintain a sense of historical continuity in a struggle that has defied the most aggressive advances of bigotry and hate (p. 31).

Later, segregated schools, including reservation and boarding schools for Native American children, continued to provide few opportunities for upward social mobility, systematically undermined indigenous language and culture, and rendered children of color relatively powerless. For decades, the popular eugenics movement provided a convenient rationale for policies and practices which discriminated against African American, Latino, and Native American children (Lubeck & Garrett, 1990). Such "castelike minorities" (Ogbu, 1978) have been systematically disenfranchised through the use of literacy tests, poll taxes, segregation, and gerrymandering. Busing and other desegregation efforts have been undermined by the persistence of the "white doughnut ring" of suburban White flight (Moss, 1992), and the "savage inequalities" of school funding have been well documented (Kozol, 1991). Terms such as "culturally disadvantaged" have been present in the early childhood literature since the early 1960s, and have become code words for poor children of color. This concept of cultural deprivation blamed mothers and, indeed, entire cultural groups for their failures (Lubeck & Garrett, 1990).

It is important to recognize the multiple, often parallel, histories of the construction of the "at risk" paradigm across disciplines addressing children, families, and schooling. Bloch (1987, 1991), Bremmer (1974), Caldwell (1974), Kagan (1989), Sears (1975), Spodek (1984, 1991), Zigler and Gordon (1982), and other scholars have written about the history of early childhood education and care, and their relation to social reform movements. Such discussions often focus on the influential role of the social meliorists (Kliebard, 1986) who established early public schools, infant schools, and kindergartens for poor and immigrant children, among other efforts at "child saving." Quotes from such initial "early interventionists" typically painted extremely grim pictures of the home and neighborhood life of urban poor children. The accuracy of these descriptions of the conditions of many children in the industrial period, for example, is not at question, so much as the location of "blame" for the circumstances, including "poor parenting," and other concerns of the early social meliorists, (often) obscuring the role of the state and social institutions.

The arguments of such reformers were often framed in the need to strengthen the moral fiber of children, prevent crime, and build the future labor force of the society, which had been viewed as having limited abilities to support the poor or even punish the lawless. These are family and contemporary themes, indeed. Another familiar theme was an emphasis on "fitting in" or assimilation, which assumed the model or successful American to be Anglo-Saxon, English speaking, upwardly mobile, and middle class.

The reproductive function of schools in reinforcing the societal status quo, including the patriarchal, racist, classist, ethnocentric, heterosexist, and ableist aspects of the dominant society, has been the subject of much theoretical and ethnographic work in the past two decades. The connection between the many roles schools play in assimilation and acculturation to the dominant, caste-like system and the history of the "at risk" construct is an important one which will be revisited in a later section of this chapter.

REFRAMING THE QUESTIONS AND SHIFTING THE PARADIGM

We have to change our own mind. . . . We've got to change our own minds about each other. We have to see each other with new eyes. We have to come together with warmth.
  —Malcolm X (as quoted by bell hooks, 1992)

As discussed earlier, the way in which basic questions related to children and families are framed, within the context of education, is critical both to our understanding of the cultural and political meaning and significance of constructions such as the popular "at risk" label, as well as to the framing of questions which may be able to move us from a position of unexamined assumptions to a search for new paradigms, vantage points for observation and critical analysis, and more caring and culturally responsive ways to educate young people. Such reflection is, of course, relatively meaningless if not followed with action impacting on praxis.

In this section I raise a number of questions and issues, some of which were listed in our Introduction, starting with the question, Who is at risk? It is important to consider where much of the current discussion in professional education circles and in the popular media locates the deficiencies or blame for the growing numbers of those considered "at risk" for school failure and other problems. Are children and their families the ones who are truly at risk and to blame? What are the responsibilities of schools and the individuals and groups within them who are perpetuating the classism, racism, sexism, ableism, ageism, and other forms of structural, yet ever changing, oppression? Must families be responsible for getting all children "ready" for schools, or should schools be responsible for being "ready" for increasingly diverse and often marginalized children? What are the benefits to children and what are the long-term costs of this label and the programs created to mediate its predicted outcomes?

An "institutional deficiency" paradigm (Laosa, 1984), though not a new analysis of alternative ways to conceptualize the at risk "problem," is relevant to the question of who is at risk. One theory of institutional deficiency which was first argued in the 1970s and continues to gain support in the literature is the "theory of incompatibilities" (Cardenas & Cardenas, 1977). This structural theory attributes the school failure of African American, Mexican American, and poor children to "incompatibilities of characteristics of minority children and the characteristics of typical instructional programs" (p. 1). This analysis shares several assumptions with the cultural compatibility theory, as articulated by Tharp (1989), Delgado-Gaitan (1990; 1993), Delgato-Gaitan & Trueba (1991), and Trueba, Jacobs, and Kirton (1990). Cardenas and Cardenas (1977) further assert that "an instructional program developed for a white, Anglo Saxon, English-speaking middle class school population cannot be and is not adequate for a non-white, non-Anglo Saxon, non-English-speaking, or non-middle class population" (p. 1).

Cardenas and Cardenas group examples of these home/cultural and school/dominant culture incompatibilities into the following five categories: poverty, culture, language, mobility, and social perceptions. Proposed reforms include "changing the instruction to fit the child," as mentioned above in the argument for getting schools ready for all children. Among the predecessors of this paradigm were several earlier reforms being heard again recently in the context of the "at risk" debate, including alternative schools, freedom or progressive schools, bilingual or bidialectal instruction, multicultural education, performance-contract systems, open schools, non-graded primary schools, culturecentric (e.g, Afrocentric) programs, and other alternative forms of education (Laosa, 1984; Winborne, 1991).

If the responsibility is located in the schools themselves—and in the prevailing politics and policies, as well as in the day-to-day constructions of various race, class, gender, and other relations—rather than in the "victims" of poor educational practices, what kinds of different directions might our search for solutions or policies take? Rather than blaming the victims, including the struggling and caring single parents, recent immigrant and refugee families, and children living in poverty, how can we make the very system which too often contributes to these problems more accountable and more responsive to the needs of such challenged and often marginalized individuals and families? A few brief examples follow.

The Chicago City Schools have been struggling with school reform that, since the fall of 1989, places parents and communities in an unprecedented leadership role through locally elected Local School Councils (LSCs), governed largely by parents. In a publication documenting local impact of the reform efforts, *Catalyst: Voices of Chicago School Reform*, highlights from diaries of parents elected to LSCs were included. Many of the themes dealt with the disrespect which African American and language-minority parents had experienced from teachers and administrators and with their intentions to make a difference for their communities and particularly their children. Although a number of frustrations were aired in these parents' journals, several parents spoke with confidence and pride.

> We parents are now full-fledged decision makers at our schools. This does not make a lot of people happy. Some teachers, some staff, and the principal did not want to see inexperienced, uneducated parents give them advice on how to educate our children. My plea to most is: We are educated, smart, talented, and energetic. Our experience is our children. We know best what their needs are because we love them, we raised them, and we care for them from day to day. (*Catalyst*, 1990, p. 30)

Another integrally related question concerns how children, and parents who hold membership in one or more "high risk" groups feel about being increasingly visible bearers of the "at risk" label. As Tyack (1989) states, "labels are not neutral; they contain assumptions about the problem and the remedy." Being labeled "at risk" is certainly not neutral and must be weighed carefully for its relative potential for possible and needed assistance or intervention and its potential for damage, disempowerment, or further marginalization.

It would be naive to assume that children are unaware of having this label applied to themselves or their family and community. Much like the image of "broken home," the connotations of being "at risk" are many and do not contribute to the healthy self esteem and sense of cultural identity called for, ironically, by many reports on "at risk" children. I have talked with children in urban schools who are painfully aware of their participation in special programs for "at risk kids," including programs which are labeled, as such, by signs on the door of the room where they get special services! "At risk" has become an increasingly loosely used label. The rush to a diagnosis and the related, ever changing prescriptions, may indeed be putting our young "patients" at far greater risk in life by often less than subtle messages that such children are not sufficient, have a high likelihood of academic and personal failure, and have questionable or even damaging families.

The race and class bias, blaming, and "othering" in many contemporary intervention programs targeted at "at risk" children and families are evident. Examples include Wisconsin's "Learnfare" program, which has also been proposed and enacted in other states, in which families' welfare payments are cut in direct proportion to the number of unexcused absences of their child(ren). More recently, Wisconsin has also implemented "Bridefare," in which mothers receiving AFDC benefits are "rewarded" for marrying the father of their child(ren). In West Virginia and Indiana, a driver's license penalty program has been enacted, in which youth under eighteen years of age lose their driver's license if they drop out of school. It would not be illogical to argue that such programs for "at risk" youth serve to put not only these young people, but their families, at even greater financial and emotional risk and serve to reinforce the stigma and marginalization of being part of the "underclass." With welfare reform being once again on the national agenda, themes such as "Two years and you're out" are also reflected in proposed policies, further reflecting the "othering" evident in many state public assistance policies and limitations.

The racism, classism, and sexism implicit in these and other such programs for people living in poverty and their children are evident. Such programs and welfare reform initiatives put family life under surveillance, use threats and punishment for non-compliance, and promote the conviction that "poverty is a private affair," best understood within a "politics of conduct" (Polakow, October, 1993). In recent testimony before Congress, Valerie Polakow (October, 1993) put it this way:

> This public discourse of Otherness currently promotes a view of welfare reform that puts them back to work, forces them to take family responsibility, and develop economic self sufficiency. Yet there is no state accountability in such policies which coerce women to work or do service; for the state provides only the barest minimum of support services to assist women who are forced to adhere to such require-

ments. Obey or be cut! The bitter and desperate lives . . . created out of such welfare reform policies—from Workfare, Learnfare, Bridefare, Healthfare, and the Social Contract— contribute to the *unmaking*, not the making, of a viable family. (p. 1)

As a mother of children in a Chicago school stated (in *Catalyst*, 1990), "I've always felt if teachers disrespect the parents, do not like the parents, then how are they able to teach the children?" (p. 30). Other parents' journals reflected the lack of respect shown to children and the related assumptions made by teachers and other staff about their home life. One mother and Local School Council member describes a teacher who "treated parents with disrespect at first, and then with a kind of cynical dishonesty. Actually, this teacher's treatment of parents was the least of his disrespect. He did not read the readings, gave inaccurate tests and was weeks late in assigning term papers" (p. 36). A Chicago school counselor put it this way: "Half the kids have horrendous home problems, the least of which may be divorce"; and an LSC member summed it up by saying, "If our school fails I wonder if there is hope anywhere. We have so much going for us, and yet the problems loom large" (p. 30).

These brief quotes from Chicago parents illustrate not only some of the concerns that parents have, but also reflect the vision that sustains their struggles to maintain an "at promise" view of children surrounded by tough realities of neighborhood and family. Yet, as I have suggested elsewhere (Swadener & Niles, 1991), a vision of what "could be"—of children and families "at promise"—is at the heart of empowering teachers and policy-makers to acknowledge, understand, and confront the severe problems faced by many U.S. families.

QUESTIONS, DILEMMAS, AND POSSIBILITIES FOR RECONSTRUCTING THE DISCOURSE OF RISK

Ultimately, we cannot afford to look for either vindication or validation that comes from outside us. We must rebuild our communities, but first we must rebuild our minds.
    —*Bebe Moore Campbell, 1993*

Perhaps one of the best ways to consider parent and community perspectives on the "at risk" debate and related issues is through an inquiry grounded in several questions which are left intentionally open ended to encourage reflection. In keeping with a vision for creating more democratic classrooms and practices, each question is followed by a "what if" inquiry (Swadener, 1990; Swadener & Niles, 1991). This section will pose questions and point directions for policy in the following areas: (1) family and community perceptions and involvement, including issues of class and privilege, and (2) curriculum and school climate implications.

Family and Community Issues

One of the strongest themes in the literature on successful parent involvement and empowerment is the notion of *success for all* which includes the assumption that all children can learn and achieve school success (Davies, 1991). Davies suggests that no child should be labeled as a likely failure due to economic, social, or racial characteristics of family or community. What might the full implementation of such an "at promise" view of children entail?

What messages are we sending parents—particularly low income parents, single parents, and dual-career working parents? What do labels such as "at risk" communicate to families? Many programs are labeled "at risk" or for "troubled youth," further stigmatizing children and families. What if we replaced "at risk" with "at promise" and provided enrichment programs and special activities and opportunities similar to those frequently advocated for "gifted" children?

How can we involve parents in non-trivial decision making and in more powerful roles in their children's education? What about parents who have strong negative feelings about schools and dominant power relations, who speak limited English, who do not want holidays celebrated in public schools, or who tell us they do not care? What if educators conveyed an "at promise" vision with parents and caregivers and involved them in seeking needed change?

To what degree are we, as educators and community members, discussing some of the issues facing so-called "functional" or "traditional" families, including the loneliness or "affluenza" that many economically privileged children bring with them to school (Edelman, 1991), or the confusion and alienation that many children who have multiple caregivers and frequently changing child care arrangements grow up with? Of similar concern are the "hurried children" (e.g., Elkind, 1983), who have been described as suffering from the neglect of affluence. While deconstructing the rhetoric of risk, it is equally important to interrogate the "master script" (Lorde, 1984) assumption of superior experience and knowledge gained by White children in suburban schools (Arnold & Swadener, 1993). "Affluenza's" damaging effects on children of privilege include neglect (e.g., lack of time with parents or extended family, fragmented activities, and hurried lives), an overabundance of material wealth, encouraging accumulation, with self-worth becoming overidentified with materialism, adding to the pressure on affluent youth to measure up, score well on tests, and perform competitively both inside and outside of school.

In her book *When the Bough Breaks*, Sylvia Ann Hewlett (1991) cited a study of five thousand eighth graders in California that concluded it was the affluent children who spent the largest amount of time on their own, apparently because their parents' careers were so time-consuming. Do we recognize the signs of such hurried, yet often lonely, children and understand some of the pressures on young children to grow up quickly, perhaps even being denied a childhood? What if we really care about—in fact love—all the children in our schools? How might this cause us to reconsider our definition of "risk" and our construction of the likelihood of failure?

Many "parent empowerment" programs, as part of school reform and site-based management initiatives, assume that schools are waiting for what parents have to give them and that parents will be candid and confident in their relations and communication with schools (Swadener & Niles, 1991). How valid and realistic are these assumptions? What assumptions do teachers make about parents' relationships with schools and teachers? What if we turned schools over to parents or at least involved them in more substantive and less superficial ways? What if schools were opened up for more uses in the community and for more hours of the day and months of the year?

What are some of the difficulties associated with parent "training" initiatives, which often emphasize making homes more like schools and parent-child interactions more structured and academically oriented or more "school-like"? How might schools be made more "home-like" and the home and community cultural patterns better reflected in classrooms—particularly in the early years of schooling?

Are teachers, caregivers, and other stakeholders aware of the growing information on differences between working-class and upper-middle-class families, in terms of different views of parent involvement, the importance of grades, or the roles of parents in their children's education (e.g., as described in Annette Lareau's (1989) book *Home Advantage* or Mara Sapon-Shevin's (1994) book *Playing Favorites*)? What if more alternative schools, within school districts and communities, were available so that parents could have an equitable choice in curriculum and educational environment? (This should not, however, be interpreted as an argument for vouchers or the rapidly growing privatization movement in U.S. education.)

School Climate and Curriculum Issues

What if current graded, competitive, and increasingly test-driven and individualistic school practices were replaced by non-graded nurturant environments, where children were taught by the same teacher, pending mutual agreement, for several years and where standardized tests were banned in the primary years? Much attention has been given, for example, in school-based reform efforts and related literature, to the detracking of curriculum and the use of portfolio/performance-based assessments and more parent—and student—involvement in setting individual student goals.

What if we devoted the same energy we are now devoting to finding better identification and early interventions for "at risk" children to changing curricula and teaching practices to those which are more culturally sensitive, inclusive, and relevant to all children? What kinds of family literacy, across different income and cultural groups, have been particularly successful (e.g., Delgado-Gaitan, 1990; Taylor & Dorsey-Gaines, 1988)? Do teachers realize the variety of ways in which children learn literacy skills, even in the poorest families? How can we build on these strengths and provide the types of support that parents and children will truly find empowering? How can we better listen to—and *hear*—families we now label as "at risk"?

How can we provide more culturally inclusive and responsive learning environments, curricula, and practices in our classrooms, teacher preparation programs, and parent involvement activities?

How might we be contributing to the miseducation or even "educational and assessment abuse" (Taylor, 1991) of some children? What if teachers and teacher educators were required to show evidence of multicultural literacy and sensitivity in addition to the mastery of "general knowledge" drawn primarily from Eurocentric, masculinist traditions? What if those of us who are monolingual were considered "at risk" in a multilingual nation and world?

Are labor issues and history, particularly as they relate to current unemployment and race and gender equity issues, part of our social studies curriculum? How could family or neighborhood oral histories bring these issues alive for young people? What if community and global struggles for social change became the heart of the social studies curriculum?

What if traditionally oppressed groups, who are indeed the global majority or "first world" and are soon to be the majority in the United States, defined, boycotted, and eventually declared a moratorium on the "at risk" label as a bankrupt construct which perpetuates a deficit and racist model and a caste system in U.S. schools and communities? How might the "at promise" metaphor help us create a more just reality?

CONCLUSION: POSSIBILITIES FOR VIEWING CHILDREN AND FAMILIES "AT PROMISE"

[The birth of my daughter] revealed to me the
need to see the past as connected to the future.
The story had to show hope, as well as the
promise that tradition and family and life
would always sustain us, even in the middle of
dramatic change.
                                        —Julie Dash, 1992

The preceding series of "what if" questions is intended to provide the basis for the alternative perspectives discussed in this concluding section of the chapter, as well as in other chapters in this volume. A point worth addressing first, however, is the issue of whether the term "at risk" is ever justified or serves children and families. This, after all, is what all of these other theoretical, semantic, and cultural arguments boil down to. Will changing or modifying terminology alter praxis or remove the threatening and damaging life circumstances often experienced by children? How does this construct help or hinder children's possibilities for fulfilling their potential, developing positive self-esteem, identity, and cultural pride, and what sorts of pain and failure may it prevent? Much as Shirley Kessler (1990, 1991) argues for reconceptualizing early childhood education beyond child development and "developmentally appropriate practice" to an ethic of caring, combined with education for democracy, I would argue for creating such a context of *caring* for children and families—a caring which transcends labels and prejudgments embodied in terms such as "at risk." I feel this must be coupled with authentic respect for cultural, linguistic, gender, class, and other aspects of human diversity. As deceptively simple as it may seem, we need to treat all children like human beings, without "at risk," "doomed to fail," or other adjectives or qualifiers—limiters—added. "Human beings at promise," needing our care, confidence, and faith: This may indeed be the only way to begin to transform a "nation at risk" to a future generation "at promise."

Perhaps the time has finally come to move beyond the dominant culture assumptions and deficit-model thinking that have so separated students and educators alike, particularly as they create barriers to building the sort of culturally inclusive alliances which authentic change will require. Such alliances for children can begin to transcend the internalized oppression which is a major byproduct of the deficiency model embodied in the construct "children and families at risk."

Noted writer and Holocaust survivor Elie Wiesel (1989) discussed the ethics of caring in the following way:

> In a moral society, people listen to each other and care about the other person. No person may be sacrificed for any goal. . . . A primary difference between an immoral society and a moral society is that in an immoral society, people don't listen. [They] know everything, know the question, know the answer to the question. Cliches are used. But in a moral society, there is a sense of wonder at the presence of someone else. I am free because other people are free. No cliches are used. . . . (p. 3)

The notion of children and families being "at risk" has indeed become a cliche in a number of professional and public discourses, just as it is in Michelle Fine's (1988) description of "at risk" as "kitsch." We do children, families, and entire groups of people a disservice in our persistent overuse and trivialization of this construct.

By suggesting an alternative "at promise" view, I have attempted to convey the importance of considering the possibilities in *all* children and the promise of partnerships with parents and community members of diverse backgrounds. This view locates outside the family many of the problems faced by children and families so that attention can be focused on the larger contexts within which families struggle and change must occur (Swadener & Niles, 1991). By viewing parents and children as "at promise," we enhance the possibilities of constructing authentic relations where we actively *listen* to and learn from one another.

Given the challenges of facing racism, classism, sexism, and other forms of oppression in education, including the policy, curricular, and teacher development work that must be done to fight such underlying sources of miseducation and disempowerment, it seems rather fruitless to spend so much time, energy, money, and intellectual leadership in developing clearer, and ever more inclusive, identification procedures for determining who should be considered "at risk." Viewing *all* children as facing great challenges and yet "at promise," and doing the hard curricular, structural, personal, and relational work required, can move us beyond the persistent deficit model and closer to the realization of a caring community for young people and their families. Such reconceptualization is a critical first step toward the transformative changes in praxis and policy necessary to facilitate the promise of *all* children.

REFERENCES

Arnold, M. S. & Swadener, B. B. (1993). *Savage inequalities* and the discourse of risk: What of the white children who have so much green grass? *The Review of Education, 15,* 261–272.

Blackwell, P., Buell, M. J., & Burns, M. S. (1991, October). *Cocaine-exposed children: The bio-underclass?* Paper presented at the Reconceptualizing Research in Early Childhood Education Conference, Madison, Wisconsin.

Bloch, M. N. (1987). Becoming scientific and professional: An historical perspective on the aims and effects of early education. In T. S. Popkowitz (Ed.), *The formation of the school subjects.* (pp. 25–62) Basingstoke, England: Falmer Press.

Bloch, M. N. (1991). Critical science and the history of child development's influence on early education research. *Early Education and Development, 2*(2), 95–108.

Bremmer, R. H., Ed. (1974). *Children and youth in America: A documentary history. Vol. 2: 1866–1932.* Cambridge, MA: Harvard University Press.

Burchell, G., Gordon, C. & Miller, P. (Eds.). *The Foucault effect: Studies in governmentality.* Chicago: University of Chicago Press.

Castell, R. (1991). From dangerousness to risk. In G. Burchell, C. Gordon, & P. Miller (Eds.). *The Foucault effect: Studies in governmentality.* (pp. 281–298). Chicago: University of Chicago Press.

Caldwell, B. M. (1974). A decade of early intervention programs: What have we learned. *American Journal of Orthopsychiatry, 44*(4), 491–496.

Campbell, B. M. (1993). Black must be beautiful again. In H. R. Madhubuti (Ed.), *Why L.A. happened: Implications of the '92 Los Angeles Rebellion* (pp. 259–264). Chicago: Third World Press.

Cardenas, B., & Cardenas, J. A. (1977). *The theory of incompatibilities: A conceptual framework for responding to the educational needs of Mexican American children.* San Antonio, TX: Intercultural Developmental Research Association.

Catalyst: Voices of Chicago School Reform. (1990). Chicago school reform: A beginning. Vol. 1(1), February. Chicago, IL: Community Renewal Society.

Coles, R. (1989, September). *The moral lives of children.* Keynote address for lecture series on Human Values and Contemporary Ethical Issues, Kent State University.

Council of Chief State School Officers (1988, November). *A guide for state action: Early childhood and family education.* Washington, D.C. Council of Chief State School Officers.

Cravens, H. (1993). Child saving in modern America 1870s-1990s. In R. Wollons (Ed.), *Children at risk in America: History. concepts. and public policy* (pp. 3–31). Albany, NY: State University of New York Press.

Cuban, L. (1989). The "at risk" label and the problem of urban school reform. *Phi Delta Kappan, 70,* 780–801.

Dash, J. (1992). *Daughters of the dust: The making of an African American woman's film.* New York: The New Press.

Davies, D. (1991). Schools reaching out: Family, school and community partnerships for student success. *Phi Delta Kappan, 72*(5), 376–382.

Defert, D. (1991). "Popular life" and insurance technology. In G. Burchell, C. Gordon, & P. Miller (Eds.). *The Foucault effect: Studies in governmentality.* (pp. 211–234). Chicago: University of Chicago Press.

Delgato-Gaitan, C. (1990). *Literacy for empowerment: The role of parents in children's education.* London: Falmer Press.

Delgato-Gaitan, C. (1993). Researching change and changing the researcher. *Harvard Educational Review, 63*(4), 389–411.

Delgado-Gaitan, C., & Trueba, H. (1991). *Crossing cultural borders: Education for immigrant families in America.* London: Falmer Press.

Delpit, L. D. (1986). Skills and other dilemmas of a progressive Black educator. *Harvard Educational Review, 56*(4), 379–385.

Delpit, L. D. (1988). The silenced dialogue: Power and pedagogy in educating other people's children. *Harvard Educational Review, 58*(3), 280–298.

DuBois, W. E. B. (1903). *The souls of Black folks.* Quoted in West, C. (1993). *Race matters.* Boston: Beacon.

Edelman, M.W. (1987). *Families in peril: An agenda for social change.* Cambridge, MA: Harvard University Press.

Edelman, M.W. (1990, March). *SOS America! A moment of opportunity and danger.* Presentation to the annual conference of Children's Defense Fund, Washington, D.C.

Edelman, M. W. (1991, May/June). Kids first! *Mother Jones,* p. 32.

Edmonds, R. (1979). Some schools work and more can. *Social Policy, 9*(5), 28–32.

Elkind, D. (1983, July). The curriculum disabled child. *Topics in Learning and Learning Disabilities,* 71–78.

Ellsworth, E. (1989). Why doesn't this feel empowering? Working through the repressive myths of critical pedagogy. *Harvard Educational Review, 59,* 297–324.

Ewald, F. (1991). Insurance and risk. In G. Burchell, C. Gordon, & P. Miller (eds.). *The Foucault Effect: Studies in governmentality.* (pp. 197–210). Chicago: University of Chicago Press.

Fine, M. (1988, September). Of kitsch and caring: The illusion of students at risk. *The School Administrator,* 16–23.

Fine, M. (1990). Making controversy: Who's "at risk"? *Journal of Cultural Studies 1*(1), 55–68.

Fine, M. (1993). A diary on privatization and on public possibilities. *Educational Theory, 43*(1), 33–39.

Foster, M. (1989, March) *Effective teaching practices for differing learner contexts: Illustrative cases.* Paper presented at the annual meeting of the American Educational Research Association, San Francisco.

Frymier, J., & Gansneder, B. (1989). The Phi Delta Kappa study of students at risk. *Phi Delta Kappan, 71*(2).

Graue, M. E. (1992). Meanings of readiness and the kindergarten experience. In S. Kessler & B. B. Swadener (Eds.) *Reconceptualizing the early childhood curriculum: Beginning the dialogue* (pp. 62–90). New York: Teachers College Press.

Greene, M. (1986). In search of a critical pedagogy. *Harvard Educational Review, 56,* 427–441.

Grotberg, E. H. (Ed.). (1976). *200 years of children.* (DHEW Publication No. OHD–77–30103). Washington, D.C.: Government Printing Office.

Hale-Benson J. E. (1986). *Black children: Their roots, culture and learning styles* (rev. ed.). Baltimore, MD: Johns Hopkins University Press.

Heath, S. B. (1983). *Ways with words: Language, life and work in communities and classrooms.* Cambridge: Cambridge University Press.

Hewlett, S. A. (1991). *When the bough breaks: The cost of neglecting our children.* New York: HarperCollins.

hooks, b. (1992). *Black looks: Race and representation.* Boston: South End Press.

Kagan, S. (1989). The care and education of America's young children: At the brink of a paradigm shift? In F. J. Macciarola & A. Gartner (Eds.), *Caring for America's Children.* New York: The Academy of Political Science.

Kessler, S. A. (1990, April). *Reconceptualizing early childhood education.* Paper presented at the annual meeting of the American Educational Research Association, Boston.

Kessler, S. A. (1991). Early childhood education as development: Critique of the metaphor. *Early Education and Development, 2*(2), 137–152.

Kliebard, H. (1986). *The struggle for the American curriculum.* London: Routledge and Kegan Paul.

Kotlowitz, A. (1991). *There are no children here: The story of two boys growing up in the other America.* New York: Doubleday.

Kozol, J. (1991). *Savage inequalities: Children in America's schools.* New York: Crown Publishers.

Laosa, L. (1984). Social policies toward children of diverse ethnic, racial, and language groups in the United States. In H. W. Stevenson & A. E. Siegel (Eds.), *Child development and social policy* (pp. 1–109). Chicago: University of Chicago Press.

Lareau, A. (1989). *Home advantage: Social class and parental involvement in elementary education.* London: Falmer Press.

Lather, P. (1991). *Getting smart: Feminist research and pedagogy with/in the post modern.* New York: Routledge.

Leifield, L. (1992). Personal communication.

Levin, H. (1989). Financing the education of at-risk students. *Education Evaluation and Policy Analysis, 11,* 47–60.

Lightfoot, D. (1993). *"Where are the kids?": A look at Proyecto Motivacion.* Unpublished paper. University of Wisconsin-Madison.

Lorde, A. (1984). The master's tools will never dismantle the master's house. In *Sister outsider* (pp. 110–113). Freedom, CA: The Crossing Press.

Lubeck, S. (1985). *Sandbox society: Early schooling in black and white America.* New York: Falmer Press.

Lubeck, S. (1988). Nested contexts. In L. Weis (Ed.), *Class, race and gender in American education* (pp. 43–62). Albany: State University of New York Press.

Lubeck, S., & Garrett, P. (1990). The social construction of the "at-risk" child. *British Journal of Sociology of Education, 11*(3), 327–340.

Martin, T. (1993). From slavery to Rodney King: Continuity and change. In H. R. Madhubuti (Ed.), *Why LA. happened: Implications of the '92 Los Angeles rebellion* (pp. 27–40). Chicago: Third World Press.

Moraga, C. (1981). La Güera. In C. Moraga & G. Anzaldua (Eds.),*This bridge called my back: Writings by radical women of color* (pp. 27–34). Watertown, MA: Persephone Press.

Moss, B. (1992). *School desegregation: Enough is enough.* Columbus, Ohio: Danmo Publishing Company.

Noddings, N. (1984). *Caring: A feminine approach to ethics and moral education.* Berkeley, CA: University of California Press.

Ogbu, J. (1978). *Minority education and caste.* New York, NY: Academy Press.

Page, R., & Valli, L. (1990). Curriculum differentiation: An introduction. In R. Page & L. Valli (Eds.), *Curriculum differentiation* (pp. 1–15). Albany, NY: State University of New York Press.

Pellicano, R. R. (1987). At risk: A view of "social advantage." *Educational Leadership, 44*(6), 47–49.

Placier, M. L. (1993). The semantics of state policy making: The case of "at risk." *Educational Evaluation and Policy Analysis, 15*(4), 380–395.

Polakow, V. (1992). Deconstructing the discourse of care: Young children in the shadows of democracy. In S. Kessler & B. B. Swadener (Eds.), *Reconceptualizing the early childhood curriculum: Beginning the dialogue* (pp. 123–148). New York: Teachers College Press.

Polakow, V. (1993). *Lives on the edge: Single mothers and their children in the other America.* Chicago: University of Chicago Press.

Polakow, V. (1993, October). *Welfare reform and the assault on daily life: Targeting single mothers and their children.* Testimony given to the U.S. Congress, Women and Welfare Reform: Women's Poverty, Women's Welfare: A Policy Conference to Break Myths and Create Solutions (Chairs: Congresswomen Patsy Min, Lynn Waters, Lynn Woolsey, and Congressman Ed Pastor),Washington, D.C.

Popkewitz, T.S. (in press). Policy, knowledge and power: Some issues for the study of educational reform. In P. Cookson & B. Schneider (Eds.). *Transforming schools: Trends, dilemmas, and prospects.* NY: Garland Press.

Reed, A., Jr. (1992). The underclass as myth and symbol: The poverty of discourse about poverty. *Radical America, 24*(1), 21–40.

Reyes, M. L. & Halcon, J. J. (1988). Racism in academia: The old wolf revisited. *Harvard Educational Review, 58*(3), 299–314.

Sapon-Shevin, M. (1994). *Playing favorites: Gifted education and the disruption of community.* Albany, NY: State University of New York Press.

Sears, R. R. (1975). Your ancients revisited: A history of child development. In E. M. Hetherington (Ed.), *Review of child development research, 5,*1–73.

Simmons, R. K. (1988). *The crucial element in the development of black children: A guide for African American parents Part I.* Chicago, IL: African American Images.

Slavin, R. E. (1989, March). *Disadvantaged vs. at-risk: Does the difference matter in practice?* Paper presented at the annual meeting of the American Educational Research Association, San Francisco.

Soto, L. D. (1992). Success stories. In C.A. Grant (Ed.) pp. 153–164. *Research in multicultural education: From the margins to the mainstream.* New York: Falmer Press.

Spodek, B. (1984, April). *The past as prologue: Exploring the historic roots of present day concern in early childhood education.* Paper presented at the annual meeting of the American Educational Research Association, New Orleans.

Spodek, B. (1991). Reconceptualizing early childhood education: A commentary. *Early Education and Development, 2*(2),161–167.

Steiner, G. Y. (1976). *The children's cause.* Washington, D.C.: Brookings Institution.

Swadener, E. B. (1990). Children and families "at risk": Etiology, critique and alternative paradigms. *Educational Foundations, 4*(4),17–39.

Swadener, E. B., & Niles, K. (1991). Children and families "at promise": Making home-school-community connections. *Democracy in Education, 5*(3), 13–18.

Taylor, D. (1991). *Learning denied.* Portsmouth, NH: Heinemann Educational Books.

Taylor, D., & Dorsey-Gaines, C. (1988). *Growing up literate: Learning from inner city families.* Portsmouth, NH: Heinemann Educational Books.

Tharp, R. (1989). Psychocultural variables and constants: Effects on teaching and learning in schools. *American Psychologist, 349–359.*

Trueba, H., Jacobs, L., & Kirton, E. (1990). *Cultural conflict and adaptation: The case of Hmong children in American society.* New York: Falmer Press.

Tyack, D. (1989, March). *The mismatch between schools and students who don't fit them.* Paper presented at the annual meeting of the American Educational Research Association, San Francisco.

Walsh, D. (1987, November). *"Redshirting" in kindergarten.* Paper presented at the annual meeting of the American Anthropological Association, Chicago.

West, C. (1993). *Race matters.* Boston: Beacon Press.

Wiesel, E. (1989, April). *Building a moral society.* Lecture at the Provost's Forum, Kent State University, Kent, OH.

Wilson, B. J. & Reichmuth, M. (1984, April). *Early screening programs: When is predictive accuracy sufficient?* Paper presented at the annual meeting of the American Educational Research Association, New Orleans.

Wilson, W. J. (1987). *The truly disadvantaged: The inner city, the underclass and public policy.* Chicago: University of Chicago Press.

Winborne, D. G. (1991). Perspectives on children "at risk": Cultural considerations and alternative educational approaches, in J. J. Harris III, C. A. Heid, D. G. Carter, Sr., & F. Brown (Eds.). *Readings on the state of education in urban America.* (pp. 251–265). Bloomington, IN: Indiana University Center for Urban and Multicultural Education.

Wollons, R. (Ed.). (1993). *Children at risk in America: History, concepts, and public policy.* Albany, NY: State University of New York Press.

Woodson, C. G. (1933). *The miseducation of the Negro.* Washington, D.C.: Associated Press.

Zigler, E., & Gordon, E.W. (1982). *Daycare: Scientific and social policy issues.* Boston, MA: Auburn House.

2

Mothers at Risk

In the early 1980s a film entitled *Whatever Happened to Childhood?* won an Emmy Award. The film remains a stunning indictment of the breakdown of the American family and its residual consequences: a dramatic increase in crime, including murder, among children, the rising numbers of young adolescents having sex and involved in drugs and alcohol, and the shocking increase in the number of unwed young mothers. Children, we learn, are exposed to much more violence and sex on television; 400,000 attempt suicide each year; fully half of all American children can now expect to spend at least some time in a single-parent home. Over half the mothers of children under the age of six are working.

These "facts" certainly bear scrutiny. Yet the filmmakers never take an overt stance on the images that bombard our senses. Rather, the sequences subtly move from juvenile detention center to school to home, and it is mainly the children on the screen who interpret their import. The children tell us that parents have absolved themselves of responsibility for them, that older children have had to become parents to younger children, that no one is there anymore for the kids. From the mouths of babes, teachers, and other professionals, we learn:

• There are not any parents there to show them that there's good stuff on TV.
• No one is waiting when I get home.
• [When parents divorce] they find themselves available, single, attractive, and employable. They forget they are parents. Older children have to become the parents.
• Parents are not really concerned about what their kids are doing anymore.

The interpretation that forms the subtext in the documentary is that no one is there for children, because parents (read mothers) are too concerned about themselves. Teachers don't care. The traditional family is gone, and kids are losing hope. The conclusion, never made explicit, seems simple: Mothers have forsaken home and hearth, and so the very foundation of society has been undermined. Only if the family is reinstated and mothers stay home and care for children once again will the pernicious consequences of their absence be remedied.

Upon reflection, it becomes evident that much of the power of the film rests in its exclusions. Mothers themselves are noticeably absent. Following a lengthy segment that depicts two preschool-age children sitting on a couch, flipping through stations on the remote control until they, grinning, come across what is obviously an "adult" film, we hear their young mother speak vaguely about the increase in sex and violence on television. A second mother is fifteen, the parent of an infant she had carried too long to abort. The only other mother in the documentary is helping her child—a "skinhead"—make t-shirts with the word "Anarchy" written on them. She tells us that, if her children want to do drugs, particularly hard drugs like LSD, she wants them to do so at home. The absence of other mothers underscores the film's central theme: Most mothers are no longer around.

Related to mother absence is the fact that alternative interpretations of the "facts" are neither entertained nor suggested. For the most part, mothers have no voice. It is as though *this* rendering is simply self-evident and indisputable. The camera leads us, as though by logic, to the home, and the absence of the mother there, both from the camera lens and in the minds of the children, serves as evidence that she is, indeed, gone.

This film is an example of what Lyotard (1984) has called a "metanarrative," and it is exemplary of the type of "text" that is increasingly being studied by social and political scholars concerned with ways in which the symbolic universe comes to be dominated by a particular view.[1] Specifically addressing education, Wexler (1987) argues that forms of social symbolic practice—the production of meanings that constitute both our shared and subjective realities—need themselves to become objects of study.

The notion that any rendering is a partial one and one which inevitably has political implications is beginning to revolutionize the social sciences. In the eighteenth century, Comte and other early social theorists believed that social theory could advance society. The social order was a knowable reality that could be discerned, truth could be revealed, and solutions to society's problems could be "discovered." Where "modernists" (postpositivists, critical theorists, etc.) later sought frameworks that would provide alternatives to positivism, "postmodernists" have mounted a still more pointed critique by questioning the very existence of frameworks or "structures" that are timeless and universal. The reality we share is one that is historically and temporally situated.

Social science, far from being a rational and linear process pulling us ever closer to consensus, has instead become ever more fragmented. The various explanatory frameworks that have arisen have come to be viewed instead as discourses that represent alternative *constructions* of reality, constructions that privilege the interests of some and marginalize those of others. For an increasing number of social theorists, a universalist, acontextual, and value-free science is no longer tenable.

In a recent testament to the "incredulity of metanarratives," Polakow (1993) describes a reality quite different from the one depicted in *Whatever Happened to Childhood?* After first demonstrating that the myth of domesticity represents a recent and delimited state at best, Polakow deconstructs myths of childhood and of the family and enables the voices of young single mothers to be heard. Especially significant is her portrayal of sexist, classist, and/or racist beliefs and practices that have confined single mothers and their children to a "zone of deviance and moral suspicion" (p. 5). Polakow's mothers describe what it is like to have little choice about giving birth at a young age; what it is like to be homeless with children, to lose benefits because your job earns a few dollars over the maximum allowed; what it is like to have a sick child when you have no insurance and cannot afford to see a doctor; what it is like to have no way to improve your situation, because every avenue is blocked. She aptly names the stories of these mothers "narratives of endurance and survival" (p. 41).

For Polakow, the problem is not one of individual indifference or failure but rather of political economy, of restrained and ineffectual public policy. Her book provides a forum in which single mothers describe the frustrations and limitations of their lives "on the edge," the constant struggle to provide for their children in a country in which fathers are not made accountable and public policy is aimed at minimizing costs and assigning blame.

This chapter argues likewise that it is mothers who are "at risk," for increasing numbers are in extreme economic and social circumstances that make it unlikely that they will be able to care for children in ways that have been mythologized to be normal and optimal. Pitted against enormous odds, and despite often heroic efforts, many women simply have too much responsibility and too few resources. In the first section, crucial elements of the current crisis facing young families and their children are explored. In the second, recent statistics—the "facts"—on the "at risk" status of mothers and children are examined. Specifically, I examine key factors that are believed to have ill effects for children.

In the third section, I look at how these facts are being constructed and interpreted within contemporary political discourse by describing assumptions or themes that have guided the two major policy agendas in the United States—conservative and progressive/liberal. The conservative agenda, and especially the ideology of the New Right, is shown to inevitably result in maternal culpability, while the progressive policy agenda has been an effort to redefine the problem as one of institutional, rather than individual, failure. While progressives do attempt to tinker with or alter the existing system, however, both the magnitude and severity of the current crisis suggest that what is needed is a much more fundamental questioning and reframing of the basic ideological premises and institutional structures that constitute society. It is this topic that shapes the final discussion

THE CRISIS

In professional and policy circles, children and families "at risk" have become topics of increasing concern. Twenty-five percent of American children have been classified as "disadvantaged," with this proportion expected to rise over the next several decades (Pallas, Natriello, & McDill, 1989). One-third of school-age children is currently "at risk" for school failure (Levin, 1989).[2] Increasingly, the "at risk" status of children has become a rallying cry for a variety of educational reforms, including school restructuring (e.g., Cuban, 1989) and expansion (e.g., Council of Chief State School Officers, 1988; NCDPI, 1988).

States define risk status according to a number of indices (Morado, 1989). In some, preschool children are considered to be at risk for educational failure if they are from low-income families. In others, children with limited English proficiency, readiness deficiencies, or combinations of characteristics are identified. The state of Michigan, for example, lists more than two dozen variables thought to indicate risk status. These include family income, single-parent family, migrant work, and evidence of abuse or neglect.

In general, the "at risk" label alleges that a child suffers some environmentally induced deficiency. It stands in contrast to a "disability," which indicates a genetic or biological cause. In both cases, however, by implication or design, mothers are presumed to be the *source* of the problems children experience. If a child does not fare well, emotionally, socially, or academically, it is the family—but the mother specifically—who is implicated. If a child is born out of wedlock, born to a teenage mother, lives in a female-headed household, or is welfare dependent, it is presumed to be the mother's fault. On the "master list" of empirical indicators of pathology, Reed (1992) argues, "most—four of Wilson's [*The Truly Disadvantaged* (1987)] six, for example—are observable only in women" (p. 36). Alternatively, a mother can damage her child by failing to get adequate prenatal care or by passing on defective genes. The mother either has not provided the child with a positive home environment, or she has induced some biological deficiency. The presumption is ubiquitous. Grubb and Lazerson (1982) declare that "parental incompetence has been blamed for every imaginable social problem: poverty, juvenile delinquency, poor school performance, child abuse, moral failure, and the decline of Western civilization" (p. 222).

Much of the criticism of mothers, however, is muted. In this era of political correctness, it has become fashionable to allude to problems or to rename them. In a statewide survey of school superintendents and principals, for example, administrators associated the "at risk" status of children with poverty, minority status, single parenting, and maternal employment (Lubeck & Garrett,

1989, 1990).[3] They made reference to the cause of problems, however, largely through innuendo:

> We have large numbers of children who come from homes with no emphasis on education. . . . Large numbers of youngsters come into school with absolutely no background, either academic or social. . . .Many of our five-year-olds come to kindergarten with minimal experiences and marginal skills, partially due to poor parenting skills. Many parents are "drop-outs" and lack the know-how and ability to provide quality preschool experiences for their child [sic]. . . . Many of our homes do not offer children the support needed to develop emotionally, socially, and academically. (Lubeck & Garrett, 1990, pp. 336–337)

When problems were construed in this way, it was usually argued that school personnel should come to the rescue:

> Many children are not ready for kindergarten. With so many working parents, I think three- and four-year-old programs are the answer to many school problems. . . . As usual, the schools must take up the slack because no one else can or will. . . . To break the chain of illiteracy and poverty, a parent education component should be a requirement. . . . The sooner we get them the better. (pp. 336–337)

In these examples, mothers are not attacked directly but rather through reference to the poor home environments they provide or to their children's "minimal experiences and marginal skills" (p. 336).

Good mothering is considered to be a critical determinant of children's normal development in our society, yet mothers have not played such a pivotal role in children's lives historically—nor do they do so today in many societies after the first two (breast-feeding) years. Scholars have noted that the family as a nuclear unit did not exist two centuries ago. It has been argued that it was capitalism that divided society into the public (male, productive) and private (female, reproductive) spheres (Zaretsky, 1973).[4] Men were to provide economic support, while women would meet the social and emotional needs of husband and children.

The domestic role of the mother became increasingly psychologized after the Industrial Revolution, when women's self-definition and children's well-being came to be intimately linked. As

Chodorow (1978) writes, "our language, science, and popular culture all make it very difficult to separate the need for care from the question of who provides that care" (pp. 35–36). She sees the role of the mother to be culturally mediated rather that biologically determined. The notion that mothers are crucial to their children's welfare is one that is historically situated and has psychological, social, political, and economic ramifications.

> Women's mothering is central to the sexual division of labor. Women's maternal role has profound effects on women's lives, on ideology about women, on the reproduction of masculinity and sexual inequality, and on the reproduction of particular forms of labor power. Women as mothers are pivotal actors in the sphere of social reproduction. (p. 11)

Thus, for many women, mothering defines one's conception of self, one's role in relation to others, and one's "place" in the social order; as such, it can be a source of satisfaction, of inequity, and of oppression.

By unraveling the presumptions behind many educational reform initiatives and policy guidelines or the circumlocution of school principals and superintendents, the largely Western middle-class myth of domesticity is unveiled. In this rendering, society is grounded in the nuclear unit; family comprises a working father, a nurturing mother, and their progeny. The mother must keep the father involved and interested in the family and ensure that her children develop physically, socially, emotionally, morally. If society is now falling apart, the social dissolution can be explained by the intractable and willful behavior of women who have put their own interests before those of others: women who have children at too young an age, women who have children out of wedlock, women who divorce, women who raise children alone, women who work, women who need welfare to get by. In this seamless construction, many of society's ills narrow to one source—the individual who does not do her duty and who thus must be vilified.

RISK FACTORS

In both the popular press and professional journals, several factors are seen to contribute to the "at risk" status of children, including poverty, single parenting, racial/ethnic group identity, and maternal employment.[5] Their significance is highlighted in recent reports:

- By 1991 more than one in five American children (21.8 percent)—including nearly one in four children younger than six—was poor. The total number of poor children reached 14.3 million, 4.0 million more than than in 1979. (Children's Defense Fund, 1992, p. 25)
- Over the last decade, the percent of children living in single-parent families has increased from 21.3 to 24.1 percent. In 1990, almost 13 million children, 2 million more children than in 1980, lived in these primarily female-headed families. (*Kids Count Data Book*, 1992, p. 12)
- 31 percent of *all* children under six in 1989 were minorities. However, 59 percent of *poor* children were minorities. (National Center for Children in Poverty, 1992, p. 2)
- Today, approximately 10.9 million children under age six, including 1.7 million babies under one year and 9.2 million toddlers and preschoolers, have mothers in the paid labor force. (National Commission on Children, 1991a, pp. 21–22)

Poverty. Increasingly, society's wealth is being concentrated in older Americans and in childless families, the so-called DINKS (Double Income, No Kids), while those families with children have experienced what has been described as "staggering declines in . . . annual earnings . . . between 1973 and 1990" (Children's Defense Fund & Northeastern University, 1992). Nelson (1992) maintains that "Families today have fewer resources to provide for their children, less time to devote to their nurturing, fewer informal supports and more anxiety about their children's futures" (p. 4). Recent survey results echo this contention. The vast majority (88 percent of parents who participated in a National Commission on Children (1991b) survey expressed their conviction that it is far more difficult to be a parent today than formerly. Eighty-seven percent said they had difficulty making ends meet, while 81 percent believed that parents and children no longer spend enough time together (p. 9). For parents in poverty these general stressors can be magnified.

One American in seven was reported to live below the poverty line in 1989. Children constitute the largest group of those in poverty because economic, political, and social changes are disproportionately affecting young families (Edelman, 1989). The crux of the dilemma has been described in an update of a publication aptly entitled *Vanishing Dreams* (Children's Defense Fund & Northeastern University, 1992):

> The current generation of young adults is no less educated, motivated, or responsible in most areas of life than its predecessors. As a group, they are more likely to complete high school, enroll in college, delay childbearing, and prepare for their futures than the generations before them. But in fundamental ways, the rules of the game have changed. Young Americans now are less able to build an early foundation for their own economic security, form stable families, provide adequate support for their children, or have hope and confidence in the future. In the process, they as a group increasingly are falling further behind older Americans. (p. 1)

The report examines data from the U.S. Bureau of the Census and the Bureau of Labor Statistics to document this trend. Young families, defined as those whose head is younger than thirty, are considered to be the "crucible" of the next generation, for most American children are born into such families. The report's key findings reflect how many have been adversely affected by recent change:

- After adjusting for inflation, the median income of young families with children plunged by nearly one-third—32 percent—between 1973 and 1990.
- These income losses have affected virtually every group of young families with children: white, Black, and Latino; married-couple and single-parent; and those headed by high school graduates as well as dropouts.
- As a result of these income losses, the poverty rate for children in young families doubled—from 20 percent in 1973 to a shocking 40 percent in 1990.
- . . . the child poverty rates for young Black families (68 percent), young Latino families (51 percent), young female-headed families (77 percent), and young families headed by high school dropouts (64 percent) are astronomical.
- Nearly three-fourths of the increase in the number of young families with children living in poverty has occurred outside the nation's central cities. (p. 2)

The authors of the report attribute these catastrophic consequences, not only to changes in the economy and in family composition, but also to government policies that have failed to respond
to changing conditions.

   Single Parenting. Both the number and proportion of children
living in female-headed households have increased due to divorce
and out-of-wedlock births. The U.S. divorce rate is the highest in
the world (Beller & Chung, 1991). Approximately one million children witness the divorce of their parents each year, while one child
in ten lives in the home of a relative, friend, or foster parent—or in
an institution (*Kids Count Data Book*, 1992, p. 10). Nearly one-
third of the children born in 1989 were born to single mothers,
twice the number only twenty years ago. Today fully one-fifth of
American children—nearly 13 million—lives in a single-parent
family (U.S. Bureau of the Census, 1989). It has been projected that
one-half of all American children will spend some period of time
in a female-headed household (Bumpass, 1984).

   Although the reasons for these changes are varied, the consequences for children have been devastating. Female-headed households are far more likely to be poor than other types of families
(Garfinkel & McLanahan, 1986), a phenomenon characterized as
"the feminization of poverty" (Pearce, 1978). Most two-parent
families will not experience poverty (Ellwood, 1988), yet, since the
mid- 1980s, more than 60 percent of mother-only families with
young children have been poor (Kamerman, 1985).

   Government policies have not been aimed at ameliorating
the negative social, economic. and educational consequences ema-
nating from such changes. The burden of raising children continues to be borne disproportionately by women. Many fathers do not
help to support their children, so that the poverty rate for families
not receiving child support is more than double the rate for families that do receive it.

   Many mothers are themselves disadvantaged in the work-
place because of the lower wages accorded "women's work" (for
example, see Reskin & Hartmann, 1986). One recent study argues
also that women are thrust onto welfare and frequently remain
there, not because they don't want to work, but because working
does not help to make them any better off: "The essence of the
trap," Jencks (1992) maintains, "is that, although welfare pays
badly, low-wage jobs pay even worse" (p. 225).

   Racial/Ethnic Group Identity. By the turn of the century,
fully one-third of the American population will belong to an eth-

nic, racial, or linguistic "minority" group (African American, Latino/Hispanic, Native American, Asian) (American Council on Education, 1988). Although the mean incomes of all families, with the exception of the most well off, have declined, the incomes of African American and Latino/Hispanic families have been and continue to be substantially lower than those of Whites. Edelman (1989) notes, "Nearly half of Black children, almost two-fifths of Hispanic children, and nearly one-seventh of white children in the United States are poor" (p. 23), while Sidel (1986) writes: "There is currently significant discussion about whether the phenomenon we are seeing—increasing numbers of women and children making up the ranks of the poor—is really the feminization or the 'minoritization' of poverty" (p. 22). The factors appear indeed to be confounded. Between 1959 and 1981, the number of African American children living in mother-only families more than doubled; between 1972 and 1981, the number of poor Latino children living in female-headed households doubled as well (p. 16).

Maternal Employment. In 1948, 11 percent of all women with children under the age of six were employed; in 1990, the comparable figure was 60 percent (U.S. Bureau of the Census, 1990, cited in Children's Defense Fund, 1992, Table 2.1, p. 16). Most (51 percent) mothers of infants now return to work within a year of their children's birth (U.S. Bureau of the Census, 1988). Since nearly half (47 percent) of the workforce will be women by the year 2000 (Jones, 1987), their labor force participation has become essential to the economic welfare of the nation. Nonetheless, little has been done to address the disjuncture between work and family life—and the absence of the mother from the home continues to be construed as a risk factor for children, particularly for those who are poor, minority, and/or living in single-parent homes.

POLITICAL AGENDAS

Conservative and liberal/progressive agendas have defined both the nature of social problems and their possible solution in different ways. Indeed, from their differing vantage points, not only family policy but the very nature of the risks described above have been seen to have different meanings and to warrant different responses. Steiner (1981), for example, discusses the implications of family policy for liberals and conservatives:

Family policy, in liberal circles, is understood to mean economic assistance and social services that will put a floor under family income and lead the way to self-sufficiency. There is a tendency for conservatives to read a different meaning into national programs directed to the family, a reading that equates family policy with acceptance of indolence, promiscuity, easy abortion, casual attitudes toward marriage and divorce, maternal indifference to child-rearing responsibilities. If family policy means accepting these behavior patterns, indeed facilitating them by minimizing resulting economic hardship and social stigma, conservatives want none of it. (p. 17)

The section that follows investigates themes embedded within conservative and liberal/progressive family policy agenda. The "metanarratives" of the respective discourses are then examined to clarify how the risk factors described above are interpreted. The conclusion explores the consequences and limitations of both.

The Conservative Agenda

In recent years, conservative and liberal politicians have been able to forge some degree of consensus around issues such as child care, health care, and welfare reform. For the purpose of contrasting the conservative-liberal extremes, however, the discussion below will center on the conservative "New Right."

According to the ideology of the New Right, increasing numbers of children are at risk because of the breakdown of the American family (see, for example, Bauer, 1986). The "problem" is narrowly conceived as what happens in the home—and it is, in large part, a problem attributed to women.

Several themes recur in this conservative rhetoric. First, the concept of "family values" links the welfare of children to mothers and to the roles they are able or willing to play. Mothers should marry and stay married, live in nuclear families, care for children, and refrain from working outside the home when their children are young. Conservatives emphasize the value of the traditional model of family: two parents, several children, and a division of labor in which the father is employed and the mother bears primary responsibility for home and progeny. Since the traditional nuclear family is seen to be the type of family that optimizes the development of children, other forms are neither recognized nor encouraged. Those not molded by this ideal are considered deviant and blamed for society's ills.

Second, societal problems are attributed to individual failure, that is, to individuals who refuse to work, to fathers who fail to support their wives and children, and to mothers who are inadequate or irresponsible child rearers. A third theme asserts that the primary function the family serves is the bearing and rearing of children, with the major concern the best interest of the children. It follows that responsibility for children should remain in the family. Parents, rather than the public, should be responsible for children.

From this perspective, many of the problems and risks discussed above are blamed on aberrant individual behavior. Conservatives point to the stream of immigrants, particularly to those from Europe, who for decades landed on these shores and, through struggle and sacrifice, improved their lot in life. Their success proves that America is the land of opportunity, that people who are willing to work hard can "make it." Murray (1984) mounts a yet more pointed critique, claiming that the welfare system itself has worked against the very ideals our society espouses by rewarding those who do not work and penalizing those who do.

Archconservatives believe that the lessening of the social stigma associated with bearing and rearing children outside of marriage has resulted in dramatic increases in out-of-wedlock births. Women today are less likely to remain in unhappy marriages, while increasing numbers of poor Black women will not marry men who are unable to support them or their children (Staples, 1985). Free health care, food stamps, free or low-cost housing only make it easier for women with children to make it without men—or so the rationale goes. Thus, these programs, by their very nature, would seem to contribute to the problem rather than to its solution.

In addition, changes in family structure are seen to be instrumental in causing poverty. Since women have a choice about whether or not to have a child, social policy should encourage them to make the "right" choice. Single parenting should be discouraged at all costs; if government has any role to play, it should be in providing *dis*incentives to out-of-wedlock childbearing and rearing. Single parents should not be subsidized, abortion should be outlawed, and unmarried women who become pregnant should be encouraged to put their children up for adoption.

Conservative rhetoric constructs the "other" as marginalized racial and ethnic minorities, living in ghettoized inner cities. "These people" seem to bear children without any concern for their welfare. Mothers are unschooled and may be substance abusers; fathers are absent. Recent immigrants may be poor and unable to help their children enter the mainstream of society. Thus, the conservative response is what Jencks (1992) calls the "make 'em suffer" strategy; If people suffer, unwanted behavior will not be reinforced. According to this logic, the appropriate policy response is to eliminate or seriously curtail welfare—and to restrict immigration from the Caribbean, Latin America, the Far East, and Africa, while at the same time encouraging immigration from Western Europe. Finally, public policies such as family leave and subsidized child care are seen to encourage maternal employment and foster public, rather than personal, responsibility for the welfare of children.

Liberal/Progressive

Progressives tell a different story. Table 3.1 compares recurring themes in conservative and liberal/progressive family policy agendas.

Progressives support a broad conception of family. Fewer than 10 percent of American families currently live up to the conservative ideal of a nuclear unit in which the father works and the mother remains at home with the children (Rossi, 1978). Families, therefore, must be considered in all their diversity, including, but not limited to, the nuclear model. Families have a variety of configurations: mother-only or father-only homes, grandparent(s) and grandchildren, stepfamilies, extended families. The 1990 Census estimates that nearly 30 percent of families no longer conform to the Bureau's broad definition of family as a group of people related by blood, marriage, or adoption and sharing the same household. Although there is agreement that diverse families should be supported, some liberals draw the line at accepting gay and lesbian marriages and families as legitimate.

Secondly, the vicissitudes that families are experiencing are not seen to be due so much to individual failure as to social and economic changes beyond the control of individuals. Where conservatives champion the status quo, striving to maintain the social order—and its inequities—progressives urge a more active role for government in redressing the injustices that inevitably arise within a capitalist economic system. Social policies are needed which help people to get training and find work, and safety net programs need to exist for those who are unable to earn enough to provide for their children.

Table 3.1
Recurring Themes in Family Policy Agendas

Conservative	*Liberal/Progressive*
Celebrates traditional family in which the father is breadwinner and the mother takes care of home and children	Supportive of a broader conception of family; "families," not simply "family"
Families are the building blocks of society; society's ills are attributed to the failure of individuals to fulfill their roles and responsibilities for children	The stressors families experience are not a result of forsaking conservative ideals; families are being buffeted by social and economic changes beyond their control
The primary function of the family is the bearing and rearing of children; the primary concern must be the best interest of the children	Needs of children and parents are of equal importance
Responsibility for children must remain private	More public responsibility needed

Sources: Bauer, 1986; Scanzoni, 1991; Grubb & Lazerson, 1982

Finally, there is some concern to balance the interests of children and adults (Scanzoni, 1991). The assumption that families exist *primarily* for children is questioned. People may elect not to have children or to limit family size. Scanzoni argues that the mother-child bond is not the preeminent concern; rather, all ties within the family are important. He sees "the developing child in a matrix interacting with three additional developmental realities [the developing adult, the developing adult primary relationship, and the developing child/adult relationship] that are equally significant both scientifically and practically" (p. 15 and Figure 2).

Since it follows that the greater the well-being of the adult the greater the well-being of the child, policy (and thus programs) must be aimed at simultaneously enhancing the well-being of both, not merely the children. (p. 16)

Each is inextricably linked to the others, so that neither the needs of the child nor the needs of the adults can be advanced without regard for the needs of the other.

Progressives see critical indicators of risk for children to be a call to action. Poverty destabilizes families and has adverse consequences for children. Thus, the response for the last several decades has been to support a welfare system in which the government provides poor mothers with benefits and subsidies to ensure that they have food, clothing, medical care, and shelter. Welfare was not, in itself, seen as the problem; long-term welfare dependency, however, was.

Liberals find the conservative injunction to simply "work harder" absurd. They note that available jobs are low paying, offering little opportunity for advancement. Many of the poor are children who cannot fend for themselves, and their parents often lack the education and resources necessary to maximize their opportunity. Single mothers are often caught in a no-win situation: the jobs they can get are too poorly remunerated to enable them to both pay bills and cover the high cost of child care. Lacking child care, others *cannot* work.

Currently, welfare benefits are discretionary, and there is wide variability across states in the amount of support available. Critics argue that the system is punitive and does not reinforce and reward efforts to become independent and personally responsible. Recent reforms aim to put welfare mothers back to work when their children are at ever younger ages—with child care subsidized at relatively low levels. What assistance is given has been minimal, and the method of service delivery, too often, mean-spirited.

Liberal critics have also challenged the conservative claim that welfare benefits have contributed to marital disruption. However, they too register caution that social policies should not *encourage* female-headed households (Garfinkel & McLanahan, 1986). Since most Americans do not favor extreme measures such as insisting that partners marry or put their babies up for adoption, Ellwood (1988) suggests that government has only a few levers: information, education, and moral guidance, strengthening two-parent families, giving less and expecting more from single parents, or expecting more from absent parents (pp. 75–79). He argues that the least compelling argument can be made for making life harder on single parents; the other three are where government needs to intervene. At the same time, however, he doubts that government can reverse changing patterns in family formation: "Just as there is little evidence that the government caused many of the trends, there is little to suggest that it can do much to answer them" (p. 79). Nonetheless, initiatives have included media campaigns against teenage pregnancy, expanded and improved sex education classes, efforts to maintain abortion rights, and the garnishing of wages to ensure that child support payments will be made.

Unlike the conservative depiction of the poor as largely made up of members of Black, Latino, Native American and other ethnic groups, there has been some liberal acknowledgment that the majority of the poor are White. Since members of racial, ethnic, and linguistic minority groups do encounter greater prejudice and disadvantage, however, progressives have advanced antidiscrimination policies in education and employment as efforts to ameliorate longstanding inequities.

Finally, rather than seeing women's work as an impingement on and threat to the family, liberals have been generally supportive of child care subsidies, family and medical leave, and other initiatives that promote maternal employment. Some have claimed that women's greater autonomy will have positive effects on children; ideally mothers will have greater self-esteem, and parents will share childrearing responsibilities and treat one another as equals. Although a progressive family policy agenda remains inchoate, its features have been broadly sketched and simply stated:

> As a nation, we urgently need a sustained commitment to an array of coherent family policies that are relevant to the circumstances of today's families and that are dedicated to the premise that families should be supported in meeting the needs of their children. Above all, we need to forge a new partnership between community institutions and family, and between work and family—a partnership that can enable and encourage families to succeed in their most irreplaceable functions: raising healthy, secure, and productive citizens for the future. (Nelson, 1992, pp. 4–5)

Although there has been some meeting of the minds on current policy issues at the federal level, gross distinctions between conservative and liberal policy positions remain and can be observed in only a cursory review of recent reports. The recommendations made by the Committee on Economic Development (Research and Policy Committee of the CED, 1991) are based on economic, rather than moral, reasoning. The problem—and goal— is to make children into productive citizens. The recommendations allude to parental failure, assume that individuals themselves—and volunteers (Bush's "thousand points of light")—must be responsible for improving the situation, deride "big government" and look to the state, rather than the federal government, for any assistance that might be required. No particular legislation is advocated.

By contrast, the recommendations of the progressive Children's Defense Fund (1992) mirror the conviction that society has a moral responsibility to take care of its own. The goal is "to assure that every child has a Fair Start, a Healthy Start and a Head Start" (p. 4). These recommendations depict people as victims of change and call for immediate (federal) government involvement to remedy the situation. Specific policies are suggested. A child support assurance program would aim to make absent parents financially responsible for their children but also provide a government safety net when this is not possible. A national health insurance plan and full funding of Head Start are also advocated.

Vacillating between such extremes, Congress has been able to mount only a halting response to the massive changes that are occurring in society. Public policy initiatives, in effect, have done little more than extend or alter an already inadequate and piecemeal approach.

DISCUSSION AND CONCLUSIONS

National statistics on the risk status of mothers and children are used in interpretive contexts—conservative and progressive— which define the nature of problems and their likely resolution in very different ways. Like the film *Whatever Happened to Childhood?*, these political agendas themselves tell partial stories and offer partial solutions.

In what remains one of the most probing analyses of "how Americans fail their children," Grubb and Lazerson (1982) trace the process by which serious consideration of social and economic inequity gets translated into a concern with individual deficiency:

The structural inequalities of a capitalist society create barriers to stable family life and to decent childrearing conditions for poor, lower-class, and minority children. These inequities in turn generate the pressure for the state to alleviate poverty and to provide some semblance of equal opportunity. But structural inequalities simultaneously generate the public attitudes and political pressures that prevent the state from discharging these responsibilities. Public responsibility for children is thereby reduced to remedial programs that usually prove insufficient and children's institutions that are consistently unable to redress the problems they were created to solve. (p. 96)

The authors maintain that, despite increasing public action and accountability, a myth of private responsibility for children has dominated discussions of a range of policy issues. According to the doctrine of *parens patriae*, the government only intercedes when parents are thought to have failed their children. And, indeed, standard political discourse too often frames the problems of women "on the edge" in terms of individuals—recalcitrant or victimized—who need to be either penalized or assisted.

In cycling down to determine the root cause of society's ills, researchers and policy-makers alike have found women—particularly those young, poor, and minority—an easy target. Actions supposedly intended to "assist" have been premised on a sort of elaborated Dreikurs scheme that penalizes people for "bad" behavior and rewards them for "good." Recent initiatives for getting people off welfare illustrate the rightward swing in ostensibly liberal sentiments. Some are meant to be punitive or to control the behavior of those who seemingly cannot control themselves:

- New Jersey has begun cutting benefits for women who have children while on welfare; the euphemistically titled Family Development Act would do the same at the federal level.
- Wisconsin and other states have advocated paying lower welfare benefits to unwed teen mothers as a disincentive to early childbearing.
- A Kansas state legislator has made the case that welfare costs can be contained by requiring poor women to wear Norplant birth control implants.

Others see "good" in forming nuclear units in the traditional mode:

- Wisconsin has devised Bridefare, a plan to reward women who marry in order to get off welfare.
- Wilson (1987) advocates that a public policy goal should be to make men "marriageable," an effort Reed (1992) has described as a "macroeconomic dating service." (pp. 34, 36)

Traditionally defined expectations for women remain, and these are compounded—and confounded—by race and class prejudices which implicate women in the reproduction of not just children, but poverty itself.

This blaming of individuals serves numerous purposes. First, it provides an easy, relatively powerless, target for public scorn ("Them") and allows those ("Us") who are neither poor, unmarried, divorced, minority, nor working in a job that provides little flexibility to be self-congratulatory. Indeed, it follows that, if "they" are responsible for their ill fortune, "we" must surely deserve all the good things that have come our way. Secondly, the "Us" and "Them" distinction makes it clear who it is that has the right to speak and who is to be spoken of, relieving the "Us" of any responsibility to listen and to try to understand what is happening from "their" point of view. Finally, by focusing on the players, one need not consider how the rules of the game are unfair, nor how the playing field is anything but level.

Yet many of the factors that most impact families exist "above the heads" of those currently held responsible. It is not simply that the rich are getting richer and the poor poorer. Thirty-seven million Americans have no health insurance. Basic pre- and post-natal care is inaccessible to many, and child immunization rates are lower than in many poorer nations. Birth control information is not widely available, and contraceptives can be too costly for low-income women to afford. Medicaid funds cannot be used for abortion, virtually ensuring that poor women will not have the same rights as women who are better off. Child support enforcement has been inadequate at best, leaving a majority of single mothers responsible for raising children with little or no assistance from fathers. Welfare is insufficient and the procedures for acquiring it demeaning. Housing subsidies are limited, and food stamps, in many states, do not provide an adequate diet. Women and children increasingly make up the ranks of the homeless. Widespread gender and racial discrimination continues to exist, limiting both educational and employment opportunity. Quality child care can be too costly for many to afford, and public funds for child care are limited. Head Start accepts only 35 percent of eligible children and segregates them according to class and frequently race. Finally, work settings remain organized according to traditional conceptions of parental roles. Federal family and medical leave is unpaid and available only to those in relatively large firms. Few companies offer *paternity* leave, sick leaves to care for children, flexible hours, job sharing, cafeteria-style benefit plans, or part-time work with benefits (Lubeck & Garrett, 1991). American policy-makers, unlike those in Sweden and some other European nations (Haas, 1991; Kamerman, 1991), have made virtually no effort—beyond child support enforcement—to foster shared parenting.

Focused as we are on individuals, on efforts to recapture the past, and on the need to create distinctions between "Us" and "Them," we fail to address the deep-seated ideological and institutional barriers faced by women in our society, particularly by those who are poor and trying to raise children alone against almost overwhelming odds. As long as discussions remain within the conservative-liberal conundrum, significant change is unlikely to occur.

Instead, the "at risk" ideology, the myth of domesticity, and the discourse of difference all need to be challenged on multiple fronts. Is the behavior of poor people a sign of pathology? Reed (1992) proposes a counterclaim:

> [T]he behavioral tendencies supposedly characterizing the underclass exist generally throughout the society. Drug use, divorce, educational underattainment, laziness, and empty consumerism exist no less in upper status suburbs than in inner city bantustans. The difference lies not in the behavior but in the social position of those exhibiting it. (p. 33)

And other questions arise: Is poverty driven by individuals who don't want to work or by a lack of jobs that pay a wage sufficient to provide for a family? How do handouts substitute for opportunities? How does public—and corporate—policy help to maintain a society with such extremes of poverty and wealth? If fully half of all American children will be reared in female-headed households, can they, in truth, be characterized as non-normative? If, as Ellwood (1988) suggests, the government cannot reverse trends in family formation and if the least compelling argument can be made anyway for making life harder for single parents, why do so many recent initiatives do precisely that? How might other individuals and institutions be enlisted in support of children? How does the very construction of public policies reinforce gender, race, and class prejudice? How can we stop blaming and start building? In her commitment to the "natural resources" that women embody, it is perhaps Adrienne Rich (1978) who makes the most eloquent plea for replacing the language of risk with a language of renewal and of possibility:

> I have to cast my lot with those
> who age after age, perversely,
> with no extraordinary power,
> reconstitute the world.

NOTES

1. "A metanarrative refers to a grand overarching narrative—a transcending validity that is part of a 'metadiscourse'" (Polakow, 1993, p.190).

2. Slavin (1989) argues that the term "disadvantaged" signals concern for *poor* children and leads to programs for *populations* of children. The use of the term "at risk," by contrast, identifies *individual* children who are performing below grade level or likely to be. As such, the term has a broader referent, including, but not limited to, poor children. In actual usage, however, the terms are frequently used interchangeably.

3. A representative sample of principals and all school superintendents in the state was surveyed regarding their preferences for prekindergarten programs. School administrators were asked to provide factual information on their districts and schools, as well as to express their opinions about types of programs, desired staffing, adult/child ratios, organization, and financing. Fully 93 percent of all superintendents and 84 percent of all principals surveyed responded (Lubeck & Garrett, 1989).

4. Hartmann (1975) and Ferguson and Folbre (1981) hold that this division predates the transition to capitalism.

5. For example, both the Pallas et al. study and school administrators in the Lubeck/Garrett study associated the "at risk" status of children with several characteristics: poverty, single-parent families, racial/ethnic group identity, and limited maternal education ("dropouts"). The Pallas team also cited "non-English language background," while the principals and superintendents in the Lubeck/Garrett study instead made frequent reference to working mothers. The rate of female labor force participation in North Carolina is among the highest in the nation. Because of space constraints, two factors—limited maternal education and non-English-speaking family—will not be discussed here.

REFERENCES

American Council on Education (1988, May). *One third of a nation.* Commission on Minority Participation in Education and American Life.

Bauer, G. (1986). *The family: Preserving America's future.* Washington, D.C. The White House Working Group on the Family.

Beller, A., & Chung, S. (1991). Child support and the feminization of poverty. In E. Anderson & R. Hula (Eds.), *The reconstruction of family policy* (pp. 179–190). New York: Greenwood Press.

Bumpass, L. (1984). Children and marital disruption: A replication and update. *Demography 21,* 71–82.

Children's Defense Fund. (1992). *The state of America's children: 1992.* Washington, D.C.: Children's Defense Fund.

Children's Defense Fund & Northeastern University's Center for Labor Market Studies. (1992). *Vanishing dreams: The economic plight of America's young families.* Washington, D.C.: Children's Defense Fund.

Chodorow, N. (1978). *The reproduction of mothering: Psychoanalysis and the sociology of gender.* Berkeley: The University of California Press.

Council of Chief State School Officers. (1988, November). *A guide for state action: Early childhood and family education.* Washington, D.C. Council of Chief State School Officers.

Cuban, L. (1989). The "at-risk" label and the problem of urban school reform. *Phi Delta Kappan, 70*(10), 780–801.

Edelman, M. (1989). Children at risk. In F. Macchiarola & A. Gartner (Eds.), *Caring for America's children* (pp. 20–30). New York: The Academy of Political Science

Ellwood, D. (1988). *Poor support: Poverty in the American family.* New York: Basic Books.

Ferguson, A., & Folbre, N. (1981). The unhappy marriage of patriarchy and capitalism. In L. Sargent (Ed.), *The unhappy marriage of Marxism and feminism: A debate of class and patriarchy* (pp. 313–338). London: Pluto Press.

Garfinkel I., & McLanahan, S. (1986). *Single mothers and their children: A new American dilemma.* Washington, D.C.: The Urban Institute Press.

Grubb, N. & Lazerson, M. (1982). *Broken promises: How Americans fail their children.* Chicago: University of Chicago Press.

Haas, L. (1991). Equal parenthood and social policy: Lessons from a study of parental leave in Sweden. In J. Hyde & M. Essex (Eds.), *Parental leave and child care: Setting a research and policy agenda* (pp. 375–405). Philadelphia, PA: Temple University Press.

Hartmann, H. (1975). *Capitalism and women's work in the home.* Ph.D. Dissertation, Yale University.

Jencks, C. (1992). *Rethinking social policy: Race. poverty, and the underclass.* Cambridge, MA: Harvard University Press.

Jones, R. (1987). New directions in employment and training policy: A federal perspective. *Policy Studies Review, 6*(4), 777–781.

Kamerman, S. (1985). Young, poor, and a mother alone. In. H. McAdoo & J. Parham (Eds.), *Services to young families.* Washington, D.C.: American Public Welfare Association.

Kamerman, S. (1991). Parental leave and infant care: U.S. and international trends and issues, 1978–1988. In J. Hyde & M. Essex (Eds.), *Parental leave and child care: Setting a research and policy agenda* (pp. 11–23). Philadelphia: Temple University Press.

Kamerman, S., & Kahn, A. (1989). The possibilities for child and family policy. In J. Machiarola & A. Gartner (Eds.), *Caring for America's children* (pp. 84–95). New York: The Academy of Political Science.

Kids count data book: State profiles of child well-being. (1992). Washington, D.C.: Center for the Study of Social Policy and the Annie Casey Foundation.

Levin, H. (1989). Financing the education of at-risk students. *Educational Evaluation and Policy Analysis, 11,* 47-60.

Lubeck, S. (1989). A world of difference: American child care policy in cross-national perspective. *Educational Policy, 3*(4). 331–354

Lubeck, S., & Garrett, P. (1989). *Pre-kinderarten programs in North Carolina: Preferences of superintendents and principals.* Raleigh, NC: Report to the North Carolina General Assembly.

Lubeck, S., & Garrett, P. (1990). The social construction of the "at-risk" child. *British Joumal of Sociology of Education. 11*(3), 327–340.

Lubeck, S., & Garrett, P. (1991). Child care in America: Retrospect and prospect. In E. Anderson & R. Hula (Eds.), *The reconstruction of family policy* (pp. 191–202). NewYork: Greenwood Press.

Lyotard, J.-F. (1984). *The postmodern condition: A report on knowledge.* Minneapolis: University of Minneapolis Press.

Morado, C. (1989). State government roles in schooling for 4-year-olds. *Theory into Practice.* 28, 34–40.

Murray, C. (1984). *Losing ground: American social policy, 1950–1980.* New York: Basic Books.

National Center for Children in Poverty (1991). *Five million children: 1991 update.* New York: Columbia University School of Public Health.

National Commission on Children (1991a). *Beyond rhetoric: A new American agenda for children and families.* Washington, D.C.: National Commission on Children.

National Commission on Children (1991b). *Speaking of kids: A national survey of children and parents.* Washington, D.C.: National Commission on Children.

Nelson, D. (1992). *Introduction. Kids count data book: State profiles of child well-being.* Washington, D.C.: Center for the Study of Social Policy and the Annie Casey Foundation.

North Carolina Department of Public Instruction (NCDPI). (1988, December). *Proposal for pilot programs for three- and four-year-old children in the public schools.* Raleigh, NC: NCDPI.

Pallas, A., Natriello, G., & McDill, E. (1989). The changing nature of the disadvantaged population: Current dimensions and future trends. *Educational Researcher,* 17–22.

Pearce, D. (1978). The feminization of poverty: Women, work, and welfare. *The Urban and Social Change Review,* 11(1), 28–36.

Polakow, V. (1993). *Lives on the edge: Single mothers and their children in the other America.* Chicago: The University of Chicago Press.

Reed, A. Jr., (1992). The underclass as myth and symbol: The poverty of discourse about poverty. *Radical America,* 24(24), 21–40.

Research and Policy Committee of the Committee for Economic Development. (1991). *The unfinished agenda: A new vision for child development and education.* New York: Committee for Economic Development.

Reskin, B. & Hartmann. B. (Eds.). (1986). *Women's work, men's work: Sex segregation on the job.* Washington, D.C.: National Academy Press.

Rich, A. (1978). Natural resources. In *The dream of a common language: Poems 1974–1977.* New York: W. W. Norton & Co., Inc.

Rosewater, A. (1989). Child and family trends: Beyond the numbers. In J. Machiarola & A. Gartner (Eds.), *Caring for America's children* (pp. 4–19). New York: The Academy of Political Science.

Rossi, A. (1978, August). Who is the real family? *Ms.*

Scanzoni, J. (1991). Balancing the policy interests of children and adults. In E. Anderson & R. Hula (Eds.), *The reconstruction of family policy* (pp. 11–22). New York: Greenwood Press.

Sidel, R. (1986). *Women and children last: The plight of poor women in affluent America.* NewYork: Penguin.

Slavin, R. (1989, March). *Disadvantaged vs. at-risk: Does the difference matter in practice?* Paper presented at the annual meeting of the American Educational Research Association, San Francisco, CA.

Staples, R. (1985). Changes in Black family structure: The conflict between family ideology and structural conditions. *Journal of Marriage and the Family. 47,* 1005–1014.

Steiner, G. (1981). *The futility of family policy.* Washington, D.C.: The Brookings Institution.

U.S. Bureau of the Census. (1988). *Fertility of American women. June 1987.* (Current Population Reports, Series P-20, No. 427). Washington, D.C.: U.S. Government Printing Office.

U.S. Bureau of the Census. (1989). *Household and family characteristics: March, 1988.* (Current Population Reports, Series P-20, No. 437). Washington, D.C.: U.S. Government Printing Office.

U.S. Bureau of the Census. (1992). *Statistical abstract of the United States 1992* (112th ed.) Washington, D.C.: U.S. Governments Printing Office.

Wexler, P. (1987). *Social analysis of education: After the new sociology.* London: Routledge & Kegan Paul.

Wilson, W. J. (1987). *The truly disadvantaged: The inner city, the underclass, and public policy.* Chicago: The University of Chicago Press.

Zaretsky, E. (1973). *Capitalism, the family, and personal life.* New York: Harper & Row.

3

The Politics of
Who's "at Risk"

The language of "risk" is upon us, piercing daily consciousness, educational practices, and bureaucratic policy-making. Scholars, practitioners, and activists have been quick to name, identify, and ossify those who presumably suffer at the mercy of "risk factors." It satisfies both the desire to isolate these people, by the Right, and to display them, by the Left. This essay waves a reminder: The cultural construction of a group defined through a discourse of "risk" represents a shaved and quite partial image. It is an image that typically strengthens those institutions and groups which have carved out, severed, denied connection to, and then promised to "save" those who will undoubtedly remain "at risk."

With the image of "youth at risk" comes the litany of threats now saturating the popular, policy, and academic literatures. The arguments go as follows: Unless public education in the United States improves . . . the Japanese will conquer the international marketplace . . . hardworking Anglo-Americans will be swallowed by non-white, noneducated, nonworkers . . . too few will be able or willing to support "us" through Social Security payments . . . city streets will grow increasingly unsafe . . . out-of-wedlock births will swell . . . And on it goes.

The one-liners ring so familiar because they chant so ritualistically. Filling public talk, shaping public policy, they traumatize and inhibit public imagination. This is the shaping of discourse. This is the making of controversy. And this is the perversion of possibility. Perhaps no field surpasses public education as the space into which public anxieties, terrors, and "pathologies" are so routinely shoved, only to be transformed into public policies of what must be done to save "us" from "them."

This essay peels through the constructed and impacted layers of debate which give ideological shape to today's Dropout Problem. This analysis of the borders of the debate surrounding (and, therefore, creating) "dropouts" distinguishes between those concerns which have been fronted as the central controversies of the Dropout Problem and those concerns which have been trivialized or silenced.

We begin by eavesdropping inside a debate about dropouts printed in the pages of *The Public Interest*, summer 1989, between former Assistant Secretary of Education Chester Finn and Rutgers Professor Jackson Toby. Within the narrow space opened by the conservative discourse on education, Finn and Toby find themselves in opposition, which they seem to think quite ironic. Toby writes:

> We are brothers-in-arms in the educational-excellence movement. Apparently he [Finn] thinks it is easier than I do for adults to coerce young people to do what we consider good for them. I agree that coercion works for at least three quarters of the fourteen to eighteen year olds. They want to live up to our expectations. Hence we can force them to remain enrolled or persuade them to do so without coercion, as Japanese high schools demonstrate. The remaining quarter constitutes the problem. (1989, p. 136)

Toby wants to lower the compulsory age limit for high school students, enabling their early exit and ridding schools of adolescents who simply don't want to be there. Finn worries about giving adolescents too much say about departing from school, and he writes, instead, in support of a strategy that was first implemented in West Virginia and is now popular elsewhere:

> [The] recently enacted "no pass, no drive" law denies driver's licenses to dropouts under the age of eighteen [exceptions are made for hardship cases]. This law is reportedly drawing dozens of youngsters back to school, though not necessarily for the sheer love of learning. . . . The underlying idea, of course, is to make life at least mildly unpleasant for prospective dropouts by exacting an immediate cost of the sort that most adolescents will have to pay. (1989, p. 132)

The contours of this debate position "adolescent choice" (let youngsters leave high school as early as they wish) against "adolescent coercion" (punish those who leave, as an incentive to stay). The sense of democratic and educational possibility within this ideological slice is remarkably slim and not at all about the individual or collective needs and desires of adolescents. It withers rapidly away from any image of collective educational engagement, inquiry, passion, democracy, or critical excitement in the minds of secondary school students.

Jackson Toby does not want to "keep bodies in" that don't wish to be there. And Chester Finn does not want to let those bodies out. The two men barter over these bodies as public property, while the minds, passions, and critiques of those most likely to drop out are rendered simply irrelevant to the arguments posed. For Toby, these young women and men constitute the worrisome 25 percent. And for Finn, they are, as he has written elsewhere, a "manifestation of linked social pathologies and inherited characteristics" (1989, p. 16). Either way, they are not "us." And they are not even very closely related to us. To the extent that a connection between us and them is acknowledged, it is not in the creation of urban decay—for there they have led themselves astray—but in our rehabilitation of them, who survive "at risk." We turn now to the popular and policy debates which currently shape the Dropout Problem.

PUBLIC AND SUBJUGATED CONTROVERSIES SURROUNDING THE DROPOUT PROBLEM

We live in a country in which 25 percent of adolescents fail to graduate from high school. Urban adolescents drop out at rates estimated to be up to 60 percent of Blacks and Latinos in the comprehensive high schools of New York City, Boston, and Chicago. And in urban areas, only 35 percent of all dropouts and 25 percent of female dropouts return within two years for a GED or a diploma (Kolstad & Ownings, 1987). The remainder of this essay takes as its task the analysis of the Dropout Problem as represented in public discourse. It offers an analysis both of those issues which surface as public controversies and those which remain subjugated. Issues which have been constructed to make controversy offer a sharply individualized lens on the Dropout Problem. Those which have been subjugated reveal far more about deep social interdependencies and the shallowness of proposed "solutions." This essay offers a cultural journey through the ideological constructions and constrictions of "youth at risk."[1]

*Controversies about Individuals: Issues That Float up
into Public Discourse*

Measurement.

MR. STEIN, *Comprehensive High School principal, at the first Parent-Teacher Association meeting of the year: Welcome to high school. We are proud to announce that 80 percent of our graduates go on to college.*
                                        —*September*

I jotted that down in September, not knowing why it would be useful—but anticipating that, by June, it would be. After all, I was a researcher interested in high school dropouts in this urban high school. I conducted an archival cohort analysis of 1,430 incoming ninth graders to assess their high school survival rate and discovered that only 20 percent of the incoming ninth graders ever graduate. Indeed, it is true that 80 percent of the 20 percent go on to college. That's 16 percent of the cohort.

Perhaps the greatest public controversy around high school dropouts surrounds questions of measurement (see Mann, 1986). If we are to assess the depth of the problem, understand the need for differential intervention, and hold schools, communities, and cities accountable, then it makes good sense to standardize a way of thinking about the scope of the dropout problem. And so we do certainly need to consider whether we calculate dropout rates within a static or a cohort frame; whether we "count" home instruction, GEDs, or imprisoned youngsters as "on register" or "dropouts"; whether we include special education placements and GEDs in aggregate graduation rates. These issues fill the measurement debate. While they are by no means frivolous, measurement itself has grown into a national fetish. Debates about the magnitude of the problem have become, for some policy-makers, districts, land advocates, the focus of policy debate, with urban low-income estimates ranging from 40 percent to 60 percent. Given the magnitude of the problem and its disproportionate effect on low-income youths, the question of "how big"—as a national fetish—diverts more attention to measurement than to children and education. A parallel diversion characterizes the debate over national standards focused more on "how high" than how we get from here to there.

Early versus Late Intervention.

GUIDANCE COUNSELOR *at an urban high: By high*
school, it's already too late. Look at their
incoming records, and you can predict who's
going to drop out. You need to start young,
before school. We need to get to them before
they are turned off to school—that happens at
home.

This is offered to me as an argument for early intervention, and an explanation of why transformations of high schools are too late.

This second major public controversy involves *when* to intervene to reverse students' biographies of academic failure. Early intervention and later intervention are posited as if oppositional. In times of urban and rural bankruptcy, whose children are being asked to "choose"? The evidence on early intervention is unambiguous. From Head Start to Ypsilanti, the data confirm the prophylactic effects of early intervention on academic achievement, retention, delinquency, and college attendance rates. Indeed, the Committee on Economic Development has recommended the public and universal provision of preschool experiences for all (1987).

At meetings among urban administrators concerned with the Dropout Problem, however, the debate inevitably turns to where limited public monies should be targeted. The artificial choice accepts that public education for low-income ethnics is *no one's* priority, and it pits little people (about whom romance and a sense of hope swoon dramatically) against adolescents (about whom most are highly-ambivalent). If we opt for little, we write off the current generation of urban adolescents (who are parents of the next generation). We legitimate the illusion that "at risk" adolescents cannot be "turned around" academically and that the correction needs to be in the student, not in schools, the economy, and race and class arrangements. We produce a generation of low-income youngsters who will lack jobs, skills, and options and will do what adolescents without skills so often do: parent, get involved in criminal wage-producing activities, and/or enroll in one of the proprietary schools which have dropout rates of 70 percent or more (Fine, 1987). The controversy over early versus later intervention derives from a contest over fiscal crumbs, an acceptance of genocidal budgets for low-income public education. This debate is, in the final analysis, an ideological and material diversion that gets educators, parents, and advocates fighting *within* districts, ignoring the dwindling stream of dollars coming forth at all.

Promotion/Retention and Tracking.

URBAN DISTRICT SUPERINTENDENT: *We need standards, and a promotion policy assures that standards are in place.*
ADVOCATE: *But all the evidence suggests that promotion policies only encourage kids to stop trying and perhaps facilitates their dropping out!*
SUPERINTENDENT: *What about the positive effect on the kids who are not flunking out? You don't measure that!*
                         —*Conversation among educators.*

TANYA: *I stopped tryin' after they held me over. Felt real bad, stupid you know, how would you feel?"*
PATRICE: *I understand why they doin' it, want to know it's a degree worth somethin' but it hurt somethin' bad. 'Nough to make me drop out and just stop carin'.*
                         —*Conversation among adolescents.*

A third public controversy involves the now popular implementation of promotion/retention policies. At specified academic levels, students in many districts are tested with standardized instruments, and if they do not pass the examination, they are retained in grade or tracked down. In these policies, the aim is to halt the social promotion of students who aren't learning at "appropriate pace" and to limit the negative influence of such students on their "age-appropriate" peers. It is justified as an effort to contain and resolve problems before they accumulate into a lifetime of academic failure. Yet evidence has been collected over the past decade from across the country which confirms that neither retention nor tracking enhance learning substantially or in a sustained way. They assuredly increase the likelihood of dropping out (Labaree, 1983; Shephard & Smith, 1989; Wheelock, 1993). As policies for tougher promotion standards are put in place across the country, and as efforts to detrack are resisted, we are *again* obligated to ask whose "risk" is being lessened and whose is being exacerbated (see McDill, Natriello & Pallas, 1987)?

   Discipline/School Violence.

ASSISTANT DEAN *in charge of discipline: I see my job as the pilot of a hijacked plane. My job is to throw the hijacker off, even if that means bodily.*

   The fourth public controversy concerns discipline, suspension, and expulsion. We know from the National Coalition of Advocates for Students that nationally African American and Latino students are significantly more likely to be suspended, placed in special education, and expelled than are White students, and that social class mediates this relationship. And we know from ethnographic evidence (Fine, 1993) that suspension substantially increases the likelihood of further absenteeism, ultimate failure, and dropping out. It is the rare educator who has the time or energy to welcome back a student who has been suspended or even out for an extended period of time for a "good" reason.

   Over the past decade we have heard little about alternatives to suspension and expulsion, some about the creation of special placements for violent (and in some communities "pre-violent") adolescents, and much about urban schools as jungles, infested with violence and lack of discipline. Note the rapid popularity of Joe Clark of Paterson, New Jersey, and the proliferation of metal detectors at the front doors. While violence inside schools, communities, and homes cuts across social classes and racial/ethnic groups, low-income students and their kin are particularly vulnerable to institutional and interpersonal violence and to the absence of legal protection from that violence.

   But while violence is a significant social issue, the move to identify "pre-violent" adolescents or "passively violent" youths and to create special schools for them represents a strategy of blaming individual students (which may need to be done for a few, but not upwards of 40 percent), rather than a strategy for educating urban youths. Another false and diversionary dichotomy has been created by obscuring the question of how to create educational contexts which nurture students' relationships, enable creative conflict, and inhibit violence (Zane, 1994).

Minimum Age of Exit.

ADMINISTRATOR *for a major urban school district, speaking to a group of advocates: Isn't it just your middle-class values that make you think we should keep kids until they are seventeen? Why not let them leave at fourteen? Become a carpenter or contractor apprentice? They are entitled to come back up to age twenty-one. But let them go if they don't want to stay.*
ADVOCATE: *What would you do if your child said that he wanted to drop out of high school at fourteen?*

A fifth controversy concerns minimum age of exit from compulsory education, echoing the Toby-Finn debate. Ironically phrased in the language of student rights, it has been argued that adolescents should be "allowed" to leave high school prior to age sixteen or seventeen (depending on state mandates) rather than "forced" to stay. Perhaps in a world in which meaningful employment, Job Corps, Peace Corps, Citizens Conservation Corps, apprenticeships, or public service opportunities were available equitably to adolescents in ways that enabled education, housing, health care, experience, adequate income, and a strengthened sense of one's own competence—perhaps then I would be happier about "allowing" adolescents to leave high school early. But as it stands, the recommendation is suspect. What are low-income adolescents going to do once they are "allowed" to leave, while their more affluent peers are sent to a school counselor when they ask to drop out (see Fine, 1986)? They are merely extricated from public responsibility—off the public school register, with their mother's public welfare rolls subsidies reduced proportionately. The "incentive" seems likely to work precisely, and adversely, along lines defined by class and race.

"Alternatives."

CHIEF I: *Given that the comprehensive high schools, or equivalents, are going to remain inside urban areas, what we need to do is*

develop alternative settings for youths at risk,
so that they have some choices.
CHIEF II: *But not in the urban areas. We need to*
create as many opportunities as possible to get
kids out of city schools and into suburban set-
tings.
—*Discussion between chief state*
  school officers

"Alternatives," exceptions, or magnets are often wonderfully "successful" for the participants (depending upon measures of success). As a district policy, however, alternatives alone usually enable access for a limited number, resulting in the substantial neglect of that majority of students who remain in non-alternative schools. Further, they may necessitate waivers—rather than policy change—or require psychological (often racial) "assimilation" rather than institutional transformation.

All adolescents deserve and desire what are usually the conditions of "alternatives"—small, intact, and personal spaces in which to engage their peers, adults, communities, and texts. We know that the success of alternative schools is attributable, in part, to a small size which enables personal contexts for empowered and empowering teachers (Foley & Crull, 1984). But the proliferation of alternatives for "at risk" students simply removes a small group of students from large comprehensive high schools while, at the same time, preserving (bolstering) those schools. The question we are left with is how innovation and alternative models can saturate and transform the mainstream, thereby challenging and invigorating it, rather than supporting the mainstream from the problematic margins.

As in any area of innovation, the creation of alternatives, even positive alternatives, may accommodate a few, but it more fundamentally acts as a holding pond for the "mainstream" and thereby enables urban education to remain fundamentally unchanged.[2]

Controversies of Structural Interdependence:
Subjugated, Silenced, and Not Floating Up

Public obsession with the issues of measurement, early intervention, promotion, suspension, minimum age of exit, and public alternatives (schools or degrees) for "at risk" youth dominate public discourse on what can be done about high school dropouts. My own work suggests that while these issues clearly feel central to public education, a series of subjugated controversies, concerning the structural interdependencies of "us" and "them," also deserve policy attention. These issues may suffer from a lack of vocal advocates or from constituencies of parents and advocates too tormented, disempowered, frightened, or alienated to keep trying to agitate for change inside public education. I raise these controversies to resurrect the arguments and to invite popular and policy debates on these issues.

Equal Opportunities versus Outcomes. The first unarticulated controversy concerns the historic, ideological, and legal distinctions between equal opportunities and severely unequal outcomes (Apple, 1982; Bowles & Gintis, 1976; Ryan, 1981). Public education in the United States has historically been differentially accessible, based on a youngster's social class, race/ethnicity, language, gender, disability, and legal status of parents. But it is fair to say that today all children inside the United States—even those of "undocumented workers"—have legal access to a public education. Questions of equity no longer sit at the doorway of public schools. Still, children, on the basis of social class, race/ethnicity, gender, and geography, receive substantially different educational experiences and reap sharply distinct outcomes. Questions of equity must be interrogated today inside schools, and at their exits. The notion of equal opportunity rings hollow without analyses of outcomes. We must ask, again, what constitutes equality. Lawsuits over finance equity in New Jersey and Texas and quality of education in Alabama begin to raise these concerns systemically.

The Ideological Public-Private Split. The second subjugated controversy involves the artificial severing of the "public sphere" from the "private sphere" inside public education. Relatively undisputed among educators and policy-makers is an acceptance that public schools can't "do it all." Students' "private" affairs, therefore, cannot be school business.

We survive in the culture in which this ideological public-private distinction is held to be precious, while assumed to be universally understood and shared (Eisenstein, 1989), as feminist scholars have argued. But one need not spend a lot of time inside a low-income urban public school to notice the weighty presence of state and corporate interests and the attenuated interests of community, labor, advocacy, social change organization, and families. This latter collection of interests, collapsed into "the private," is expelled from public education's purview, while AT&T representatives lecture students on the work ethic, Shearson Lehman opens an Academy of Finance, the military recruits, Wilfred Academy of Beauty displays its promises on Career Day, and "right to life" advocates come to speak to hygiene class. During the Persian Gulf invasion, supportive buttons and flags were distributed in schools, while resisters were often considered inappropriately "political." If we conceptualize public schools as a space for the practice of critique and expression of democracy and for the interrogation of social inequity, then we must admit that there is nothing wrong with the presence of these private and state bodies inside schools—except insofar as public interests are expelled. In this case, what is called democracy is in fact the hegemony of private and state interests which thrive on the "privatization" and marginalization of public concerns.

School-Community Relations. The third subjugated controversy involves the relationship of low-income schools to low-income communities. My travels through a series of urban comprehensive middle and high schools convince me that while exceptions are obvious (especially in Chicago and the New Visions Schools in New York City), public schools in low-income neighborhoods often represent themselves as the means for low-income students to "escape" their local communities—sometimes as a way to save "those students" from "those parents." Obviously problematic, insofar as this position nurtures both racism and classism, it is also patently ineffective pedagogy. It undermines that which adolescents bring to their schools and classes and that which their parents/guardians could bring. Fundamental to a strong school-community relationship are certain beliefs: that schooling is a vehicle for activating individual enhancement as well as social critique, community, and social change; that school-parent-community collaboration will strengthen adolescents' commitment to schooling; and that low income parents and communities are precisely the "public" and the constituency to whom public schools are accountable.

With some important exceptions[3] (notably in Chicago, see Fine, 1993), little is being said or done by policymakers or educators that truly incites parental participation, empowerment, and critique (Epstein, 1988). To the extent that parent involvement is noted as "essential" to school improvement, the strategy is typically one in which parents are trained as homework monitors or "better parents"—not as collaborators, sources of critical information, innovators, or critics. Even many one-time liberals have given up on "those parents" (perhaps now that "those parents" in cities are disproportionately African American, Latino, and low-income). Unless this power differential that marks the relations between schools and low-income communities is addressed as controversial and inside public policy, the relationship will continue to be educationally bankrupt.

"Options" to High School Graduation. The fourth subjugated controversy involves the proliferating structural ring of "options" for dropouts: proprietary schools, GED programs, the military, and (more recently) job-readiness programs. In my ethnographic work at Comprehensive High School, and since, these four "options" emerge as those most frequently sought after by high school dropouts. Emerging from comprehensive high schools as "discharges," seventeen-year-old adolescents are for the most part alive, energetic, creative, and motivated. They are trying to figure out how to create a life for themselves, their existing (or planned) children, and sometimes for their mothers as well. Intrigued by all that they hear about GEDs, proprietary schools, and the military, they are never educated to the realities. The folklore, furnished and fueled by peers and educators, obfuscates evidence that:

In New York State, less than half of GED test-takers typically pass the examination.

In New York State, the Department of Education released a report on proprietary schools that documented 70 percent dropout rates; the fact that these schools earn significantly more from students who enroll and do not complete than from those who do complete their educations; and evidence of unethical and unrealistic promises and abysmal postprogram placement rates in what are often temporary or probationary positions.

Nationally, many high school dropouts may get into the military (although most will fail the entrance examination), but they are much more likely than other soldiers to be less than honorably discharged within six months; female dropouts will not be allowed into the military at all, at least during "peacetime" (see Fine, 1990).

Public schools inside urban areas fundamentally and uncritically bolster these "alternatives" as "second chances," without informing students of the problematic aspects of these "options." Public schools, in fact, volunteer bodies to these institutions by enabling recruitment through advertising and the solicitation of names. Moreover, the public sector subsidizes all three efforts—most particularly proprietary schools—substantially.

Given the dismal consequences of these three "alternatives" for most low-income adolescents,[4] why do we not feel compelled to inform students, to investigate recruitment, advertising, and financing, and to hold public schools accountable for the numbers of their students who are "allowed" or encouraged to flee to these "alternative" institutions?

The generic issue of the collapsing economy for low-income workers remains fundamentally subjugated. The proprietary schools and the military continue to represent themselves as the "last institution willing to serve low-income Black and Latino adolescents." And no counterevidence emerges publicly. The wealth earned by the proprietary schools, the questionable exchange rate of the GED, and the automatic waiving of civil rights of those who enter the military seeking jobs, training, glamour, and travel are topics that are silenced inside public schools and policies.

REFLECTIONS ON "YOUTH AT RISK"

[Social ideology is] real in that it is the way in which people really live their relationship to the social relations which govern their conditions of existence, but imaginary in that it discourages a full understanding of these conditions of existence and the ways in which people are socially constituted within them. . . .
—Belsey, 1980

We find ourselves faced with the fundamentally silenced question: Who benefits from the ideological and material construction of "youth at risk?" In recent debates around public education, the term has gained not only popularity but promiscuity. An adolescent may be "at risk" if she exhibits high absenteeism, has been retained in grade, performs poorly in class, indicates a "pre-violent" disposition, is pregnant, has a learning disability, lives in a single-mother household, or simply arrives from Puerto Rico.

To position these students as "at risk" bears potentially two very distinct sets of consequences. The benevolent consequence is that their needs could in fact be attended to. But the notion "at risk" inside the dropout literature also offers a deceptive image of an isolatable and identifiable group of students who, by virtue of some personal characteristic, are not likely to graduate. As Foucault would argue, the image betrays more than it reveals. Diverted away from an economy that is inhospitable to low-income adolescents and adults, particularly U.S.-born African Americans and Latinos, and diverted from the collapsing manufacturing sectors of the country, housing stock, and impoverished urban schools, our attention floats to the individual child, his/her family, and those small-scale interventions which would "fix" him/her as though their lives were fully separable from ours. Like the notion "underclass," "at risk" does far more damage than good.

> Underclass is a concept that muddies debate and inhibits the formulation of constructive policy. It reflects the centuries' old preoccupation with dividing poor people into categories of moral worth. As a modern euphemism for the undeserving poor, it reinforces the tradition of blaming the victim. By stigmatizing them, it insults those it designates. It also works against their best interests, for it fosters political divisions among the working class and poor, who need each other as allies, and, through its concentration on the behavior of a relatively small number of people clustered in inner cities, deflects attention from the problem of poverty and minimizes its extent. The word underclass has little intellectual substance. It lacks a consistent, defensible theoretical basis. It is not a "class" in any of the usual senses. Most definitions, in fact, substitute varieties of bad behavior for the criteria customary in stratification theories. Nor can the social scientists who use it, let alone the media, agree on a definition. (Katz & Sugrve 1993, p.20)

This essay has elaborated the floating range of controversies surrounding what is popularly represented as the Dropout Problem. Those controversies divert social attention to individual children and adolescents, their families, and their communities. As Catherine Belsey would argue, these controversies indeed represent "real" issues. More dangerously, however, at the same time they are imaginary. They reproduce existing ideologies, shave off alternative frames, and recommend as "natural" those programs of reform which reproduce and sediment class, race, and gender stratifications.

Those controversies which have been subjugated and silenced, in contrast, would turn our critical concern onto the very ideological and material distinctions that privilege those already privileged and disadvantage those already disadvantaged. They force our attention to the existing tapestry of social inequities woven through structural interdependencies of class, race, and gender. They ask us to interrogate within schools long-sustained distinctions between "public" and "private" spheres; between the liberal rhetoric of equal opportunity and radical demands for equal outcomes; between what we permit "our children" to do and where we send "those children" in the name of helpful alternatives.

Simply said, "youth at risk" is an ideological and historical construction. While the numbers and their skewed class and racial distributions are intolerable, and the academic and economic consequences incurred are severe, we must remember that today more students graduate from high·school than was true fifteen years ago. Today, however, they will not as easily find work, housing, community, or support, particularly if they are low-income and/or of color. The U.S. Department of Labor documents the differential consequences of dropping out for White males and females and Black males and females. For dropouts age twenty-two to thirty-four, 15 percent of White men live in poverty compared to 28 percent of White women, 37 percent of Black men and 62 of Black women. While 31 percent of Black female graduates live below the poverty line—half the proportion of Black female dropouts—this is still twice the rate of White male dropouts. The absence or presence of a high school diploma does not disrupt the much more encrusted structural interdependencies of class, race/ethnicity, and gender inequities.

The Dropout Problem is a real issue, but more profoundly it too has been appropriated as an ideological diversion. We can and must improve public schools to retain and critically educate a greater percentage of students, particularly low-income students. But at the same time, the degree must have exchange value across class, race, and gender lines; the economy must be rich for all; housing, child care, health care, and social services must be designed to accommodate all urban dwellers. While these conditions remain as they are, the Urban Dropout Problem continues to be exploited, cast deceptively as the central cause of the erosion of city, state, and national strength. In such contexts, the construction of the "at risk" adolescent distracts and it allows voucher advocates to wave "dropouts" and "violence" as a terror tactic to encourage privatization and segregation. Fundamentally, the notion of "risk" keeps us from being broadly, radically, and structurally creative about transforming schools and social conditions for all of today's and tomorrow's youths.

NOTES

1. The work derives from research I have conducted across the growing terrain of urban high school dropouts from 1980 through the present. This research program, if I can offer it some post-hoc coherence, has involved quantitative evaluation research comparing dropouts and stay-ins at an alternative high school in the South Bronx (Fine, 1983); a year-long ethnographic analysis of a comprehensive high school (C.H.S.) in upper Manhattan (Fine, 1986); consultation with diverse urban school districts sprinkled across the northeast corridor; legal testimony I have delivered before the New York City Council, the New York State Legislature, and the Legislature's minority caucus; extensive involvement with advocacy groups nationally; and participation in a series of policy-making sessions, including the 1987 Summer Institute of the Council of Chief State School Officers (Fine, 1988).

2. Chester Finn explains that most high school dropouts ultimately return to school within a few years and some even earn a GED, relying upon the Census Bureau survey data which reveal that 86 percent of the adult population (aged twenty-five to twenty-nine) have completed at least four years of high school by 1985. Finn concluded that the gap was explained by an alternative: earned GEDs. But he is far more optimistic than others about educational rebound of high school dropouts. Andrew Kolstad and Jeffrey Ownings (1987), researchers from Finn's own department, conducted a longitudinal analysis of a sample of dropouts from the High School and Beyond data set. Of the 28,000 sophomores in the original cohort—which excluded all adolescents who dropped out prior to the tenth grade—Kolstad and Ownings' analysis draws on approximately 2,000 dropouts included for follow-up. Of these, 40 percent had completed diploma or certificate requirements within two years of when they should have graduated from high school. Disproportionately, however, the returning dropouts were those who had dropped out as seniors (41 percent versus 27 percent who were sophomores), were White (41 percent vs. 30 percent of Hispanics and 33 percent of Blacks), of high income (53 percent of high income compared to 37 percent of medium and 30 percent of low income), and from the suburbs (42 percent versus 35 percent urban). Kolstad and Ownings report that in urban areas, 42 percent of males returned and graduated, but only 25 percent of female dropouts earned a diploma or certificate by the time of the follow-up. For Blacks and Latinos—but not for Whites—males return and graduate at rates approximately 10 percent higher than females. The race, class, and gender discrepancies, confounded by geography, demand attention for any analysis of "at risk" youth.

Former Assistant Secretary Finn also failed to acknowledge the differential financial consequences of a GED and a standard high school diploma. A report commissioned by the American Council on Education (Passmore, 1987) concludes that while young adults with GEDs are economically better off than those with neither degree nor diploma (on outcomes including labor force participation rates, employment, and wages), young adults with high school degrees are substantially better off than those with GEDs. The typical GED recipient would have earned in 1985 about $780 more than a youth without a GED or diploma, but $1,340 less than a youth with a high school diploma. In the absence of a discussion of differential rates and differential outcomes, Finn's argument obscures more than it enlightens about "at risk" youth. Relying on the GED "alternative" as solution, by the end of the essay Finn reveals his embedded assumptions, and priorities, about us and them.

3. For information on parent organizations, see The Parent Empowerment Project sponsored by the National Committee for Public Education in Baltimore; the Center for Responsive Education in Boston; the organizing initiated by Designs for Change in Chicago; and the activism sponsored by numerous individual advocacy organizations across the country.

4. There are many fabulous GED programs for adolescents and adults, but most GED educators agree that a standard diploma has greater exchange value than a GED and may be easier to acquire (Passmore, 1987).

REFERENCES

Apple, M. W. (1982). Curricular form and the logic of technical control: Building the possessive individual. In M. Apple (Ed.), *Cultural and economic reproduction in education* (pp. 247–274). Boston: Routledge and Kegan Paul, 1982.

Belsey, C. (1980). *Critical practice.* London, New York: Methuen.

Bowles, S., & Gintis, H. (1976). *Schooling in capitalist America.* New York: Basic Books.

Committee on Economic Development, Research and Policy Committee. (1987). *Children in need: Investment strategies for the educationally disadvantaged.* Washington, D.C.: Committee for Economic Development.

Eisenstein, Z. (1989). *The female body and the law.* Berkeley: University of California Press.

Epstein, J. (1988). *Schools in the center: School, family, peer, and community connections for more effective middle grades school and stu-*

dents. Mimeographed draft prepared for the Carnegie Task Force on Education of Young Adolescents. John Hopkins University.

Fine, M. (1983). Perspectives on inequity: Voices from urban schools. In L. Bickman (Ed.), *Applied social psychology annual* (Vol. 4) (pp. 217–245). Beverly Hills: Sage Publications.

Fine, M. (1985). Dropping out of high school: An inside look. *Social Policy*, (Fall), 43–50.

Fine, M. (1986). Why urban adolescents drop into and out of public high school. *Teachers College Record*, 87, 393–409.

Fine, M . (1987). Silencing in the public schools. *Language Arts, 64*(2), 157–174 .

Fine, M (1988). Deinstitutionalizing educational inequity. In Council of Chief State Officers (Ed.), *At risk youth: Policy and research, pp. 88–119.* New York: Harcourt, Brace & Jovanovich.

Fine, M. (1991). *Framing dropouts: Notes on the politics of an urban high school.* Albany: State University of New York Press.

Fine, M. (1994). Working the hyphens: Reinventing self and other in qualitative research. In N. K. Denzin & Y. S. Lincoln (Eds.). *Handbook of Qualitative Research.* (pp. 70–82). Thousand Oaks, CA: Sage Publications.

Fine, M., & Rosenberg, P. (1983). Dropping out of high school: The ideology of school and work. *Journal of Education, 165*, 257–272 .

Finn, C. E., Jr. (1989). The high school dropout puzzle. *The Public Interest,* 87, (Spring), 131–134.

Foley, E., & Crull, P. (1984). *Educating the at-risk adolescent: More lessons from alternative high school.* New York: Public Education Association.

Katz, M., & Sugrve, T. (1993). *History and the underclass debate.* SSRC document.

Kolstad, A. J., & Ownings, J. A. (1987, April 16). *High school dropouts who change their minds about school.* Washington, D.C.: U.S. Department of Education, Office of Educational Research and Improvement, Center for Statistics, Longitudinal Branch. (Mimeographed).

Labaree, D. F. (1983). *Setting the standard: The characteristics and consequences of alternative student promotional policies.* Philadelphia: Citizens Committee on Public Education in Philadelphia.

Mann, D. (1986). Can we help drop-outs: Thinking about the undoable. *Teachers College Record, 87,* 307–323.

McDill, E., Natriello, G., & Pallas, A. (1985). Raising standards and retaining students: The impact of the reform recommendations on potential dropouts. *Review of Educational Research, 55* (4), 415–333.

Passmore, D. L. (1987, September). *Employment of young GED recipients.* GED Research Briefs 14. Washington, D.C.: American Council on Education.

Ryan, W. (1981). *Equality.* New York: Pantheon Books.

Shephard, L., & Smith, M. (Eds.). (1989). *Flunking grades: Research and policy on retention.* New York: Falmer Press.

Toby, J. (1989). The high school dropout puzzle. *The Public Interest, 87,* (Spring), 134–136.

Wheelock, A. (1993). *Crossing the tracks.* New York: New Press.

Zane, N. (1994). When discipline recedes. In M. Fine (Ed.), *Chartering public reform.* New York: Teachers College Press.

II. Children and Families at Promise

ELIZABETH QUINTERO
MARY KAY RUMMEL

4

Voice Unaltered:
Marginalized Young
Writers Speak

INTRODUCTION

> To awaken to life, even life with its uncertainties and blank
> walls, is what we want of our students and ourselves. It is
> important to communicate to young people that the world is
> an unfinished task. . . . An object, classroom, neighborhood,
> street, field of flowers shows itself differently when encoun-
> tered by different spectators . . . the reality of that object or
> classroom or neighborhood or field of flowers arises out of
> the sum total of its appearances. Thinking of those specta-
> tors as participants in an ongoing dialogue, each one speak-
> ing out of a distinct perspective and yet open to those
> around, I find a kind of paradigm for what I have in mind.
> —Greene, 1992b

This study investigates the writing of young children—specifically females and children from culturally and linguistically diverse families—using a methodology that combines reflections of unique detail and metaphor as strong indication of voice. The purpose of the study is to use the authentic voices of the children to convince teachers of the potential of young girls and children from culturally and linguistically diverse families. This potential must be the point of departure for development of curriculum, teaching practice, and resulting evaluation design. Elbow (1981) describes writing with voice as writing into which someone has breathed. Voice, for him, has nothing to do with the words on the page, only with the relationship of the words to the writer, . . . the words contain not just an explicit message, " 'the sun glints down a pathway of ripples,' but also some kind of implicit message about the condition of the writer. . . ." (Elbow, 1981, p. 299). We educators need to learn to recognize, encourage, and respond to the power of the convergence of writer and word expressed by Elbow (1981). Through *attention to children's voices*, the authors contend, cultural and linguistic factors will remain an integral part of all instruction and serve as a guide for the process adaptation and teachers mediation of knowledge advocated by Reyes (1993).

The theoretical framework of the study is one which uses a theoretical triangulation combining critical theory, feminist literary theory, and symbolic interactionism. The application of this theoretical and methodological framework elicits evidence of female and marginalized voice in children, before this voice has been "socialized away." The authors contend that this dramatic evidence supports a classroom context that encourages and enhances these voices in a generative transformative way and helps to deconstruct the myth that children who represent diversity are "at risk." Rather, the voices show unique strength and potential.

All children know and care about the social and cultural meanings in their lives. They love, laugh, get angry, and get scared. As Oakes and Lipton (1990) advise, personal and communal milieux are rich as a point of departure for virtually any subject of study. For example, in a family literacy class children wrote about what is important in their lives:

Child O: Angel es m fnd [sic]. (Angel is my friend.)
Child A: I love my grandma.
Child V   I like truck to go camping

Child E:	Los quiero mucho mis amigos [*sic*]. (I love my friends a lot.)
Child M:	Me enojo cuando mi mama me castiga [*sic*]. (I am angry when my mother punishes me.)
Child AM:	I like my dad because he plays with me.
Child V:	I get scar of monsters [*sic*]. (I get scared of monsters.)
Child O:	I'm met wen d dog bt me [*sic*]. (I'm mad when the dog bites me.)

The authors concur with Swadener and Kessler (1991) when they point out that there is a relationship between ". . . what we teach in school and the unequal outcomes of schooling based on social class, race, language or dialect, and gender (p. 87). Polakow (1993) vividly points out how public schools are "a mirror reflection of public perceptions of the poor" (p. 107), thus perpetuating the tragic misconception of minority and poor children.

The work samples of this study were combined from two literacy projects. One literacy project was in Minnesota. The Community Programs in the Arts and Sciences (COMPAS) Dialogue Program was a four-year initiative to improve the teaching of writing in the St. Paul public schools. It brought together professional writers who worked for the COMPAS Writers-in-the-Schools Program and teachers from St. Paul schools. The purpose was to establish a collaborative long-term relationship designed to help teachers develop new skills and ideas, to use writing as a teaching tool, and to encourage teachers to become familiar with the writing process through their own writing. COMPAS accomplished this goal through a multifaceted, year-long effort that linked classroom teachers with professional writers who demonstrated and modeled writing techniques and strategies, nurtured teachers' individual writing, and drew teachers into support groups to enhance the use of writing in the classroom. The Dialogue Program in St. Paul consisted of three phases of activity:

1. Each year, an autumn institute was offered that consisted of four day-long workshops that brought teachers together outside the classroom and gave them an overview of the program. The institute used program writers as staff to present the writing process and showcase techniques and uses of writing that would be emphasized throughout the year.

2. The writers served a total of six weeks in residency in each school. These six weeks were spread out over the school year to emphasize the generative, drafting, revising, and evaluative aspects of the writing process and to give teachers time to practice teaching the writing process between periods of writer residency.

3. A teachers' seminar group, consisting of all faculty involved in Dialogue plus the writer, met weekly during the residency periods. The purpose of these meetings was to allow teachers time to develop lesson plans and share classroom activities, as well as to encourage them to practice their own writing skills.

The institute and the in-school seminar deepened interaction between the writers and teacher. Dialogue focused on two areas of the curriculum, language arts and social studies. Writing genres were flexible and included poetry, fiction, personal essay, journals, and journalism as appropriate to grade level. Because the professional writers involved in the program were creative writers, there was an emphasis on expressive writing. These writers were selected by COMPAS for their proven experience in teaching writing in the classroom and for their ability to work successfully with teachers.

The other literacy project was a bilingual family literacy project in El Paso, Texas, consisting of parents and children learning together. Groups met after school in neighborhood school buildings. The project was designed to provide participatory literacy and biliteracy (Spanish and English) development opportunities for families in El Paso's culturally and linguistically diverse community and was dedicated to outreach in critically active ways to the community of the participants. The philosophical and theoretical perspectives demanded attention to and respect for experiential knowledge (including culture and language), knowledge of power (including facts and systems), and critical competence (including transformational action). The instructional design consisted of a series of learner-generated thematic lessons written by the staff with constant input by the participating parents and children. The themes were addressed through a flexible, five-step model:

• Initial Inquiry—an oral language activity which encourages group dialogue

- Learning Activity—a concrete, hands-on experience activity done in family teams
- Language Experience Approach Activity—a writing activity done in family teams
- Storybook Demonstration—storytime that encourages interaction
- Home Activity Suggestion—activities for the whole family to do at home

The theoretical priorities of the project design were critical theory, whole language theory, and symbolic interactionism. These theories guided the praxis which dictated the instructional design according to three underlying premises, all of which are solidly grounded on past research in the fields of literacy and language acquisition. These premises are:

1) parent involvement and its positive effect on children's lives,
2) the holistic approach to the acquisition of literacy skills, and
3) the acceptance of code-switching in the classroom as an effective teaching and learning strategy.

THEORETICAL PERSPECTIVES

This study embraces three theoretical perspectives: critical theory, feminist literary theory, and symbolic interactionism. The analysis of the children's writing is done using a triangulation process in which the writing is categorized into examples showing critical theory and feminist literary theory and then combined to illustrate symbolic interactionism.

Critical theory is embraced as it applies to the process of conscientization as Freire (1985) envisioned for adults and as it applies to children. Freire defines conscientization (based on the Brazilian conscientização), as "the process by which human beings participate critically in a transforming act" (p. 106). He goes on to say that "Conscientization thus involves a constant clarification of that which remains hidden within us while we move about in the world, though we are not necessarily regarding the world as the object of our critical reflection" (p. 107). In some literacy projects and early childhood programs serving linguistically and culturally diverse children, it has been found that children, with encouragement and acceptance, do gain self-confidence to do their own reading and writing. They will voice their own reality in terms of culture, social issues, and cognitive development when it is valued as a sharing of knowledge (Quintero & Macías, 1991; Wong Fillmore, 1990). They participate critically in the context of becoming true multicultural learners, and they reject being forced to extinguish one culture in the interest of gaining knowledge of another or denying any aspects of their own development.

For example, a fourth-grade girl so sick with asthma she couldn't lift her head from the desk uses her language in powerfully personal ways that exhibit conscientization. She is too young to bring about external change in her life, yet by voicing her pain she validates her feelings and lays groundwork for future transformations.

> God Why?
> God why do you
> take people away
> and hurt their family
> why?
> Well at least you
> can let them live longer
> especially babies
> Why is my life
> miserable ?
> Why do I only
> live with my mom ?
> Why do I have
> so many brothers and sisters ?
> Why can't my mom
> and dad live together?
> Why didn't they get married ?
> Why do you make me
> suffer from asthma?
> Will you let me grow out of it?
> Why do I act like this?

Giroux (1991), a critical theorist, connects critical theory to literary theory in the context of voice:

> There is a politics of resistance in which difference is explored through the category of voice. Central here is the need to engage voice as an act of resistance and self-transfor-

mation, to recognize that as one comes to voice one estab-
lishes the precondition for becoming a subject in history
rather than an object. . . . Instead of talking about literacy,
radical educational theory would have to educate teachers
and administrators to speak and listen to many languages and
ways of understanding the world. (p. 22)

The authors believe that educators must engage children's voices
and acknowledge their resistance and efforts at self-transforma-
tion. The children in the study speak of their understanding of the
world. If we respect children, we must listen.

Proponents of a feminist approach to teaching writing focus
on writing as a means for women to find personal and political
voice (Ritchie, 1990; Lassner, 1990; Cooper, 1989). They explain
the lack of differences between male and female writing found in
many genres of writing, especially those expository forms most
closely connected to "school writing," as the result of suppression
of authentic female voice by the demands of constant adaptation
to an imposed standard of a male-dominated society. In a recent
comparative study of college-age male and female writers gender-
linked effects were quite undramatic (Rubin & Greene, 1992). This
is in marked contrast to the work of Kamler (1992), who found in
young children many stylistic differences at all levels of text when
she studied writing development in an Australian kindergarten
classroom. Kamler proposes that the practice of writing constructs
the gendered identity of the writer even though most writing
research has attended to the development of children rather than
girls and boys separately. (Graves, 1983; Calkins, 1991).

While such studies have acknowledged the importance of
social context in the process of learning to write, they have not
examined the socially constructed nature of the written texts children produce. In the present work, as in that by Kamler (1992), language is viewed as a representation and construction of culture and
as a resource for making meanings under social constraints of specific kinds. Children engaged in using language are viewed as constructing their world through language while their language is
simultaneously constructing them through its use. Thus, the literacy endeavor seen through these children's writing in terms of
voice involves individual transformations and transformations in
context of various groups of people.

A sociological theory that discusses human interactions in
terms of meanings is symbolic interactionism. This theory main-

tains that meaning is made when people interact (Blumer, 1969). Bloch (1991) explains that this type of symbolic science "focuses on intersubjectivities that are created through interactions between people, their discourse, and the interpretations of meaning within specific contexts" (p. 97). Symbolic interactionism in this study was embraced as the link between critical theory (conscientization) and feminist literary theory and the synergistic combination of the two. Symbolic interactionism is not only the acknowledgment that meaning is constructed as people interact (Blumer, 1969), but also, as this study emphasizes, this interaction is a means to focus a critical perspective and keep in the forefront of all analysis and action the intersection of race, ethnicity, class, and gender. These children's work samples show combined critical social context with the contexts of the "regular" school, the local community, and the families of the participants.

RESEARCH METHODOLOGY

In this chapter two aspects of voice will be described and analyzed in children's writing: the use of unique, even quirky, detail often in the form of metaphor (Wolf, 1988) and unique detail as it critically describes the sociocultural context of the child. Both of these literary elements are carriers of the explicit and implicit messages described by Elbow (1981). For example, unique detail such as "Me siento triste cuando mi mama no me deja ir con mi amiga (I feel sad when my mother doesn't let me go with my friend)" tells us the explicit message about the situation but also an implicit message about the mother's relationship with the child, the child's range of feeling, and the child's social development. Metaphor as a form of unique detail particularly provides the possibility of communicating what cannot be literally expressed. The two-year-old who says "When I say timber, nothing falls" is expressing a feeling of helplessness that he would not be able to express in literal language (Rummel & Dykstra, 1983). We make the world familiar with metaphor, Maxine Greene (1992a) says, "We feel less powerless when we can name and explain." This empowerment is the essence of critical transformation. In her work, Greene emphasizes the power of metaphor for transformation—both personal and communal.

The authors contend that the goal of writing instruction is personal and political empowerment. Thus, it is important to

encourage the unique voices of girls and boys who are from culturally and linguistically diverse families. Poet Audre Lorde (1984)
speaks to this notion of difference as a referent for critique:

> Those of us who have been forged in the crucibles of differ-
> ence—those of us who are poor, who are lesbians, who are
> Black, who are older—know that survival is not an academic
> skill. It is learning how to stand alone, unpopular and some-
> times reviled, and how to make common cause with those
> others identified as outside the structures in order to define
> and seek a world in which we can all flourish. It is learning
> how to take our differences and make them strengths. For the
> master's tools will never dismantle the master's house. They
> may allow us temporarily to beat him at his own game, but
> they will never enable us to bring about change. (p. 112)

Teaching children to suppress their voices in order to help them
survive, as described in studies of adult writers (Rubin & Greene,
1992), will never bring about change.

In describing the research methods used in this study, the
meaning of the gender label itself needs discussion. Gilligan (1982)
believes that it is an empirical fact, not some biological imperative, that locates women's epistemology among women. Males
who are socialized might acquire knowledge in the same manner,
and what is often considered women's language is also used by
men in a sociopolitically marginal role (Lakoff, 1973). The work of
Rubin and Greene (1992) calls the above psychological gender-role
orientation. In the present study we analyzed the writing of both
girls and boys who are from diverse backgrounds, largely African
American and Mexican. We are applying feminist literary theory
to children from marginalized groups.

Some writing samples analyzed in this paper are poems written by children from grades one through four. These writing samples can be analyzed for metaphors that tell us about the individual child's sociocultural context. In the present study, metaphor is
defined as analogical, "a thinking process or operation in which a
relationship between a thought-feeling complex and a well-under-
stood object or situation is found and expressed in words" (Khatena, 1972).

Other writing samples are from children participating in the
bilingual family literacy project in El Paso, Texas. Some of the
samples analyzed represent oral writing dictated by five year-olds

and transcribed by an adult. This oral composition, described by
Calkins (1986, p. 35) as "early forays into writing," is recognized in
the field as writing (Phinney, 1993). In other cases, the samples of
young children were written as squiggles on pictures and transcribed by an adult. This also is considered writing (Temple et al.,
1993). Regardless of the form, the work samples of the children
represent both class work and home activities done cooperatively
with parents and other family members.

Children's work from diverse marginalized groups across age
and geographical context was purposefully brought together to
show the dynamic potential of voice. Metaphors are analyzed
using classifications of analogy first developed by Gordon (1961)
and used to study metaphors in children's writing by Rummel and
Dykstra (1983). The terms "analogy" and "metaphor" are used
interchangeably in this study.

The work samples were categorized according to:

Symbolic analogy: A poetic image that has representational quali-
                    ties: What does it state about the child's view
                    of life?
Fantasy analogy: The use of imaginary phenomena in the com-
                    parison process: What is the social reality
                    behind the construction of the fantasy?
Personal analogy: The process of identifying oneself with an
                    object oneself with an object, process, or other
                    person in order to get a new viewpoint: Who
                    does the writer identify with, and what is the
                    extent of that identification?

Three aspects of critical transformation were also analyzed in
conjunction with the metaphor analyses. These critical categories
were 1) social context of the self; 2) social context of family; 3)
social context of community.

DISCUSSION

Symbolic Analogy and Sociocultural Context

Symbolic analogy or metaphor, because of its representational
qualities, gives us insight into a child's perception of life. The
poem, "Life," written by a fourth-grade student, shows metaphor
as a means by which a child can simultaneously create and pro-

claim who she is. This child's use of symbolic metaphor reveals a personal stance toward life. In terms of social context, it defines her in relation to community. It also is an example of the transformation described previously by Greene (1992b). In the poem, the child moves from self to others to a holistic view of life, making her world familiar with her own metaphoric power.

Life

I'm a heart, pounding in my chest.
I'm a winter breeze, chilling people as they walk by.
I'm a letter, writing to people, cheering them up.
I'm life, coming and going.

In the following poem, the writers use of symbolic metaphor also vividly names his thoughts, intentions, and actions toward life. This child relates his life interactions to family context. The child's words describe a critical event in dealing with death.

Life has been like a messy room for me.
Like I had lost some thing,
and I had to put everything
up where it was.
Like when I lost
my father, I just went into shock.
I was putting my life back together
over and over,
but something again and again
kept knocking it down
over and over again.
And I'm finally gettin'
that room clean.
So get me the broom
and the dust pan
because I want to have
a better life for you all
and when I finally pick up that final
batch of dirt
then I will have
a clean sparkling room.

This seven-year-old writer uses symbolic metaphor to challenge her environment. Images of personal power show young children's exploration of dynamics of self in relation to the world.

> My name is lightning.
> I scare kids and
> my god is Zeus
> and I cause fires sometimes.
> My name is sun.
> I make the planets hot
> and anything that comes near
> me will be fried.

In the bilingual family literacy class, the participants had been discussing "things that fly." Many children wrote about desires to travel on planes or in space ships. This five-year-old chose a different route:

> I like to be a bat and go to a tree [*sic*].

The symbolism he used permitted him to be something other than a boy in a vehicle and to go someplace different from where he was.

In the next writing sample, the tree image is an example of unique detail that is realistic, immediate, and a useful resource in the five-year-old's cultural context. In a complex sense, the tree's use is to take care of and protect her immediate communal world. The child, a participant in a bilingual family literacy project, is responding to the question, "¿Para qué sirven los arboles?" (How are trees useful?)

> "Para secar la ropa y para darle sombra al carro."
> (To dry our clothes and to provide shade for the car.)

In the last poem for this section, a child recreates the event of her birth in universal and mythological symbols. In the poem she and her family are central to a mythological view of the universe.

> On the day I was born the earth shook and the angels wept.
> On the day I was born the sky turned green, the clouds turned
> orange.

On the day I was born, they discovered Atlantis.
And books overflowed my house.
On the day I was born the earth was clean and there was peace.
On the day I was born my family scampered to see me.
On the day I was born the sun fell in love with the moon.

Fantasy Analogy and Sociocultural Context

The following writing samples represent the child's construction of fantasy by using imaginary phenomena in the creation of images. This is the most common form of metaphor used by young children (Rummel & Dykstra, 1983). A child's fantasy writing can tell us much about her/his personal, family, and community contexts. It is a way of nurturing the ability to summon up an "as if," as Greene calls it (1992a), a sense of "what is out there, what I can reach if I try." It is a way of doing what Greene suggests, "helping students find language to bring dreams into being, language that introduces them to the experience of going beyond."

The next poem, also describing "the day I was born," is a fantasy analogy in contrast to the symbolic analogy above. This child's fantasy about her birth also uses the power of metaphor to connect herself, her family, and her world. It is a fantasy set in the natural world as opposed to the mythological world described above.

On the day I was born
The sun shown
Bright n' high.
The birds started singing.
My mom and dad
Started to cry
'Cause they were so happy
I came.
On the day I was born
All the land animals
Started to gather
All around my room
To see me.
The rivers flowed
More than ever.
It rained

But after that
A beautiful rainbow appeared.
And my mom and dad
Said the rainbow was perfect
And so am I.
They said I made their lives happy.
On the day I was born
I made the sun show bright.
And made my mom and dad cry.
On the day I was born
Everyone was on my side.

In one of the bilingual family literacy classes, the teacher, in a lesson about community helpers, was trying to elicit traditional responses (such as policeman and fireman) to the question: What community helper would you like to be when you grow up? "A ghostbuster" was one boy's very serious response. This kindergarten child viewed the work of a ghostbuster as legitimate caring for his community. He used fantasy to actually be empowered to take care of his family, friends, and community.

Another child's writing sample from the family literacy class shows the almost constant image-making process of the young child. He drew what looked like two fried eggs (with red yolks) as eyes and a red, ketchup-made nose and mouth and wrote under the drawing:

Sometimes I wonder in my mind that when I eat eggs and put ketchup on my eggs it seem like I am drawing a funny face [*sic*].

The metaphor in "My Hands Jump" gives unique detail to the fourth-grade child's personal images and desires. She shows critical personal transformation in the sense that she is able *to be* her hands.

My Hands Jump

At night my hands
jump because they dance.
They are known to all creatures.
They jump and plie and spin
so fast you can hardly see them.

They jump into bushes and spin
 around the twisted branches and use leaves for tutus.
The wind whistles a tune
and crickets sing songs
of beauty and boldness.
Their dancing slippers
of dried bean seeds begin
to wear thin
so they come home to bed
strip off their tutus
and dancing slippers
and drift off to sleep.

In the following sample, a second-grade child is reproducing her own family experiences through fantasizing about the interaction of loons.

Loon 1: O go to bed.
Loon 2: No
1: Yes Sh
2: No
1: Don't sh
2: No
1: Go to sleep
2: No
1: sh
2: make me!
1: Be Quiet! Go to sleep
2: 1 don't want to
1: Shut up
2: make me
1: Elvis Duck is coming and if you aren't good you won't go
2: ZZZZZZZZZZZZZZZZ
ZZZZZZZZZZZZZZZZZZZ
ZZZZZ ZZZZZZZZZZZZZ
ZZZZZZZZZ ZZZZZ ShShSh

Personal Analogy and Sociocultural Context

It is personal analogy in metaphor, however, that gives us the power to overcome our personal isolation. Ozick (1989) describes this power.

Through metaphorical concentration doctors can imagine what it is like to be their patients . . . those at the center can imagine what it is to be outside. The strong can imagine the weak. Illumined lives can imagine the dark. We strangers can imagine the familiar hearts of strangers. (p. 283)

In personal analogy the child becomes something else and speaks from the point of view of that identification. Much can be learned by considering what the child identifies with and the extent of that identification. In "My Name Is Like the Wind," a ten-year-old girl identifies with something large, the wind, and sees the wind as encompassing all the community, referred to as "anything."

> My Name is Like the Wind
>
> My name is wind
> talking to the sky.
> I am wind
> looking around the world.
> I am the wind
> that has fingers that touch anything.
> I am the wind
> that blows through your body.
> I am the wind
> that talks to you when you are bad
> or in a sad mood.
> I am the wind.

In this poem, a six-year-old identifies with a fox and uses the metaphor for action outside herself.

> I am a red fox.
> I will give you berries.
> I will take you to the top of the mountain.
> I will show you the whole town.

A kindergarten student in the bilingual family literacy class had made a puppet at home for homework. When he brought the puppet back to class to show the other participants, he made no complex explanations, he put the puppet on his hand and *became* a clown. He explained to the class that he had entertained his brother at home by making him laugh with the puppet. He then wrote,

I am a paper clown and I like to laugh.

Another child used analogy not only for herself but also for a family member, creating an interaction.

Cloud Love

Mom, you are the cloud,
I am the rain.
When you get mad at me
you drop me so I rain
on little animals & people.
When you are not mad at me
you come down before
I soak into the ground—
Then we rise together.

Rummel and Dykstra (1983) found that children did not use the extended identification process of personal analogy or metaphor unless they were specifically guided to do so. That is why there are few samples from the children in the bilingual family literacy project. However, personal analogy in the form of symbolic and pretend play is integral in the cognitive and socioemotional development of young children. In the family literacy project, the four-year-old children most often revealed examples of personal analogy through their writing about their pretend play:

Yo soy Rafael [the Ninja Turtle] con mi chucks.
(I am Raphael with my numchucks.)
Soy el love bug y voy a mordir a Grandma porque le quiero.
(I am the love bug and I'm going to bite Grandma because I love her.)

CONCLUSION

The purpose of this study was to use the authentic voices of the children to convince teachers of the potential of young girls and children from culturally and linguistically diverse families and to encourage teachers to create classroom contexts in which children can use their voices to affirm their social contexts and to create new situations for themselves.

School contexts often reproduce mainstream society's biases regarding race, ethnicity, class, and gender. Yet, schools can also be a place for change. As teachers learn to read children's texts more critically they will help children learn to be resisting readers and writers of their own and other texts and explore through language new metaphors and structures that challenge (Kamler, 1992, p. 32).

If teachers want to encourage children to use language to create new images for themselves in cultural contexts, we need to know how to guide children's voices in writing through use of expressive genres, like poetry and fiction. This intervention on the part of the teacher demands an awareness that linguistic choices are socially constructed. A teacher can help children by "listening" to their voices, reading their often short communications with a sensitivity to the messages children are giving about themselves and their lives.

A sixth-grade teacher in the Dialogue Program commented during a seminar, "These writers see things in students' writing that I don't see." He was describing a sensitivity to voice that is often a result of personal immersion in the writing process. Teachers who write learn to look beyond form and mechanics in order to respond to the voice of the writer (Rummel, 1992.) Many of the teachers who participated in the Dialogue Program described growth in this ability. A fourth-grade teacher said, "My students have confidence about writing they didn't have before—and, especially, so do I. Everyone has feelings and imagination and writing is sharing that."

A direct suggestion from Atwood (1991) guides us specifically:

> There's a lack of self-confidence that gets instilled very early in many young girls, before writing is even seen as a possibility. You need a certain amount of nerve to be a writer, an almost physical nerve, the kind you need to walk a log across a river. The horse throws you and you get back on the horse. I learned to swim by being dropped into the water. You need to know you can sink and survive it. Girls should be allowed to play in the mud. They should be released from the obligations of perfection. Some of your writing, at least, should be as evanescent as play. (p. 152)

Atwood's comments are echoed by a sixth-grade teacher from the Dialogue Program:

> As a person, to be able to write down what you think for yourself and others is essential to success. And writing goes hand in hand with reading. Writing touches everything. I'm determined that my kids unlearn their fear of a piece of paper. I want them to see blank paper as a gift for setting down their next thought.

REFERENCES

Atwood, M. (1991). Nine beginnings. In J. Sternburg (Ed.), *The writer on her work* (p. 152). New York: Norton.

Bloch, M. N. (1991). Critical science and the history of child developments influence on early education research. *Early Education and Development, 2*(2), pp. 95–108.

Blumer, H. (1969). *Symbolic interactionism, Perspective and method.* Englewood Cliffs, NJ: Prentice-Hall.

Calkins, L. (1986). *The Art of teaching writing.* Portsmouth NH: Heinemann.

Calkins, L. (1991) *Living between the lines.* Portsmouth, NH: Heinemann.

Cooper, M. M. (1989). Women's ways of writing. In M. M. Cooper and M. Holzman (Eds.), *Writing as social action* (pp. 141–156). Portsmouth, NH: Boynton/Cook.

Elbow, P. (1981). *Writing with power.* New York: Oxford University Press.

Freire, P. (1985). *The politics of education* Granby, MA: Bergin and Garvey.

Gilligan, C. (1982). *In a different voice: Psychological theory and women's development.* Cambridge: Harvard University Press.

Giroux, H. (1991). The politics of postmodernism: Rethinking the boundaries of race and ethnicity. *Journal of Urban and Cultural Studies,* 1(1), 5–38.

Gordon, W. J. (1961). *Synectics: The development of creative capacity.* New York: Harper.

Graves, D. H. (1983). *Writing: Teachers and children at work.* Portsmouth, NH: Heinemann.

Greene, M. (1992a). *Imagination and breakthoughs in the unexpected.* Unpublished paper presented to the Association of Supervision and Curriculum Development. New Orleans.

Greene, M. (1992b). The passions of pluralism: Multiculturalism and the expanding community. *Educational Researcher. 22*(1), 13–18.

Kamler, B. (1992 April). *The social construction of gender in early writing.* Paper presented to the American Educational Research Association. San Francisco.

Khatena, J. (1972). The use of analogy in the production of original verbal images. *Journal of Creative Behavior. 6*, 93–102.

Lakoff, R. (1973). Language and wornen's place. *Language and Society, 2*, 45–79.

Lassner, P. (1990). Feminist responses to Rogerian argument. *Rhetoric Review, 8*, 220–231.

Lorde, A. (1984). *Sister outsider.* Freedom, CA: Crossing Press.

Oakes, J., & Lipton, M. (1990). *Making the best of schools.* New Haven: Yale University Press.

Ozick, C. (1989). *Metaphor and memory.* New York: Knopf.

Phinney, M. Y. (1993). Then you havta be three in my play: Politics of kindergartners at the writing table. *The Australian Journal of Language and Literacy* (in press).

Polakow, V. (1993). *Lives on the edge.* Chicago: University of Chicago Press.

Quintero, E. P., & Macías, A. H. (1991). Learning together: Sociocultural issues in literacy. *Educational Issues of Language Minority Students: The Journal.* Boise: Boise State University.

Reyes, M. de la Luz. (1993). Challenging venerable assumptions: Literacy instruction for linguistically different students. *Harvard Educational Review, 62*(4), 427–446.

Ritchie, J. S. (1990). Confronting the "essential" problem: Reconnecting feminist theory and pedagogy. *Journal of Advanced Composition, 10*, 249–273.

Rubin D., & Greene, K. (1991). Effects of biological and psychological gender, age cohort, and interviewer gender on attitudes toward gender-inclusive/exclusive language. *Sex Roles, 24*, 391–412.

Rubin, D., & Greene, K. (1992). Gender-typical style in written language. *Research in the Teaching of English, 26*(1), 7–37.

Rummel, M. K. (1992). *Writer-teacher collaborations: A model for change.* Unpublished paper presented at the National Council for the Teachers of English National Conference. Louisville, KY.

Rummel, M. K., & Dykstra, B. (1983). Analogies produced by children in relation to grade level and linguistic maturity. *Research in the Teaching of English, 17*(1), 51–60.

Shannon, P. (1990). Whole language and critical literacy. In K. Goodman, Y. Goodman, & L. B. Bird (Eds.), *The whole language catalogue.* (p. 53). Santa Rosa, CA: American School Publishers.

Shor, I. (1987). *Freire for the classroom: A sourcebook for liberatory teaching.* Portsmouth, NH: Heinemann.

Swadener, E. B., & Kessler, S. (1991). Introduction to the special issue. *Early Education and Development, 2*(2), 85–94.

Temple, C., Nathan, R., Temple, F., & Burris, N. (1993). *The beginning of writing.* Boston: Allyn and Bacon.

Wolf, D. (1988). *Writing. dialogue. and literacy: An evaluation of the COMPAS Dialogue Program.* St. Paul: COMPAS.

Wong Fillmore, L. (1991). *When learning a second language means losing the first. Early Childhood Research Quarterly. 6*(3), 323–347.

DONELDA A. COOK
MICHELLE FINE

5

"Motherwit": Childrearing Lessons from African-American Mothers of Low Income

With the increasing crime rates in urban communities in drug trafficking, theft, and homicide, as well as the alarming social problems of crack-cocaine abuse, unwed pregnancies, and HIV-AIDS, low-income African American families are once again being blamed for the country's current social problems (Gibbs, 1988). Politicians and the media allege that declining family values, single-mother households, dysfunctional childrearing practices, and dependency on welfare programs are the lifestyle preferences of African Americans who reside in these troubled communities. According to this narrow perspective, the adolescents who are terrorizing urban America are doing so because their single-parent households (which means mothers) have not adequately taught them the value of human life and decency. It is ironic that one of the most powerful groups of people in America, low-income

African American women (Belle, 1984; Copeland, 1982; Robinson, 1983), is seen as the power behind a whole generation capable of stunning the nation.

Blaming the families for the behavior of urban adolescents fails to acknowledge the political, social, and economic conditions in the United States that have abandoned our urban communities (Gibbs, 1988). National problems such as chronic unemployment and poverty have fueled the fires of desperation among urban residents as they strive to overcome the external barriers that impede their existence (Myers & King, 1983). The collusion to scapegoat African American families as the source of urban degeneration is reminiscent of the 1960s.

The Moynihan Report of 1965 placed the blame for the social ills of that time on the "matriarchs" who were said to be responsible for the deterioration of Black families and the Black community. Peters (1978) wrote of the research at that time:

> The Afro-American family has been of interest in the social science literature, mostly as the primary source of some of America's most perplexing problems, i.e., poverty, urban decay, slums, unemployment, school dropouts, disturbed race relations, and interracial marriage. (p. 655)

A number of research studies were conducted comparing Black and White mothers' childrearing practices, and when differences were found, they were interpreted to suggest that Black mothers were pathological or dysfunctional (Johnson, 1988). In attempting to conceptualize what seemed unique as family structures of Black families, social scientists labeled them "deviant," "deprived," "deficient," "disadvantaged," "disorganized," and "chaotic" (Boyd-Franklin, 1989; Peters, 1978). These were descriptions of "experts" viewing the family from outside, without regard for how Black families described their own functioning or the social constraints they were burdened with.

In response to these negative interpretations of Black motherhood, African American scholars and researchers have more recently challenged the methodological validity of comparison studies between races which contrasted mothers *as if race* were the only distinguishing variable (Clark, 1983; Huttman, 1991; Nobles, 1988). It was argued that powerful differences between Black and White family structures derived from differences in cultural world views, social class, material conditions, and racial

opportunity structures, all of which influence childrearing strategies (Billingsley, 1968; Nobles, 1988). More recent studies of low-
income African American mothers have studied how childrearing
practices accomplish both adaptation and resistance to oppressive
conditions of poverty and institutional racism (Portes, Dunham, &
Williams, 1986; Fu, et al., 1984; Peterson & Peters, 1985). In
response to the literature equating Blackness and/or poverty with
deficient parenting and negligent child development, various interventions have been designed to "help"—to provide childrearing
guidance and psychological support to low-income families
(Halpern, 1990).

   While low-income parents, like the rest of us, could benefit
from various forms of tangible support, once we listen to their narratives, as offered in this chapter, we can reframe the conversation.
"Deficit" and "risk" analyses have been thrust upon those women
without regard for separating the *risks* imposed by their contexts
from the *blame* cast upon them as if "they" were inadequate
childrearers. In contrast to the individualistic and damning
accounts that have been written about them, as if they were
idiosyncratically deficient in their approaches to childrearing, we
hear their critical analyses of the contexts and constraints born of
the Reagan Bush years, within which healthy childrearing was
made particularly difficult (Austin, 1992; Boyd-Franklin, 1989).

   The urban schools literature has been replete with scholarship and policies which either condemn these mothers as problematic childrearers, or, more recently, glorify them as supermoms.
We intend neither form of analytic reduction. Instead, we hope to
make visible the importance of social supports, material comforts,
a set of public institutions inclined to give your child the benefit
of the doubt, safe streets, and so on, which are significant, under-
acknowledged features of contexts which enable what is considered "good mothering" (Scheper-Hughes, 1992). We seek to identify how these women cope with the absence of these conditions
and how they negotiate the difficulties of parenting adolescents
within a set of public institutions designed to both disempower
and blame them and their children.

   This essay, in brief, offers a dissection of victim-blaming ideologies which surround and infiltrate these women and their families and a reframing of these women and their families through
contextual analysis. We begin, and end, with the presumption that
as long as schools are separated from or fortresses against children's families and communities, the deficit-ridden analyses of

these women and their childrearing strategies will persist, and the social and economic conditions which have dramatically disadvantaged them will slip off the analytic hook. In this essay we report on a group of African American mothers who, if their voices could be heard, could teach all of us something about the "motherwit" that is required to raise children in an urban community that is stricken with poverty, unemployment, drug trafficking, and constant threats and occurrences of violence. As Robinson (1983) argues, "we have much to learn from a woman in the poorest Black community, or one who succeeds despite incredible stress" (p. 142).

Drawing on cases from twelve mothers whose children attend a middle school in the inner city of Baltimore, this paper reveals how deeply caught these women are between institutions which stand as evidence of their "inadequacies" as parents, and children who carry all the conflicting messages of racism and classism inside the U.S. "underclass." If the tasks of motherhood, are to encourage individual growth and offer children protection, then these women suggest to us that protection is almost impossible to assure, and growth is most difficult to facilitate, within urban poverty. And yet these women struggle to do both. As determined as they are to protect and shape their children's behaviors, they recognize the importance of communicating growth through acceptance, encouragement, support, and an understanding of their children's emotional development. They recognize, further, that the public institutions and policies designed "for their good" carry deeply ambivalent messages about them and their kin. These narratives of "motherwit," voiced in contexts of federal and often familial abandonment, suggest that radically different policies are needed to replace the often contradictory, usually punishing ones that affect them today and threaten to affect them tomorrow.

CONTEXT OF THE CASES

We met this group of African American women while conducting an evaluation of a parent empowerment program from 1988 through 1990. Donnie is an African American counseling psychologist, and Michelle is a White social psychologist. We entered these women's lives as "evaluators interested in their perspectives on schooling and the program." The program was designed to activate low-income parents as homework-helpers, advocates for their middle school children, and partners in educational reform. As part of the evaluation methodology, we conducted audiotaped interviews of a sample of twelve mothers at the beginning and end of the project (see Fine & Cook, 1991, for full evaluation). Each mother was paid $20 for an hour-long interview, which was held either in her home or at the site of the program. In this program, "mother" is used to refer to any female caretaker including biological mother, grandmother, aunt, and other guardian. This sample was comprised of those who had been actively involved in the parent empowerment project (see Garlington, 1991, for details of project).

Through our assessing the mothers' views of the program, during our interviews we were struck by their openness in welcoming us into their homes, their involvement in their children's education, and their wisdom as they articulated their attitudes and described their practices in raising their children. While our study was not designed self-consciously to examine the childrearing attitudes and practices of low income African American mothers, our conversations revealed much about the contexts for mothering that seemed so "natural" to these women and so catastrophic to anyone living outside these contexts. We suggest that these women do not need tips on parenting nearly as much as they need radically transformed social and economic opportunities. These women long ago fell through the fraying safety net, and yet, with others, they darn the holes trying to catch the next generation of children as they are tossed.

The interviews were conducted by two teams, which included one of the researchers and one of the program staff members who had previous contact with the women. The demographic characteristics of the interview teams may have had an impact on the interview process, both in terms of the questions asked and the responses given. In addition, our race, gender, social class, educational and occupational level, and lifestyle may have influenced our interpretation and reporting of the interview data (Reid, 1992). One research team consisted of an African American middle-class female counseling psychologist who has no children, accompanied by an African American female program staff member who is a mother and has an associate's degree. The other team consisted of a White researcher who is a mother of one and an African American male program staff member who is a former teacher.

THE COMMUNITY

To understand the challenges that low-income African American women confront on a daily basis and their childrearing strategies, we examine first the community within which they reside. The women with whom we spoke lived in a community in which 42 percent of the families lived below the poverty level, with a mean income of $8,231; 21 percent of the residents were unemployed; over 70 percent of the residents had not graduated from high school; and 60 percent of the households were headed by women (National Committee for Citizens in Education, 1987).

The term "community" is applicable only with respect to geography. Little social connectedness has survived the 1980s–early 1990 assault on this urban community. The population tends to be transient, as families move around frequently in search of adequate housing. This limits the degree of trust between neighbors, as does the prevalence of drug trafficking and violence in the neighborhood. We observed several row houses which had signs posted on the door warning drug pushers to stay away. Parents and guardians in inner cities throughout the country fear for their children's safety as they reside amidst the drug scene, random violence, and drive by shootings (Huttman, 1991). Several of the mothers voiced these concerns in our interviews.

In discussing the differences between her own school days and those of her child, one woman said,

> But school was okay for me when I was going. We didn't worry about kids bringing guns in, and violence like it is now in school . . . I kind of worry about them you know, that situation, running around with guns and stuff in school.

Many mothers spoke of the violence in and around the school:

> You know, I feel like, my children aren't secure in school either. And it's getting to the point I question whether or not I should take them out. I'm one of them parents, you know, I feel like, at the rate the schools are going, I can teach my child at home. . . . But I wouldn't want to be getting off of work one day and somebody standing in front of my house telling me my child got shot by accident. Now, I'm, I'm not going to sit lightly with that at all, I'm not.

One woman voiced a policy critique concerning out of school suspensions. Her son, age eleven, had been sent home early because he got ink on his pants. She feared what could happen to him walking alone in the community.

> He's walking from [school], from . . . the area is bad. I mean, they raping little kids. They beating them up. Taking them off and everything. . . . And I feel more better if he's coming home with a bunch of kids than him out there one-thirty [p.m.] by himself.

These mothers are aware of the dangers that their children encounter in the community and the school and aware of their inability to protect them. As I (Michelle) interviewed and wrote about these women, I realized how often I assure my six-year-old son Sam that our family is safe, no one will hurt us, World War II was long ago, sleep tight. I know I can comfort him—temporarily—with the white lies of elite White skin. These women can't fantasize the bullets away; can't promise safety; can't unambivalently invite their children to report any problem to the police or a teacher. The problems are too implicating, the institutions too alienating, the threats too real.

As one mother told us:

> That is the pain. You've got [Social Services] workers who talk to you like you trash; same thing in the school system. They feel like 'cause you, 'cause you have, ask your child to get free lunch, and I guess only one's who . . . they just make you feel less than what you really are.

In addition to the typical childrearing responsibilities, these women teach their children to avoid criminal behavior, and to survive the institutional and interpersonal violence which has saturated their neighborhood (Greene, 1990).

> I'd been raped. You know, an' the doctor, when I did seen the doctor, the doctor told me he didn't, I could get rid of him, but he can't because I was kind of little far gone and plus, I was very sensitive at the time anyway . . . sensitive . . . about getting rid of, you know, a child. . . . And he said, "Well you could have done that [abortion]." But I said, doctor, by his growing, growing and growing, I said, I came to love this lit-

tle baby more and more. But I said, that's all right. I'll raise him the best I can.

Living on the deceptive borders where Dan Quayle wanted to distinguish "good," moral life from "bad," immoral life, these women know the borders to be tenuous, unpredictable and almost as untrustworthy as the federal government that created the impoverishment and abandonment around them (Austin, 1992). Their own kin flirt at the borders in order to survive. Morals, politics, and "bad people" are not clean categories, as all of the recent Washington exposes confirm.

> When I saw him getting . . . mixing with the bad crowd in the neighborhood, I pulled him in. . . . I said, now look, I'm going to tell you something. You get with the bad boys out there, you're going to go to jail. If you go to get locked up one time, I'm not going to come to get you, I'm going to leave you there, not because I don't love you. I said because it's a right and a wrong. You going to get teased, and they might say momma's boy but you get with boys think like you want the same things. Those boys hanging on the corner, they don't want anything. They only going to get jail and I don't want that for you. I said because you got a home, you got a bed to sleep in, food in the refrigerator. I might can't get, it might not be everything, but think what I'm telling you. I had to make a example to him about something. I have a son that didn't listen to me, okay. He got with the wrong crowd. . . . So I shows him, I say, see my son. Sometimes I see my son, I walk away, I won't say nothing. I said, I don't want to do that. I said it hurts because he's my son, but I don't like what he does, so he can't live with me, in my home. So I don't let him live in my home, see. So I show [him] stuff like that.

AN INTERIOR LOOK AT THE STRESSES
IN THESE MOTHERS' LIVES

Stress is an inherent part of the lives of women who live in such inner-city communities as that described above. Crime and violence are frequent occurrences in low-income neighborhoods.

These mothers are continuously faced with threatening and uncontrollable life events (Belle, 1984). In addition,

> recent studies indicate that chronic life conditions such as inadequate housing, dangerous neighborhoods, burdensome responsibilities, and financial uncertainties can be even more potent stressors than acute crises and events. Furthermore, low income women are at very high risk of experiencing just such noxious long-term conditions. Thus, low income women are more likely to experience both chronic stressful conditions and acute stressful events. (Belle, 194, p. 138)

Each of the women we interviewed chronicled her "troubles" concerning illness and health, money and bills, job layoffs or extremely long work days for minimal pay, drugs, crime, and violence. While unemployment, for instance, may be considered a stressor and employment a "support," living in poverty as a single parent means that work and its absence can be problematic or advantageous. Some wanted to work to "help afford clothes and food for us." Others said "I can't work—who would be home for my kids?"

Unlike so many single parents interviewed by Ladner (1972), Francis-Okongwu (1986), and Goodman (1991), the women in this sample felt bereft of positive social networks. Perhaps characteristic of Wilson's (1987) "underclass," these women constitute "the ones left behind." They reported being "The sickly sister who stayed in the neighborhood," "The kid they thought was slow." While these women work hard to support others, including children, parents, neighbors, and self, they could rarely identify anyone who regularly supported them. One woman told us:

> I think it bothers him [her son] because I noticed, I was real sick, he didn't want to go to school that day. He knew I couldn't, I didn't have no one go with me. . . . Okay, so he asked me, "Well, you ain't going to be able to open the door," or because I couldn't on account of my hand, I said that's all right. He said "a lot of people are going to see you out there and they're not going to help you." So that did make sense, so I took him down to the clinic and he did help me. . . .

Many women explained that their personal illnesses provoked adverse consequences for their children's schooling, particularly in terms of attendance and grades. It became desperately clear that when their balancing act slips, there is no safety net. Alone, vulnerable, and with few resources, they feel fully responsible for themselves and their children. And they know that the public "helping" institutions—schools, courts, and welfare—will blame them if there is a fall.

> You see I work ten hours a day, and I can't be, cause, society blames it on the parents a lot. And I think, I think that I'm a good parent. I don't take drugs, I drink occasionally but I don't do drugs, I don't have drugs in my house and so it's not something he's seen me, he hasn't seen me sell drugs, so I don't know what he does, but then society says well, you're supposed to know what your children doing at all times. It's not so. I take two hours to travel to work, two hours to travel back and I'm on my feet ten hours a day. So that's like fourteen hours a day I'm out of the house. So I told him, I said, cause as well as you getting into trouble too because I know ladies that, the judge done told them well, you're going to have to change your work schedule, or you're going to have to find another job because you're going to have to be somewhere around to let us know where your child is. And I think it's wrong, but that's what they say you know and they're on probation and everything. Have to pay fines because they kids didn't go to school. And he done hook school and all that stuff in my house and I've been through it. He's been, he was just put away, he's back on the streets again. So, now I tell him, it's up to you not up to me. It's up to you whether you want to stay in society and deal with it or if you want to be behind bars. . . . So far, he's been home about a month. I haven't had any trouble out of him. I done went through glue sniffing and huffing and all that, and he's not doing that any more. And maybe he's trying to get himself together, hopefully.

These extended family loyalties and strong kinship ties have been a consistent theme in the lives of African American families (Billingsley, 1968; Boyd-Franklin, 1989; Hill, 1972). For these women left behind, the loyalties seem to be imbalanced, not richly reciprocated. One woman discussed her juggling act in being a single parent, working, attending to her sick father, and raising her daughter's newborn infant:

Like I told all of them, I've told both schools. I'm a single parent, I'm working, I'm raising my own kids, now I'm taking on somebody else's kid, give me a break. You know. Then my father, like I told them, he's ill. My father's dying. And I'm just not going to sit idly by, be in school, work, and raise kids and not visit my father sometimes. . . . And my time is very limited. Now he would go back to the Citizen's home and then I have to be on my job by 1:30. Then I won't see any of my children anymore, which I don't see any of my children during the day at all, anyway. I took on a night job to make ends meet. Now Social Services is telling me now that I've taken on this gig, I have to give up my night job. . . . In order to be with him [the baby] because he needs the time. He's been in foster care for four months. . . . So initially I took him on because I had really got attached to him plus I helped bring him in the world.

Low-income African American mothers are in a position of being dependent on various societal institutions over which they have little power and less trust (Belle, 1984). Furthermore, "poor women who seek change through personally confronting such institutions often experience repeated failures" (Belle, 1984, p. 141). For instance, many of the mothers that we interviewed spoke of the intolerable way that teachers and administrators in the school treat them.

Oh . . . They're uppity. They're uppity. If you, I feel if I had not finished school, because I didn't, you shouldn't sneer at me . . . because you got a degree behind you ain't going to mean anything . . . because I might have something that's knowledgeable to help you and we are supposed to be a helper to one another. You know, not to bring me down because I don't know. If I don't know, then you come to me and show me and help me. . . . Not to turn you nose up behind my back. . . . And you find that in some schools with some of the teachers, some of the faculties down in the schools. And I believe if they come as beings as one, no one higher than the other, you can find more parents coming in, coming in helping.

These mothers don't seem surprised that institutions in the public sector—schools, welfare, or health care—display enormous disrespect for them (Fine & Cook, 1991).

Another mother fought a losing battle in trying to get medical care for her son who sniffs glue.

And I'm been trying to get him put over there in this children's home for the glue sniffing problem. And he had gotten worsened, then he'd stop and now he's gone back to it again. And they had sent me up to the . . . Medical Center to get him evaluated, a referral and I got that one. I'm supposed to have two in order to have him put away. And that's what I've been working on trying to do.

Her efforts at getting help for her son were impeded because she could not afford the second evaluation that the system demanded before placing her son in a treatment facility.

In such circumstances these women negotiate relationships with kin, public institutions, community, "peer pressures," drugs, and violence. Rarely do they think about, or give voice to, their own needs. Despite their chronic stressors and hardships, these women have a fighting spirit and proactive mindset in making a difference in their children's social and educational lives. Many of the mothers assertively interact with the school system on their children's behalf.

I have been over to [the Board of Education]. I called, I got letters, both the student's rights, parent's rights and everything,. . . because I do believe in the telephone, you know. And I works on it.

As another mother put it:

I can go up against the school anyway because I'm going to say what I want to say. . . . I might not be smartest, but I do know what I know, and I'm going to stand on firmly what I do know.

These mothers mobilize around public institutions, through strategies of resistance and surveillance. Appropriating the roles of volunteer, community organizer, and school aid worker, they welcome the opportunity to form a coalition for change.

One mother volunteered in school, until her son vetoed her involvement.

And when they were in the elementary level, I went to school with them and I stayed all day. . . . Oh, I was a parent volunteer and I still volunteer [at the elementary school]. Sometimes I held a classroom for a teacher if she had to go out right away. And most of the time, like when he had problems in his work, I was right there to help him, right in the classroom. When he come home with his homework I already knowed what he had to do and I, you know, I could help him that way. And then when he got down to [the middle school], I just stopped . . . the reason why I don't come down [to the middle school] and volunteer in a classroom and different things because I don't want his friends to think that I'm watching him.

This mother recognized the importance of her active involvement in her children's lives, as well as the positive and negative impact that her presence may have had on her children.

I've been in this, what's called a Christian New Club for four years, so far, as a parent and as a board member and a Den Mother, a coach; I'm just a little bit of everything. And I mean to me, if I don't put myself in it and to be involved in things that my kids is in, then I feel that I, my teaching and raising would be in vain because I'm not out there trying to participate, trying to show them the way, you know. It's in the home, it's outside the home too, you see what I'm saying?

As this parent empowerment program was coming to a close, many of the mothers scrambled to establish a Parents Club, in hopes of retaining some of the support that the program had been providing them. As one mother described the club:

Well, the parenting group has been established to raise funds, to try to recruit . . . or recruit other parents to be supportive of what's going on with their kids in school. If they see parents who are in the program now, then maybe we can encourage them to come on out and be more aware.

Many of the women were simply delighted to be part of a group that could raise funds, pressure the principal (and win), offer students field trips and cultural activities, and succeed in establishing a Parents' Resource Room in the school—by, for, and about parents.

Psychologist Brinton Lykes (1985) distinguishes social individuals from autonomous individuals when she writes:

> Social individuals are active and involved in circles well beyond immediate family or neighborhood. . . . They participate in a range of activities . . . which reflect both a sense of their own individuality . . . and a commitment to social change through collaborative or collective action.
>
> In contrast, autonomous individuals tend to describe their current communities . . . not in terms of human relations or interconnections. Independence and autonomy are themes. . . . There is little evidence . . . of commitment to or engagement in action for social change. (p. 37)

Listening to Lykes, we can hear many of these women as preeminent social individuals, with few resources to support themselves. By race, class, and gender—maybe in that order—they commit to collective survival. Working in circles together, they seek these connections, within and across communities and generations, "with and for" other parents who couldn't, or wouldn't, be as active as they. At the foundation of their work lies a deep understanding of the complex lives of their neighbors, a thoroughgoing commitment to community life in African American communities. The members of the Parent Group echo powerfully and passionately the words of sociologist Cheryl Townsend Gilkes:

> [F]our basic struggles . . . shape the consciousness of Black women—the struggle for human dignity, the struggle against white hypocrisy, the struggle for justice, and the struggle for survival. . . . No matter how high they rise, and no matter how diverse and how many places they go to build, Black women community workers are the ones who will come home to the community. (p.75)

VALUES AND ATTITUDES—PEERS AND SCHOOLS

Low-income parents of teens sit at the intersection of adolescent temptations and destructive external forces competing with their childrearing practices. Many rely upon tight or what may appear to be constraining parental care and nurturance strategies (Halpern, 1990; Huttman, 1991; Nobles, 1978). Given the inability to assure protection, and the knowledge that "public" (e.g., juvenile justice) institutions are waiting to capture their child, it is no surprise that comparison studies across race and income levels revealed low income African American parents to be more directive and controlling with their children and to value obedience, conformity, and respect for authority in their children's behaviors (Fu et al., 1984; Peterson & Peters, 1985). The degrees of freedom available to them, and to errors in childrearing, are very limited (Ogbu, 1987) .

These African American urban mothers keep a close watch on their children's involvements outside of the home. Protecting them from dangerous circumstances posed by criminal elements in the community and oppressive conditions in society (Clark, 1983; Greene, 1990), these mothers realize the stakes are too high to allow their children too much freedom and independence. It might cost them their lives. Our interviews revealed the mothers' desire to teach their children what may appear to be contradictory urban survival strategies—trusting and mistrusting (Nobles 1988; Ogbu, 1987). The mothers spoke of two major areas in which they needed to assist their children to "achieve more than we had," by both trusting and mistrusting—dealing with peers and dealing with schools.

"Peer Pressure"

"Peer pressure" is a constant concern to these mothers. While they voice concern that neighborhood children are stereotyped as "bad," these mothers must consider ways of protecting their children, ensuring that their children do not grow up too soon, monitoring their friends and associates, and giving their children advice on how to handle themselves when trouble does arise. "Don't fight" or "Just say no" are wholly inadequate to context. These women cannot, on a daily basis, narrate the lessons of remote liberalism so many of us try to preach from afar.

One mother has a daughter and a son in middle school. She is very involved with her children inside and outside of the home and expects them to follow a prescribed way of behaving at all times. She uses a teaching style consistent with what Peterson & Peters (1985) describe as the "correct way" to perform a task and "mandates" goals for her children's development. For instance, she is concerned that her daughter dress appropriately for her age and not rush the growing-up process.

> Yes, I say, take your time. You'll be thirteen . . . next year. . . .
> It's just a number. But if you stay as sweet as you are, and
> grow, you'll be adult soon. But you got them many years in
> between to be a little girl. . . . So they must be at her about
> the little stuff and this and this. . . .

She told us a story of a time when her daughter came outside with lipstick on, which was against the rules; she is only allowed to wear lipstick and fingernail polish in the house.

> I said, what is that on your lips honey? She said "My lipstick
> mom." I said, please, go in the house and get it off, them lips
> is too red for me . . . when you hit outside, everything should
> be clear off your nails, off your lips, wherever. I said because
> you look like a floozy, you look like a little Jezebel with all
> that stuff on.

This mother's attitude is consistent with research findings that African American mothers foster a sense of dependency and loyalty to parents in their adolescent daughters, while simultaneously fostering independence in interacting with outside influences (Fu et al., 1984). Again she is working the boundaries which are supposed to be so finely distinguished between "good mothering" and "bad" (Scheper-Hughes, 1992). Most of her teachings are centered around keeping her children out of trouble, yet she realizes that there is only so much protection she can provide for them (which gets viewed institutionally as "neglect"). Consequently, the mothers in this sample provide their children with powerful direction on protecting themselves:

> They fought in front of the door here and I told [my son] you
> know, the boys will antagonize you, try to fight you . . . and I
> don't want you out of school for fighting . . . I told [my son]
> you will have to protect yourself because I'm not there and
> maybe the faculty or some of the teachers in there, aren't
> there at the time . . . but I told him it's not going to stop
> there, it's going to all, each grade he go to, but you're going to
> have to be aware, you going to have to be alert, to know

who's going to be after and who's not going to be after. It's going to be hard. . . .

The mothers make a point of knowing the other children with whom their children associate, so as to steer them away from those who could be a bad influence on them. They have a keen eye for "sizing up" the children in the neighborhood, and a soft heart for "takin' in the ones on the street." The balance is often difficult.

He's a good kid, that's all I can say. . . . No problems at all. Just good natured . . . sensitive, no problems at all. It's just being around the right crowd, the right kids and that's hard to control for him. Yeah, and being a school or every school, it's everywhere. But just the part of just being with the wrong crowd or person, you know, I try to just let him know and explain to him that school is for learning. . . .

These mothers recognize that it is not enough to "Just say no." Their children must learn to negotiate their world such that they know how to associate with the "less than desirable" individuals in their community without offending them, yet also know *how* to escape them at appropriate times. As one mother explained, sometimes children do not escape.

Well, the ones that come here, he don't experience too much pressure from them, but I think it's the ones out in the street that I don't let come in my house; that is where he is getting most his pressure from. One of his little buddies was hooking, got put out of school yesterday and he come around here and wanted [my son] to go with him and I told [my son] he couldn't go. And, then when he finally went out, when he came back he was all messed up with that glue.

Another mother also spoke of the dangers of peer pressure for her son.

[I feel] frightened a lot of times. Because, sometimes I wish that he was just grown already. Where so much of that weight, if something happened, I wouldn't feel that it would be on me. And I pray that he reaches to be a grown man all the time. Where, I don't have the problem with him too much being in the street, you know, getting into trouble.

Negotiating Schools

The value of educational achievement has been posited as a major strength of African American families, regardless of socioeconomic levels (Billingsley, 1968; Boyd-Franklin, 1989; Hill, 1972; Manns, 1988; Scanzoni, 1985). A study of the perceptions of parenting success by African American mothers of preadolescent children revealed that the mothers were satisfied with their ability to help their children do their best in school, particularly in providing homework help when it was needed and supervising their television viewing and use of free time (Strom et al., 1990). These results are consistent with the involvement and deep ambivalence of the mothers whom we interviewed about their children's schools.

One mother discussed the parent's role in assisting children with homework:

As a parent, I think we should go down and be more observant in the classroom; find out what their kids are doing, some of the work they're doing. 'Cause work they giving there is much more different from when I was coming along. And my son bringing home math homework. . . . I said, I never had this before. . . . And he was showing me; and I said, well you learn, you get it good, because I cannot help you, you know. I said, I'm signing my name on your work, sign it that you had did it, but I don't know anything about it. . . .

Some of the mothers voiced concern over teachers not cooperating with their efforts at improving their children's academic performance. One mother complained that her daughter's English notebook "looked like it was from a physical education class," given how little written work was in it. Another mother was concerned about her daughter's reading and math classes.

But as far as the educational system, you know, it's been pretty bad. . . . In her math class, she says her teacher doesn't always help her . . . like she asks certain questions about certain things then the teacher tells her . . . you should have been listening, you know something like that, which I think

is really bad because the child . . . may had been listening you
know, but you can't take in everything. You know, if I feel
like their job is to help the child, so if the child asks a question . . . about something . . . it's up to you to answer it to
make sure they understand . . . so that when it comes test
time or whatever . . . the child is confident and they'll get
that part right.

These mothers praise their children for doing the best that
they can.

Both of my kids, I must say, I'm thankful. I'm proud of both
of them. They're bright, very intelligent. They do well in
school so far, they love it. You know, and I'm proud of them.
She, she was like Student of the Week . . . The line leader . . .
and she was so happy about that and thrilled. And so was I,
so I had to go and like get her a little present, just to reward
her and make her, you know, just to keep, keep it up. You
know, hang in there, for best, be the best you can be.

One mother spoke of her struggles with helping her son to
achieve despite an apparent learning disability.

Well, he was kind of slow, and kind of hard about catching
on, you know. And a couple of times I went up to the school
and discussed it with teachers. About this progress that he
was making. He had spinal meningitis when he was like five
months old . . . so they said, the doctors would tell me he
might develop a little slower . . . he might not see a change
until he's in school and then he starts having problems with
learning and grasping in his class. . . . When it first started
out, it was kind of rocky for him. . . . So when he started having all these problems with the, you know, the school and
learning, you know, I talked to his teachers about it, so they
took a little bit more time with him. . . . And then I help
him. He's got a brother that . . . helps him. . . .

Clark (1983) has posited that the family's main contribution
to a child's achievement in school is transmitted through the parents' disposition and interpersonal relationship with the child in
the home. The family's beliefs, activities, and overall cultural style
provide a foundation for the child's performance during classroom

lessons. It is obvious that these mothers recognize the importance of their role in their children's educational achievement and that they try to apply whatever resources they have to the task. They also know they need to convey a mild skepticism to their children so schools don't "kill their spirit just 'cause I raise some sand."

CONCLUSION

Once the focus shifts from "Are they good mothers?" to a critical analysis of the conditions and institutions within which these women mother, we hear not only the struggles and triumphs of low-income, single-parent, African American mothers, but the brutal and contradictory conditions within which our nation has forced them to nurture and develop their children (see Scheper-Hughes, 1992). Few who read this essay, if you are parents, haven't told "white lies" to your children to allow them to believe in the safety of their worlds, to protect them while they are still young. Not many have been able to raise children alone. Most resort to social supports that are available in kin or friends. More enjoy the virtue of class privilege which allows us to purchase our "supports" (legally or not). The bulk of us (especially if White and not in a custody battle) assume that public institutions represent our best interests or, at least, are not committed to taking our young away.

Imagine, instead, a context in which you can no longer lie to your child because she hears shots out the window; where public institutions, your only hope, evince a strong ambivalence, sometimes antipathy, toward you and your kin; where the most enduring public institutions are the prison and the juvenile justice systems, and the most reliable economic system involves underground drug trafficking. Imagine further that despite your best attempts to get your children to believe in "what could be," your children see little hope for themselves. The rules that you have taught them are negated routinely and flagrantly by the instant gratification that the drug world can offer. They are betrayed by inexplicable violence, homelessness, and despair; by the disrespect that public systems display to you, their mothers, and to them, your children; by anger to the point of defiance and vengeance. Then what kinds of childrearing practices would you invent?

We have asked you to shift your kaleidoscopic lens from a critical look at the behaviors of these women to a critical look at the contexts in which they are asked to mother—the contexts within which they are trying to change diapers, remain sane, comfort crying children, keep their kin alive and smiling. With this text we seek a moratorium on studies which decontextualize class/race-based childrearing strategies from the constraints and contexts in which these strategies have been developed. We suggest that parenting classes and training be offered only within broad based social movements committed to transforming the material and social circumstances of these women and their children. We challenge the social science silence on and degradation of poor women (Reid, 1992) and invite critical analysis of the dignity, "hidden transcripts of resistances," and collective struggles engaged by these women (Scott, 1992).

There is nothing inherently "at risk" about these women or their children. In the contexts of their lives, they spin creative strategies of survival, resistance, and collective struggle. Policies which punish them for their poverty or threaten to push them off welfare when quality jobs, comprehensive insurance, and accessible child care are unavailable reproduce the victim-blaming we have heard for decades. Research which fetishizes the individual woman as if she were the problem or the solution occludes and protects obscene contexts of economic inequity, racism, and social despair.

For those of us who engage in research with/on families in poverty, we need to invent narrative strategies that tell stories but do not romanticize individual tales of survival. For to do that, we too inadvertently camouflage the genocidal contexts, policies, and national agendas within which these women have been making much more than due. Indeed, they are making the mostly smiling, but still outraged, children of tomorrow.

AUTHOR NOTE

Preparation of this article was supported by the W.T. Grant Foundation. We gratefully acknowledge the assistance of the National Committee for Citizens in Education "With and For Parents" Program staff, Jocelyn Garlington, Coretha Holly, Robert Gregg, and Bill Rioux. We are especially appreciative of the time and openness shared by the mothers whom we interviewed.

REFERENCES

Austin, R. (1992). The "Black community," its lawbreakers and a politics of identification. *Southern California Law Review, 65*, 1769–1817.

Belle, D. (1984). Inequality and mental health: Low income and minority women. In L. E. Walker (Ed.), (pp. 135–150) *Women and mental health policy.* Beverly Hills: Sage.

Billingsley, A. (1968). *Black families in White America.* Englewood Cliffs NJ: Prentice Hall.

Bookman, C., and Morgan, J. (1988). *Women and the politics of empowerment.* Philadelphia: Temple University Press.

Boyd-Franklin, N. (1989). Five key factors in the treatment of Black families. *Journal of Psychotherapy and the Family, 6*, 53–69.

Clark, R. (1983). *Family life and school achievement.* Chicago: University of Chicago Press.

Copeland, E. J. (1982). Oppressed conditions and the mental health needs of low-income Black women: Barriers to services, strategies for change. *Women and Therapy, 1*, 13–26.

Crosby, F. (1991). *Juggling.* New York: Free Press.

Edelman, M.W. (1985). The sea is so wide and my boat is so small: Problems facing Black children today. In H. P. McAdoo & J. L. McAdoo (Eds.), (pp. 72–82) *Black children.* Beverly Hills: Sage.

Fine, M., & Cook, D.A. (1991). Evaluation reports: *"With and For Parents."* Final evaluation report submitted to National Committee of Citizens for Education, Baltimore.

Fine, M. (1991). *Framing dropouts:* Albany, NY: State University of New York Press.

Francis-Okongwu, A. (1986). *Different realities: A comparative study of nineteen Black and White female single parents.* Unpublished doctoral dissertation, University of Michigan, Ann Arbor.

Franklin, A. J., & Boyd-Franklin, N. (1985). A Psychoeducational perspective on Black parenting. In H. P. McAdoo & J. L. McAdoo (Eds.), *Black children* (pp. 194–210). Beverly Hills: Sage.

Fu, V. R., Hinkle, D. E., Shoffner, S., Martin, S., Carter, E., Clark, A., Culley, P., Disney, G., Ercanli, G., Glover, E., Kenney, M., Lewis H., Moak, S., Stalling, S., & Wakefield, T. (1984). Maternal dependency and childrearing attitudes among mothers of adolescent females. *Adolescence 14*, 795–804.

Garlington, J. (1991). *Helping dreams survive: The story of a project involving African-American families and the education of their children.* Baltimore, MD: National Committee of Citizens for Education.

Gibbs, J.T. (1988). *Young, Black and male in America: an endangered species.* Dover, MA: Auburn House Publishing Co.

Gilkes, C. T. (1988). Going up for the oppressed. In C. Bookman & S. Morgan (Eds.), *Women and the Politics of Empowerment* Philadelphia: Temple University Press.

Goodman, L. (1991, October). The relationship between social support and family homelessness. *Journal of Community Psychology. 19,* 321–332.

Greene, B.A. (1990). Sturdy bridges: The role of African-American mothers in the socialization of African-American children. *Women and Therapy, 20,* 215–225.

Halpern, R. (1990). Poverty and early childhood parenting: Toward a framework for intervention. *American Journal of Orthopsychiatry, 60,* 6–18.

Hill, R. (1972). *The strengths of Black families.* New York: Emerson-Hall.

Huttman, E. (1991). A research note on dreams and aspirations of Black families. *Journal of Comparative Family Studies, 22,* 147–158.

Johnson, L. B. (1988). Perspectives on Black family empirical research: 1965–1978. In H. P. McAdoo (Ed.), (pp. 91–106). *Black families.* Beverly Hills: Sage.

Ladner, J.A. (1972). *Tomorrow's tomorrow.* Garden City, NY: Doubleday.

Lykes, B. (1985). Gender and individualistic versus collectivist basis for notions about the self. *Journal of Personality, 53,* 356–383.

Manns, W. (1988). Supportive roles of significant others to Black families. In H. P. McAdoo (Ed.), (pp. 270–283). *Black families.* Beverly Hills: Sage.

Moynihan, D. (1965). *The Nero family: The case for national action.* Washington, D.C.: Office of Policy Planning & Research, U.S. Department of Labor.

Myers, H.F., & King, L. M. (1983). Mental health issues in the development of the Black American child. In G. J. Powell (Ed.), (pp. 275–306). *The psychosocial development of minority group children.* New York: Brunner/Mazel Publishers.

National Committee for Citizens in Education (1987, January). *Concept paper: Final planning and implementation of the project to increase the influence of parents in dropout prevention at Harlem Park middle school.* Submitted to the Prudential Foundation.

Nobles, W.W. (1978). Toward an empirical and theoretical framework for defining Black families. *Journal of Marriage and the Family, 40,* 679–688.

Nobles, W. W. (1988). African American family life: An instrument of culture. In H. P. McAdoo (Ed.), (pp. 44–53). *Black families.* Beverly Hills: Sage.

Ogbu, J. (1987). Variability in minority school performance: A problem in search of an explanation. *Anthropology Education Quarterly, 18,* 312–334.

Ortner, S. (1992). *Raising middle class adolescents.* Paper presented at American Anthropological Association Convention, Chicago.

Peters, M.F. (1978). Notes from the guest editor. *Journal of Marriage and the Family, 40,* 655–658.

Peterson, G. W., & Peters, D.F. (1985). The socialization values of low-income Appalachian White and rural Black mothers: A comparative study. *Journal of Comparative Family Studies, 16,* 75–89.

Portes, P.R., Dunham, R. M., & Williams, S. (1986). Assessing child-rearing style in ecological settings: Its relation to culture, social class, early age intervention and scholastic achievement. *Adolescence, 21,* 723–735.

Reid, P. T. (1992, August). *Poor women in psychological research: Shut up and shut out.* Paper presented at the American Psychological Association Convention, Washington, D.C.

Robinson, C.R. (1983). Black women: A tradition of self-reliant strength. *Women & Therapy, 2,* 135–144.

Scanzoni, J. (1985). Black parental values and expectations of children's occupation and educational success: Theoretical implications. In H. P. McAdoo & J. L. McAdoo (Eds.), *Black children.* Beverly Hills: Sage.

Scheper-Hughes, N. (1992). *Death without weeping.* Berkeley, CA: University of California Press.

Scott, J. (1992). *Domination and the art of resistance.* New Haven: Yale University Press.

Strom, R., Griswold, D., Strom, S., Collinsworth, P., & Schmid, J. (1990). Perceptions of parenting success by Black mothers and their preadolescent children. *Journal of Negro Education, 59,* 611–622.

Wilson, W. J. (1987). *The truly disadvantaged: The inner city, the underclass, and public policy.* Chicago: The University of Chicago Press.

6

Exploding the Myths: African-American Families at Promise

I tell my daughter, life won't always be fair
'cause she is Black, but to do her best anyway.
                    —A mother of five children

The words of this mother represent more than the truth of African American life in the United States. They are both a forecasting and a warning. They are a distillation of the socialization process for Black children: Survive and flourish despite the odds. Black parents are keenly aware of the social forces which present formidable challenges to the growth and development of their children. They have not been deluded into believing that their children are responsible for the ongoing social crises that the Los Angeles "riots" of 1965 and 1992 so graphically engraved on the American consciousness.

During the 1992 Los Angeles rebellion the common narrative of the status quo was that the "riot" was the result of a "poverty of values" in Black families. The point man for this position was former Vice President Quayle. The chant was quickly embraced and repeated fervently by President Bush, newscasters, reporters, and public and civic leaders. Once again, as in the decade of the 1960s, the light of ill-repute was flashed on the Black family. A large part of the public discourse involved blame, accusations, and condemnations of African American families. The "master narrative" of our time implies that African American families are inherently deprived, suggesting that they generate from within a deep-seated pathology that has no basis within their experience.

The characterization of young Black males as violent and full of rage ignores the historical and contemporary status of Black people as the victims of racial violence by Whites. Franklin (1974) recounts the "vicious" and "prevalent" rioting by mobs of White citizens against Black communities in both southern and northern states. In discussing the Los Angeles Watts riot of 1965, Franklin (1974) noted the rate of unemployment for Blacks during the mid-1960s was "114 percent higher than it was for whites" (p. 493). Factors contributing to the 1992 riot mirror the underlying causes of the 1965 riot: high unemployment, poor and crowded housing conditions, de facto segregated schools, discrimination in every arena of American life (Madhubuti, 1993).

The persistent stigmatizing of Black men as explosive and violent and Black mothers as immoral and castrating women who fail at parenting is a deliberate attempt to veil societal choices which create economic and social disparities (Jewell, 1988; Reed, 1992). The negative images assigned to African American families often blind educators and counselors to their essential substance. Instead of interacting with families and their children on their own terms, professionals often see and respond to caricatures.

This chapter, which draws on my research with African American urban mothers, will amplify their voices against the background of White dominant cultural assumptions regarding African American family life. The mothers in this study were aware of negative attitudes held by the larger society about Black families, their children, and community. They were committed to girding their children against such attitudes and the life threatening perils of social and political inequities.

One mother, when talking about her fears related to drugs and her eleven-year-old son stated, "Drugs come from *outside* of our neighborhood to kill our children. I teach my son that drugs were put here to defeat him, not to make him feel good." The wisdom and insight of this mother can be seen in the bright eyes of her son, who is a successful sixth-grader in the Major Work program (a special program for talented children in the local school district). Another mother of five males (two preadolescents and three in their early teens) talked about wanting to move from her neighborhood to get her sons away from potentially bad influences. She described her sons as "good boys" who stay out of "trouble," yet she wanted to make sure that she did everything she could to remove them from danger's path. Months later, when one of the research assistants on the project ran into this same mother in a local store, she smiled and triumphantly said, "I got my boys out of there; we moved." This woman is still adjusting to the recent breakup of her marriage, yet she had no time to grieve—she had to actively monitor the safety of her sons.

As I talked with sixty mothers of children between the ages of ten and twelve years old, I witnessed their fortitude over and over again. My purpose in talking with them was to get information on their struggles and joys as parents of Black children. I wanted to know if the strengths that Hill (1972) identified over twenty years ago are still evident in Black families in the 1990s. I wanted to know if Black homes had the same feel of love and character that was so prevalent in my home as a child and in the homes of my childhood playmates.

Rearing children in the context of economic disparities, political powerlessness, and a social and cultural ethos steeped in racism is a monumental undertaking for African American parents (Clark, 1983). Black families often regard success as sheltering their children from the pitfalls of self-destruction, such as drugs, crime, and cyclical government dependency. As a community, African Americans view success as extricating themselves from the consequences of poverty. Black families with low incomes understand the odds are that their children are more likely to end up on drugs, in prison, on welfare, undereducated, and locked in a cycle of powerlessness (Edelman, 1987). In addition, these families must face the appalling mortality statistics for young Black men that are routinely sensationalized on the evening news.

In spite of these forces, African American families are succeeding against the odds, irrespective of socioeconomic status, by instilling in their children high educational and social aspirations (Billingsley, 1992; Staples, 1993; Taylor & Dorsey-Gaines, 1988). In this chapter, I will share with you the results of my research as well as my personal perceptions of these families who are so unlike the families Bill Moyer introduced on *CBS Reports'* "Vanishing Family." The families in the study are experiencing various degrees of "success" and "distress," yet, what I noticed in all of these families were the core strengths which Robert Hill delineated more than twenty years ago. Each of these families exhibited, to varying degrees: 1) strong kinship ties, 2) a strong work orientation, 3) adaptability of family roles, 4) a strong achievement orientation, and 5) a strong religious orientation (Hill, 1972).

As a counselor educator who teaches the intricacies of family dynamics, I am often startled by the ways in which graduate students are influenced by the media and the prevailing stereotypes that drive our cultural images and influence social policy. Too often counselors and teachers believe that "at risk" and Black families are interchangeable terms. Indeed, to be labelled "at risk" is an automatic designation of deficiency and dysfunction (Arnold & Swadener, 1993; Reed, 1992). As helping professionals, we are doomed to failure and locked in an endless spiral of racist reproductions unless we expand our knowledge of the multiple realities posed by Black family life.

I am deeply concerned that those who work with Black children be exposed to a range of images that represent the abundant variations of Black experiences in the United States. Too often the stereotypes and one-dimensional portraits paraded before us on society's vast channels of communication (television, print media, movies, schools, etc.) become the defining contours of the children we have been commissioned to serve. The dangers in this for children are that they receive labels that do not tell us who they are and obscure their inherent worth. The danger for educators and counselors is that we will never learn the lesson of true social change, which means working collaboratively with those we think need our "help" and learning that we need to "help" (Dass & Gorman, 1985).

Of course, African Americans bear a disproportionate rate of poverty. A larger share of Black families and more than half of all Black children live in poverty (Staples, 1993). It is absolutely imperative that we reverse the impact of poverty in the lives of families and children (Pinderhughes, 1982). It is also important that we recognize the ways in which flat, narrow, negative images of Black families impair our ability as professionals to see the strengths of Black families. The task of ending poverty and the ways in which we view impoverished families are intricately linked. Social scientists have suggested for more than two decades that Black families model "role flexibility" across gender and generation. Yet, Black families are not applauded for their resourceful and adaptive skills, nor are they viewed as a model for many dominant-culture families who may lack such reserve. The continued focus on "pathology" and degeneracy in "the" Black family prevents us from gaining a clearer picture and finding solutions to the problems faced by all American families: role strain, rising divorce rates, drugs, higher rates of teen pregnancy, school dropouts, and premature and violent deaths due to suicide and homicide. Black families have a great deal to offer to our understanding of American family life.

THE STUDY

Reconceptualist scholars in a variety of social science disciplines have begun to study important factors in the African American experience (Cheatham & Stewart, 1990; McAdoo, 1988; Myers, 1990). Boyd-Franklin (1989) in her book *Black Families in Therapy* calls for greater exploration of the needs and diversity among Black families. In addition, Lindblad-Goldberg and Dukes (1985) point out that there is a gap in the literature on "characteristics of support systems in Black families [with] pre-adolescent and adolescent children (p. 43)." This study was designed to address these concerns by gathering descriptive data on the functioning of African American mothers and, by inference, their children.[1] Data gathered in this study contribute to our growing knowledge of interactional patterns in Black families.

A brief demographic form was created to define the sample. The instruments used were The Parent Behavior Form (Touliatos, Perlmutter, & Straus, 1989), Inventory of Social Contacts (Richardson, 1984), and the Black Parental Childrearing Orientation Scale (Arnold, 1990) (see Appendix). All data were gathered through self-report. The interviewers were the author and two African American female research assistants who grew up in neighborhoods bordering the community where the study was conducted. We usually worked in pairs to compare observations and check our impressions of a family, to increase our efficiency, and to extend our ability to observe the family in action. While one of us was asking questions and completing a form, the other might play with a child or engage the spouse in casual conversation. We gleaned a lot from these informal exchanges.

Sixty Black mothers were interviewed in their homes or in another natural setting of their choice. A few women were reluctant to let us into their homes, so we used the neighborhood McDonald's and the neighborhood branch library a couple of times, and once we met a woman on her job during her lunch hour. Ninety-five percent of the interviews were conducted in the participants' homes. Participants were asked questions pertaining to their parenting practices, social network and attitudes regarding traditional Black values in relationship to their *preadolescent child.* If there was more than one such child in the home, the interviewer selected the youngest child (based on the assumption that mothers would be most involved with the younger child). The names of children and their parents were obtained from the central office of the local school district. Mothers were contacted by mail and invited to volunteer for the study. We then telephoned to further encourage participation. If the woman agreed to join the study, an appointment was set at her convenience.

Entering an African American home for the purposes of data collection felt frightening and contradictory to me. I was afraid the people in those homes would view me as an outsider. The very thought of being turned away or dismissed struck terror in my soul. I really wanted these women to affirm that I was "ok," despite the fact that I possessed a Ph.D. and did not live in the neighborhood. I wanted them to see the importance of studying the Black family. In all but a few encounters, I was warmly received and recognized as a member of "the community," that community which comes from sharing the familiar. There was a genuineness, a realness between us; they took pride in my doctorate degree and wanted to know how I was being treated at the university. And just how many Black people were there at the university? They were very encouraging of the young women who assisted with the study. Motherly and sisterly advice was shared; we were offered coffee and tea and slices of homemade cake and pie. Sometimes we had to be careful not to allow an interview to become an extended exchange between soul sisters. Often, at some point in the interview, we moved from researcher and subject to collaborator and friend. Many times we left a home saying "Sure hope we come back to see them again." Mothers were eager to discuss their families, especially with Black women who possess the potential to understand and confirm their struggles.

The Mothers—Who Are They?

At the beginning of the twentieth century one-third of all Black women were in the labor force; 97 percent were evenly placed between agricultural work and domestic service (Newman, 1986). Not until 1970 did the percentage of Black women working in other capacities rise above the number working in private domestic service and the tobacco and cotton fields of the South. By 1980 less than eight percent of Black women worked as agricultural workers and domestic servants. Black women had made substantial inroads into higher status and paying occupations. Labor statistics dramatically state the case, in 1980, "twenty-nine percent of Black women worked in the clerical sector, up from one percent in 1940, and sixteen percent of Black women were professionals, up from five percent in 1940" (United States Civil Rights Commission, 1990, p. 2).

The women in this study represent the first generation of African American women freed from involuntary labor in the agricultural South and domestic service in the White woman's kitchen. They were born between 1946 and 1965 and grew up during the "era of rising expectations" for both Blacks and women. For the first time in United States history, the fields and scrubbing floors were not ordained, fixed components of the Black woman's fate. These were the daughters of men and women who had come north to work in the steel mills and manufacturing plants of the industrial age. The daughters who were expected to graduate from high school. The daughters who would never fall prey to the unsolicited advances of White men. The daughters who could dream of a better life.

The dream, however, was shaped by the realities of their lives. The constraining effects of race, gender, and class. While Black women made remarkable strides in the labor market they remained one of the poorest paid groups in the United States. Currently, Black women earn ninety percent as much as White women of comparable status. However, married Black women contribute one-third of their family's income, whereas White women contribute one-fourth. Roughly two thirds of Black women in the labor force are not married and are more likely to have children under the age of eighteen. Whereas, one-third of White women are not married and they are less likely to have children under the age of eighteen. Labor market discrimination against Black women and men, differences in family structure, and lack of access to structural opportunities contribute to the persistence of the relative low economic status to Black families (United States Commission on Civil Rights, 1990).

All the women in the study live in neighborhoods that have experienced an increasingly high rate of poverty—communities that were once considered solidly middle class. One neighborhood has a 39.9 percent poverty rate and the other a rate of 29.6 percent, almost four times and twice the national average, respectively (*Poverty Indicators*, 1991). Many of these families can be characterized as the working poor. Some families are straining to hold onto the trappings of middle-class life. In these families, more often than not, both parents worked; in some cases, one or both might work a second job (Table 1). The evidence of a strong work orientation (Hill, 1972) was very apparent in these families. Working to "get ahead" was talked about in matter-of-fact terms but with faith, almost like a mantra. Most of the families we visited lived in single-family dwellings. Some lived in duplexes. Most were renting. Forty-one or 68.3 percent of the women in the study were born in the metropolitan area where the study was conducted.

The women in the study, like most women in the United States, bear the primary responsibility for the socialization of their children, irrespective of marital status. Black mothers must socialize their children into a racist society while equipping them with the means to both resist racism and succeed within the limits of the system (Staples, 1993). This contradiction leads them to create a two-tier socialization process that is perplexing and at times polar in nature. When asked the question "Do you talk to your child about racism?" a similar theme arose: Understand the injustice of racism and rise above it. The following response is indicative of this unique socialization process: "I teach my son that things are not equal. You have to adjust, but be prepared and work twice as hard." Teaching young children about the inevitable consequences of racism and instilling hope and a sense of dignity is most certainly a weighty, if not burdensome, responsibility.

It seemed many women were accepting and aware of the profundity of the task, yet, they did not appear overwhelmed by the charge. Most of these women had a philosophy toward life and family that they followed. These women were confident regarding their parenting skills. The majority of the sample had a high school education; more than a third of the sample had college experience. Only a small portion of the sample did not complete high school, four women or 6.7 percent (see Table 2). The combination of life experience and formal education might have helped these women gain a balanced perspective on childrearing.

Another factor contributing to their confidence might have been their age. The average age was 36.9 years old. The age range was from 23 to 47 years old. Many of these women had successfully reared older children and felt they had conquered the pitfalls of parenting. They were still aware of the environmental dangers but appeared to engage them rather than feel defeated. They didn't have romantic notions about motherhood, just a matter-of-fact posture. Scott (1991) calls this the "habit of surviving." Some women took a great deal of pleasure in the role; others seemed to feel the weight of mothering more intensely.

The family structure was almost evenly divided into two categories: single female head of household and dual-parent status. The conditions of their status varied in origin: seven women had never married, fourteen were divorced, and three were widowed. Among the married women there were also differences (see Table 3). Thirty-one mothers talked about their relationships with daughters and twenty-nine mothers with sons. We listened to stories about marital strife and the loneliness of being the sole decision maker. We also listened to stories about marital partnership and the incredible blessings of family and friends—in some cases, both sets of stories from the same women!

These women were active and involved. Sixty-eight percent of them worked full time, another 6.7 percent worked part time. Despite holding down a job and managing a family, many women participated in church, community, and school activities.

What's Happening in These Families?

The majority of the mothers in the study have a large and supportive social network of family and friends; the mean number of social contacts was 15.6 for single women and 18.1 for married women. The difference in the means was not statistically significant. Of course, one view of single mothers is that they are isolated and without male support. However, women in this study have robust support networks comprised of men and women. They list their fathers, husbands, and boyfriends, brothers, male cousins, and neighbors as supporters or helpers. Although men are present in the lives of these women, the overwhelming amount of support, material and emotional, came from other women. Mothers, aunts, sisters, female cousins, and girlfriends were always listed as unfailing members of the system of social contact for women in this study.

Women listed their mothers as the greatest source of support more often than any other person. Mothers could be counted on for emotional support, babysitting, emergency loans, and shelter. Many women said their mother was their "best friend." Most women said their mother or their grandmother was their role model, " 'cause she took care of us kids."

Another finding that is supported by the literature was the egalitarian nature of Black families. On one Saturday morning interview, I entered the home of a participant just as her eleven-year-old son finished the dishes after cooking breakfast for himself and his parents. When I asked how she got him involved in domestic chores, she was quick to say that he sees his father cooking, and so he doesn't think cooking is for girls only. The mothers in the study reported having similar attitudes and expectations for their preadolescent children, regardless of gender. There were similar household chores, academic expectations, and use of patterns in Black families (Manns, 1981).

Mothers indicated a strong belief in firm and consistent discipline of their children. On the Parent Behavior Form, the lowest mean score was for the Lax Control scale (11.586), which indicates they exercised tight control over their preadolescent children. When asked "Do you expect your child to follow your rules," a firm "yes" was the most frequent reply. One mother stated: "I monitor what my child is doing all the time. She doesn't know that I'm watching her all the time, but you have to keep up with your kids and know who and what they are exposed to or you'll lose them."

These mothers had faith in the ability of adults to assist in the guidance and development of their children. They trusted family members and friends to correct and discipline their children. They also extended this to teachers, ministers, and other adults entrusted with the care of their children. They generally believed that they had properly trained their children to know the difference between right and wrong but that adults could and should correct them when they failed to do the right thing. Mothers stopped short of allowing corporal punishment of their children by adults outside of their very close family ties. These attitudes are very consistent with earlier findings on interactional patterns in Black families (Manns, 1981).

The mothers also indicated a faith in education as an avenue of social mobility (Hill, 1972). When asked to rate the importance of education for their child's future on a scale of one to seven, every woman gave it a rating of seven, the highest value on the scale. When asked "How do you model or teach this value to your child?" the responses varied from "They see me go to school and struggle with my homework, so they know they have to go" to "I keep them clean and make sure they go to school every day." Some women used themselves as a projective technique: "I could do more if I had an education," one woman said, and another woman said, "I point out my lack of opportunities because of my limited education."

It is important to remember these women are educated. Only four lacked a high school diploma. However, educational attainment does not correlate with economic achievement for African Americans (*Poverty Indicators*, 1991). Their efforts to stay in school and get a good job have not paid high dividends for them, yet they believe their children must attain more education in order to have a "decent life." This is expressed by one woman when she tells her children "High school is not enough, college is a necessity."

Some women had a very sophisticated understanding of how schools operated and teachers responded to their children. One woman, a twenty-nine-year-old mother of four children ranging in ages from three to twelve years old, explained to me how her children were treated in school based on gender differences.

> Girls are more adaptable to the structure in the school. Boys resist and show their personality in different ways, so they come off being behavior problems. Teachers say my son [a fifth-grader] is "behavior problem." He lacks control and discipline, while my daughter [a seventh-grader] never was called that. She is very talkative. She'll tell you this is the easiest honor roll ever. Whereas Dennis *had* to really work for merit roll. Another thing, most of the teachers are [White] females, and they have a hard time dealing with male students, who challenge authority.

Both of her children are achieving in school, but she feels her son has a harder time in the school system because of the teachers' shortcomings. She is aware that teachers do not have an "at promise" perspective of her son.

Another mother, relating how she and her husband convey the importance of education to their eleven-year-old son, talked about the obstacles posed by racism. Mrs. L said, "My son has to work hard because the world is trying to destroy Black males. I tell him how racism works—"last hired, first fired"—and that he has to work twice as hard to get ahead." She knows the society does not hold an "at promise" view of her son. Mrs. L encourages her son to read, and like several other mothers in the study, she models the value of education by attending the local community college. She also pointed out one way she helps him take responsibility for his learning: "if he doesn't get any homework from school I give him some. I don't only let the school have an agenda for him, as a parent I do too." Clearly, this woman is socializing her child to see himself as a person with promise and the ability to be active in his own learning process. And, like the woman who was quoted at the beginning of this chapter, she is warning him about the injustices of racism while exhorting him to do his very best.

A crucial component of the socialization process for Black families is the role of spirituality or the church. In most of the homes we visited, God was a real and present figure. Whether Jehovah's Witness, Muslim, or Christian, these homes had well-defined religious and spiritual practices. The Bible was often read, or attendance at Sunday school and church was a weekly occurrence. Wednesday night visits to the meeting hall or regular attendance at the mosque was spoken about with ease and conviction. Children were often held accountable for their participation in religious activities, such as choir practice or youth religious studies.

Whether attending religious services was a regular family ritual or an occasional family activity, a spiritual orientation was present. God was a constant and casual referent in conversation. Phrases such as "God will make a way," "Be thankful to God," and "Pray to God, it will work out" seemed to lace almost every woman's conversation. Children were taught to think in moral terms by invoking the presence and power of God in their lives. Sayings such as "God don't like ugly" and "Trust in God" were linked to moral lessons.

Some women were not active in church or questioned the significance of the church and religious teachings. However, these mothers still encouraged their children to participate in church activities. Some children went to church with their grandmothers, aunts, or other relatives. The presence of moral teachings was evident even in homes where organized religious activities were absent.

SIGNIFICANCE OF BLACK FAMILIES

Although Black families have been the subject of much research and scrutiny by social scientists and policy strategists, as an institution the African American family has seldom been appreciated or viewed as a resource for contributing to our understanding of healthy family functioning. Quite the contrary; Black families have been characterized as pathological, malfunctioning crucibles of social disorganization.

Among the first and most notable scholars to contradict the negative portrayal of African American families in the social science and popular literature was Andrew Billingsley. In his book, *Black Families in White America*, Billingsley (1968) made the point that Black families were not "carbon copies of white people" (p. 149). He also delineated the impact of wider social forces on the economic saliency of Black families, thereby influencing the internal dynamics of family life. Billingsley points to racism as the "most pervasive obstacle to the viability" of Black families.

Racism is deeply imbedded within the institutional fabric of American society. All the major institutions including the political, economic, educational, social, and others have systematically excluded the Negro people in varying degrees from equal participation in the rewards of these institutions. None of them works as effectively in meeting the needs of Negro families as they do white families. The keys to the enhancement of Negro family and community life are therefore institutional keys. These major institutions of the wider society must be changed so as to more adequately reflect the existence, needs and the *contributions* of the Negro people [emphasis added]. (p. 152)

Today Billingsley's words stand just as valid and unheeded as they did twenty-five years ago. Society seems even more closed and antagonistic to the viability of African American family life.

Much of the current research on the Black family has been directed toward challenging the prejudice of dominant-culture oriented research perspectives (Billingsley, 1992; Cheatham & Stewart, 1990; Jewell, 1988). The preoccupation with responding to pejorative assaults against the Black family has narrowed our vision of the gifts which the African American family has to offer all American families.

One such gift, of particular interest to educators and counselors alike, is the ability of Black families to motivate and inspire their children to succeed in the face of incredible odds. Repeatedly, mothers in this study talked about encouraging their children to go forward in spite of the barriers posed by racism. Socializing children to value their own inherent worth, to understand the injustices of racism, as well as how to effectively combat the systems of oppression they encounter daily is no small feat! If the reader were to heed the words of Billingsley (1968) and reflect on the existence of "contributions" made by African American families, their successful and unique approach to childrearing would not go unheralded.

Jenkins (1988) discusses the process of nurturing in Black families. He attributes the ability of families to help children see themselves as participants or agents in the events around them as the primary reason Blacks have been able to transcend negative role ascriptions attributed to them by White America.

> Throughout history, Blacks have used their adaptive abilities not only to respond to situations objectively and accurately— with demonstrative thinking—but also to go beyond the givens. They have used their dialectical thinking abilities to envision alternative conceptions of themselves, different from those imposed on them by a racist society. When labeled incompetent and unworthy, Blacks have often conceived the opposite about themselves, and then they have acted in competent and worthy ways. (pp. 118–119)

Others have noticed the "moral sophistication" of African American children; Bardige et al. (1988), in their study of the moral development of low-income urban youth, found that morality was an important aspect of their identity. In addition, the sample of seventy-three children and adolescents had a high level of self esteem.

It is . . . possible that inner city adolescents have special insights based on their perceived experiences of injustice, indifference, or failure to care. Not surprisingly, virtually every child and adolescent in the study was able to describe a situation in which something happened that was unfair and one in which someone was not listened to. (p. 163)

These researchers found that inner-city teens were more concerned about the repercussions of wrong decisions on their future than more privileged White middle-class teens. This finding affirms Jenkins's (1988) observation that Black children see themselves as agents, able to make choices, and participants in the design of their lives.

How Black families help their children learn to cope with a society that takes an "at risk" perspective of their presence rather than an "at promise" view of their gifts and potential is a study in group courage and determination. Specifically, more information is needed about how Black families teach children to cope and live with the contradictions posed by being a morally sound person in a society that is, at best, morally inconsistent.

IMPLICATIONS

The mothers in the study felt, on the whole, competent, supported, and secure in their family units. Although they were clearly concerned about their children, they felt they were taking needed precautions to protect and prepare their children for the future. Their families were thriving.

Our ability to serve African American families in the future rests on our capacity to view them in an "at promise" perspective (Swadener, 1990), to value their gifts, and to find ways to reverse the harmful effects of racism, classism, and sexism on Black families. Acknowledging the strengths of Black families, which Hill (1972) identified twenty years ago, and taking to heart the admonition of Billingsley (1968) would be important correctives in the effort to support and understand Black families.

The families in this study are very much like the families of my childhood memories. They were loving, supportive, hard working, challenging, child-centered, and struggling with the hardships imposed by racism and low socioeconomic status.

Table 1
Employment

Status	Number	Percent
Unemployed	15	25.0
Employed Full-Time	41	68.3
Employed Part-Time	4	6.7
Family Income level:		
$5,000 to $10,000	4	6.7
$10,001 to $15,000	7	12.3
$15,001 to $20,000	8	14.0
$20,001 to $25,000	5	8.8
$25,001 to $30,000	9	15.8
$30,001 or over	24	42.1

Table 2
Education Attainment

Educational Level	Number	Percent
Eighth to Tenth Grade	4	6.7
Completed High School	20	33.3
Some College	27	45.0
Associates Degree	6	10.0
Currently in College	1	1.7
Bachelors Degree	2	3.3

Table 3
Family Structures

	Number	Percent
Single Never Married	7	11.7
Single Divorced	14	23.3
Birthparents Together	26	43.3
Birthparents Separated	3	5.0
Birthparent with Stepparent	4	6.7
Adoptive Parents	3	5.0
Widowed	3	5.0

APPENDIX

Black Parental Childrearing Orientation Scale

Directions: The interviewer reads each question. Please, give participants time to respond and record their answer as close to verbatim as possible.

1. Rearing a Black child has its own set of rewards and problems. Can you think of any special problems you face as a Black parent?
   Any special rewards:
2. Do you talk with your child about racism? _____ Yes _____ No
   IF YES: What do you say to your child?
3. Do you feel it is more important to talk with your child about racism than it was for your parents to tell you about racism when you were a child? _____ Yes _____ No
   Could you put your answer on a scale from 1 to 7?
   1 = not important—4 - 7 = extremely important
   IF IMPORTANT: (4 or higher)—Can you tell me examples of ways in which you tell or teach your child about the importance of racism?
   IF NOT IMPORTANT: (3 or lower)—Can you tell me more about why you feel this way?
4. How important do you feel education is for your child on a scale of 1 to 7?
   1 = not important—4 - 7 = extremely important
   IF IMPORTANT: (4 or higher)—Can you tell me examples of ways in which you tell or teach your child about the importance of education?
   IF NOT IMPORTANT: (3 or lower)—Can you tell me more about why you feel this way?
5. How important do you feel it is for you to teach your child about religion or church on a scale of 1 to 7?
   1 = not important—4 - 7 = extremely important
   IF IMPORTANT: (4 or higher)—Can you tell me examples of ways in which you tell or teach your child about God or religion?
   IF NOT IMPORTANT: (3 or lower)—Can you tell me more about why you feel this way?
6. Is there anything else you want to tell us about being a mother of a Black child in today's world?

NOTE

1. The author gratefully acknowledges the funding of this research by the Urban University Program of the Ohio Board of Regents, Ohio General Assembly.

REFERENCES

Arnold, M. S. (1990). *The Black childrearing orientation scale.* An instrument created for this study. Unpublished.

Arnold, M. S., and Swadener, B. B. (1993). Savage inequalities and the discourse of risk: What of the White children who have so much green grass? *The Review of Education,* 15, 261–272.

Bardige, B., Ward, J. W., Gilligan, C., Taylor, J. M., & Cohen, M. (1988). Moral concerns and consideration of urban youth. In C. Gilligan, J. W. Ward, & J. M. Taylor (Eds.), *Mapping the moral domain* (pp. 159–173). Cambridge: Harvard University Press.

Billingsley, A. (1968). *Black families in white America.* Englewood Cliffs, NJ: Prentice Hall.

Billingsley, A. (1992). *Climbing Jacob's ladder: The enduring legacy of African-American families.* New York: Simon & Schuster.

Boyd-Franklin, N. (1989). *Black families in therapy.* New York: Guildford Press.

Cheatham, H. E., & Stewart, J. B. (1990). *Black families: Interdisciplinary perspectives.* New Brunswick: Transaction Press.

Clark, R. M. (1983). *Family life and school achievement: Why poor Black children succeed or fail.* Chicago: University of Chicago Press.

Dass, R., & Gorman, P. (1985). *How can I help?* New York: Alfred A. Knopf.

The economic status of Black women: An exploratory investigation. (1990). Washington, D.C.: United States Commission on Civil Rights.

Edelmam, M. W. (1987). *Families in peril: An agenda for social change.* Cambridge: Harvard University Press.

Franklin, J. H. (1974). *From slavery to freedom.* (4th ed.). New York: Alfred A. Knopf.

Hill, R. (1972). *The strengths of Black families.* New York: Emerson Hall.

Jenkins, A. H. (1988). Black families: The nurturing of agency. In A. F. Comer-Edwards & J. Spurlock (Eds.), *Black families in crisis: The middle class* (pp. 115–128). New York: Brunner/Mazel.

Jewell, K.S. (1988). *Survival of the Black family: The institutional impact of U.S. social policy.* New York: Praeger.

Lindblad-Goldberg, M., & Dukes, J. (1985). Social support in Black, low-income, single parent families: Normative and dysfunctional patterns. *American Journal of Orhopsychiatry. 55*, 42–58.

Madhubuti, H.R. (Ed.). (1993). *Why L.A. happened: Implications of the '92 Los Angeles rebellion.* Chicago: Third World Press.

Manns, W. (1981). Support systems of significant others in Black families. In H.P. McAdoo (Ed.), *Black families* (pp. 238–251). Beverly Hills: Sage Publications.

McAdoo, H. P. (Ed.). (1988). *Black families.* 2nd ed. Newbury Park, CA: Sage Publications.

Myers, L. (1990). *Understanding the Afrocentric world view.* Dubuque, IA: Kendall Hunt Press.

Newman, D. L. (1986). Black women workers in the twentieth century, *Sage* 3(1) 10–15.

Nobles, W. W. (1974). Africanity: Its role in Black families. *The Black Scholar,* 5, 10–17.

Pinderhughes, E. (1982). Afro-American families and the victim system. In M. McGoldrick, J. Pearce, and J. Giordano (Eds.), *Ethnicity and family therapy.* New York: Guildford Press.

Poverty indicators: Cuyahoga County, Ohio. (1991). Cleveland, OH: Council For Economic Opportunities In Greater Cleveland.

Reed, A., Jr. (1992). The underclass as myth and symbol: The poverty of discourse about poverty. *Radical America, 24*(1), 21–40.

Richardson, R.A. (1984). Interpersonal competence as a determinant of parenting in its social contexts: Social network involvement and childrearing. The Pennsylvania State University. Unpublished dissertation.

Scott, J.W., & Black, A. (1989). Deep structures of African American family life: Female and male kin networks. *The Western Journal of Black Studies, 13*(1), 17–24.

Scott, K. Y. (1991). *The habit of surviving: Black women's strategies for life.* New Brunswick: Rutgers University Press.

Staples, R. (1993). *Black families at the crossroads: Challenges and prospects.* San Francisco: Jossey-Bass.

Swadener, E. B. (1990). Children and families "at risk": Etiology, critique, and alternative paradigms. *Educational Foundations, 4*(4), 17–39.

Taylor, D., & Dorsey-Gaines, C. (1988). *Growing up literate: Learning from inner city families.* Portsmouth, NH: Heinemann Educational Books, Inc.

Touliatos, J., Perlmutter, L., & Straus, B. (1989). *Handbook of family measurement techniques.* Beverly Hills: Sage Publications.

7

Native Americans at Promise: Travel in Borderlands

I believe that the image is the great instrument of instruction. What a child gets out of any subject presented to him is simply the images which he himself forms with regard to it.
—Dewey, 1897/1959, p. 28

When information is relayed to policy-makers, they respond in terms of what is already inside their heads and consequently make policy less to fit the facts than to fit the notions and intentions formed out of the mental baggage that has accumulated in their minds since childhood.
—Tuchman, 1981, p. 189

John Dewey and Barbara Tuchman's words provide frames for the writing that follows. Let us begin by reflecting upon the images of Native Americans that we learned as children. I recall hours of watching "cowboys and Indians" on television; I remember classroom assignments where we made paper "Indian" headbands; I remember hearing and making threats of scalping and being scalped. This mental baggage from my childhood remained unquestioned for more than twenty years. I was the "average Anglo" Keith Bitsuie (Navajo): describes:

> I think the average Anglo off the street, if you try telling them how an Indian is, how they feel, why they do what they do, they just don't understand it. They think Native Americans are passive, really nonchalant, not on the ball, but in Native American culture how you treat the other person is what matters most: how you speak to them, how you talk to them, what you give them, how you take care of them, and that's how Native Americans are brought up. In the Anglo world, it's ME, I'm the universe, I am the center and I am God almost. The Anglo people just couldn't understand the Native American viewpoint on a lot of things.

The Anglo world was my only universe until Paiute, Blackfeet, Hopi, and Navajo people invited me into their worlds over the years that we worked and learned together in VISTA, Upward Bound, FIPSE, NSF, and other federal social/educational programs. Keith Bitsuie invited me to travel his world as we learned together, first in an Upward Bound program[1] and later as co-investigators in a research project (White, 1991) from which this chapter is drawn. This is borderland travel. Gloria Anzaldua (1987) explains that borderlands are present whenever "two or more cultures edge each other, where people of different races occupy the same territory, where under, lower, middle and upper classes touch, where the space between two individuals shrinks with intimacy" (preface).

Borderland travel helped me to question and unpack the mental baggage from my childhood.

This chapter invites readers into borderland travel. Keith Bitsuie (Navajo), Kee Yazzie (Navajo), Reuben Honahnie (Hopi), Cheryl Yazzie Singer (Navajo), Tallethia Chischilly (Navajo), Noreen Sakiestewa (Hopi), Robert Nash (Navajo), and Andrew Singer (Navajo) are guides for this textual travel. With Maria Lugones (1990), by "travelling to their 'worlds' we can understand what it is to be them and what it is to be ourselves in their eyes. Only when we have travelled to each other's 'worlds' are we fully subjects to each other" (p. 401).

Careful listening skills, listening that takes emotions seriously (see Narayan, 1988), are a necessary part of borderland travel. Please enter this borderland text with a willingness to listen carefully to what may be markedly different images, different experiences, and different understandings from those we have accumulated since childhood. Let us now explore cultural/institutional constructions of "mental baggage" about Native American peoples. Listen as Carol Lee Sanchez (Laguna/Sioux/Lebanese) (1984) illuminates dominant cultural images that she must continually negotiate as a Native American woman:

> To identify Indian is to identify with an invisible or vanished people; it is to identify with a set of basic assumptions and beliefs held by all who are not Indian about the indigenous peoples of the Americas. . . . To be Indian is to be considered "colorful," spiritual, connected to the earth, simplistic, and disappointing if not dressed in buckskin and feathers; shocking if a city-dweller and even more shocking if an educator or other type of professional. That's the positive side. On the negative side, to be Indian is to be thought of as primitive, alcoholic, ignorant (as in "Dumb Indian"), better off dead (as in "the only good Indian is a dead Indian" or "I didn't know there was any of you folks still left"), non-competitive, immoral, pagan or heathen, untrustworthy (as in "Indian-giver") and frightening. To be Indian is to be the primary model that is used to promote racism in this country. (p.163)

White society persistently constructs images that depict Indians as paragons and polarities, rarely as complex, living human beings. With Rennard Strickland (Cherokee & Osage) (1982), witness the circulation of images of Indians within American popular and scholarly discourses, from "savage to savior; from the devil incarnate of Puritan sermon to the nonpolluting, horseback riding television Indian of the public-service announcement and to the mystical, drug-world Indian of Carlos Castaneda's people of power; from the last of the Mohicans to the end of the trail; from the good Indian who brought corn to the starving Pilgrims to the stoic marine raising the flag on Iwo Jima" (p. x).

With Michael Dorris (Modoc) (1991) witness the terrain of literary and cinematic heroes who have "discovered" Indians: "Robinson Crusoe did it off the coast of Brazil, Natty Bumppo did it in New York State and everyone from Debra Paget (*Broken Arrow*, 1950) and Natalie Wood (*The Searchers*, 1956) to Dustin Hoffman (*Little Big Man*, 1970) and Richard Harris (*A Man Called Horse*, 1970) has done it in Hollywood" (p. 74). Kevin Costner, in his role as Lieutenant John Dunbar, is a more recent exemplar of these imaginary dances with Indians that perpetuate mythical assumptions of a "golden age" inhabited by "noble savages" who are forever annihilated. All of these images are inventions by non-Indians. They are among the plethora of perverse "othering" images (i.e., gendered others, at-risk others, pathological others, exotic others, disadvantaged others, culture-of-poverty others, etc.) that constitute an American landscape of oppression, a landscape we all continuously traverse.

The following are the many burdens incurred by Native Americans as they journey this oppressive landscape: "Statistically they remain among the poorest economically, the least employed, the unhealthiest, the lowest in education and income level, and the worst-housed ethnic group in America" (Dorris, 1981 p. 63).

It is important to note that these onerous burdens are derived from a historical legacy of colonization. As the American government actively colonized Indian lands, European schooling forms sought to colonize the minds of Indian youth in boarding schools (see Adams, 1979, 1988a, 1988b, and forthcoming; see also Senese, 1991). The following quote from Henry Price highlights how Tuchman's notion of "mental baggage" works in his policymaking efforts as commissioner of Indian Affairs in 1881:

> There is no one who has been a close observer of Indian history and the effect of contact of Indians with civilization, who is not well satisfied that one of two things must eventually take place, to wit, either civilization or extermination of the Indian. Savage and civilized life cannot live and prosper on the same ground. One of the two must die. If the Indians are to be civilized and become a happy and prosperous people, which is certainly the object and intention of our government, they must learn our language and adopt our modes of life. We are fifty millions of people, and they are only one-fourth of one million. The few must yield to the many. (Quoted in Adams, 1988a, p. 219)

As a derivative of this historical legacy, today Native Americans continue to experience the highest school dropout rate, 36 percent in 1988, and they are the only ethnic group where females drop out more often than do males (Sadker & Sadker, 1994). Examining only high school dropout rates, the rate for Native Americans is 22.7 percent, as compared to Latinos and Latinas (18.7 percent), African Americans (16.8 percent), Whites (12.2 percent), and Asians (4.8 percent) (Fine, 1991).

Equally outrageous consequences persist at the college level. Native American college enrollment has in effect declined since 1972; it has remained at approximately one percent of the total college enrollment as the total population of Native Americans has grown (Vetter, 1992). This decline is attributed to the national trend toward indifference, the federal government's increasing movement away from affirmative action, and the way institutional racism is ignored or tolerated (Tijerina and Biemer, 1987–88).

During my years as an Upward Bound program director, educators would frequently ask me, "How can you work with Native Americans? They're so resistent to education." These educators had never worked with Native American students. Their assumptions exemplify the workings of institutional racism. They exemplify how this landscape of oppression is perpetuated.

Reginald Horseman (1981) documents the pre-Marx, pre-capitalism, pre-scientific nature of racism's roots. He further demonstrates how racism maintains a tenacious grip on our cultural imagination through the beliefs of society's most enlightened and prestigious scholars. John Stanfield (1994) clarifies the contemporary institutionalized constitution of racism by explaining that "whether residents in a multiracial/multiethnic nation (such as the United States) are aware of it or not, and despite their personal preferences and political beliefs, they are socialized in their homes and schools and by the mass media and popular and material culture to assume that ethnicity defined in racial terms is normal" (p.177). He draws our attention to the particular ways social scientists institutionalize this oppression through our acceptance of "hegemonic racialized ethnic social organizations and forms of knowing and interpreting life worlds" (p. 177, also see Campbell, 1982; Stanfield, 1985; Troyna & Carrington, 1989; Gordon, Miller, & Rollock, 1990; Popkewitz, 1992.)

Vine Deloria (Standing Rock Sioux) (1978) addresses how this form of institutionalized racism damages Native Americans:

> Had the tribes been given a choice of fighting the cavalry or the anthropologists, there is little doubt as to who they would have chosen. In a crisis situation men always attack the biggest threat to their existence. A warrior killed in battle could always go to the Happy Hunting Grounds. But where does an Indian laid low by an anthro go? To the library? . . .

The fundamental thesis of the anthropologist is that people are objects for observation, people are then considered objects for experimentation, for manipulation, and for eventual extinction. The anthropologist thus furnishes the justification for treating Indian people like so many chessmen available for anyone to play with. (p. 86)

Ray McDermott (1987) draws our attention to the ways this scholarly objectification process persists in educational research with our continual asking, "What is it with them anyway? What is their situation that school seems to go so badly?" McDermott charts the various theoretical slides that have characterized the portrayal of students of color within educational discourse from "deprived (1960–); . . . curiously different in language, skills, attitudes, and overall culture (1970–)," to . . . "passively reproduced, put through the mills of inequality, and shaped into a pap form marked only by cross-generational failure (1975–)" (p. 362).

This obsession with seeing and portraying students of color within a discourse of failure typically situates "the problem" within the student. As we heard from Henry Price, the problem then becomes that the "savages" need to be "civilized." Having thus situated failure in the individual, that is, "blamed the victim" (Ryan, 1971), the more damaging educational practices trace the roots of this failure to a cycle of pathology within the students' home communities. Thus, during Price's tenure, the perceived need for boarding schools .

WRITING NEW TALES OF THE FIELD

A new tale of the field is sought here. But writing a new tale that can intervene into and against the flat, unidimensional caricaturizations of Native Americans that have persisted within ethnographic discourse since the early 1800s (see McKenney & Hall, 1836/1972) is no simple task. It is indeed risky business. As in Michelle Fine's work (1994), this is politically tense scholarship that explicitly trades on race/class privilege. I barter White privilege and my privilege as a scholar for what I intend to be movement toward social justice. Cautiously working the self-other hyphen that this work inescapably enjoins, I offer a public hearing for Native American people and simultaneously risk imperial translation. Reuben Honhanie (Hopi) contextualizes this risk of imperial translation: "We are under a microscope. A lot of people are interested in Indians, so they look at them and analyze them and analyze them again and say, 'These people are good at this, but they are not very good at this.' The reason they say that is because they have looked at them so much, whereas they haven't looked at themselves so much."

Following Elizabeth Ellsworth (1992), I write "as a non-Indian trying to refuse the Eurocentric terms of that positioning" (p. 7). Even so, I risk adding to the non-Indian legacy of othering. Writing out of shared experiences and shared friendships with co-investigators, I also risk a concomitant retreat from analysis. Rejecting accounts that romanticize Native Americans and offer up artificially constructed happy endings, I nevertheless write to provoke a sense of hope, possibility, and celebration.

This tale is drawn from detailed, subject-centered, biographical study[2] that seeks to foster "intimacy, not distance . . . stories, not models . . . possibilities, not stabilities . . . contingent understandings, not detachable conclusions" (Rose, 1990, p. 6). It is a tale drawn from direct and personal engagement with the co-investigators to explore their educational journeys from their earliest schooling experiences through college graduation. This project valorizes their successful negotiation of the constraints of postmodern educational institutions, especially postsecondary institutions historically designed for privileged White males. With Norman Denzin and Yvonna Lincoln (1994), I write this tale as a "bricoleur" engaged in pragmatic, strategic, and self-reflective methodological bricolage. This bricolage is a pieced-together, closely-knit set of practices that include six years of participant observation as first the secretary and later the director of an Upward Bound program servicing southern Utah and the Hopi and Navajo reservations in northern Arizona; three to eight hours of in-depth interviewing with each of the co-investigators; interpretation of personal and historical documents; and intensive self-reflection and introspection. This inquiry process included working collaboratively with the co-investigators to edit and revise interview transcripts to assure their comfort with and acceptance of the self stories that constitute the larger project from which this chapter is taken.

This project uses critical, interpretive, feminist sociological imagination (see Mills, 1959; Balsamo, 1990; Denzin, 1992) to illuminate how these men and women "make their own history, but not . . . under conditions they have chosen for themselves; rather on terms immediately existing, given and handed down to them" (Marx, 1852/1994, p. 287). Following the work of Larry Grossberg (1988), this research seeks to identify "the strategies and sites of affective empowerment made available in the contemporary culture forms" (p. 290). The construction of family as cultural form and survival strategy is the special focus of the reflexive narrative Kee Yazzie provides here.

Sharing John Stanfield's (1994) concern for the development of "logics of inquiry grounded in the indigenous experiences of people of color" (p. 178), I attempt to "de-Europeanize" the presentation of Kee Yazzie's narrative by evoking a narrative practice that is congruent with Native American storytelling. Kenneth Lincoln (1983) writes that Indian storytelling is "drawn from living history. Its angle of truth derives from a belief in . . . telling their lives directly. . . . To tell a story the Indian way, no less than to write, means not so much to fictionalize, as to inflect the truth of old ways still with us" (p. 222). Here I ask that readers enter Kee Yazzie's narrative "less as a point-of-view detached on the crosshairs of art" and "more as a human presence . . . taking part in the story" (p. 223). Join in his construction of living history.

KEE YAZZIE (NAVAJO), ENGINEER, ARIZONA DEPARTMENT OF TRANSPORTATION

I remember when I was pretty young, my dad would just pull the blankets off and say, "Get up—get up" and it was still dark and we would go out, even in the summertime. He didn't go by time, or a clock, he just saw over the horizon, a little light over there. He got us up and took us way up over the hill. He'd send my oldest brother way back and then my next brother, and then I would be the first one. He started us out and we would run home as hard as we could. He would line us up so when we'd come home we just about tied in the race home. We really went hard. I remember him doing that and telling us that the morning run is good for us. It brought all kinds of good blessings for us.

He also taught us that heat is good for us. Right about afternoon we had an old tire that we would take up the hill and then we would start rolling the tire down the hill and just race it all the way down the hill. That was what we did at noontime.

Winter was just the same, being exposed to the cold weather rather than hot. He thought that running in those extremes, cold and hot, was the best way for kids growing up to be strong. He told us that when he was younger, they would go out to a pond and break the ice and jump in. Or, when the first snow fell he thought we should jump into it and then come in and warm ourselves before running out to do it again. After a while you don't feel it, you just get used to it. The first snow that was what we did. Even now when I see the first snow, I usually go out and wash my face and my arms, but not jump into it.

One time my parents said they were going to go to the store and they told me to get in the truck. It seemed like that was the first time they asked me to come with them so I was really excited. I jumped in and we were off. We went down to Kayenta and that was the first time I saw that place. We went into the store and my parents got me some new clothes. We drove to where the school was, but I didn't know it was a school. There was just a lot of kids; some of them were crying and I wasn't sure what was going on. I never saw that many people before.

I guess during that time I got registered for school and then my parents kind of left me behind. I wasn't sure what was going on. I just stayed around thinking maybe they would come back. I was used to being left behind and staying at home by myself. Often when my parents would go somewhere I'd stay home and take care of the livestock. I stayed there, and that night I stood by the window and looked up at the mesa. It was really lonely. Several nights I did that, just stood there at the window and looked up at the mesa. It was very lonely for a while, and then I started to get some friends. I saw some cousins who were there, too, and we decided to hang around together.

I think my parents didn't tell me about boarding school because they probably thought I couldn't understand and they didn't want to see me hurt. They didn't want to see me cry. This is kind of a bad example, but it's like when you want to put an animal away. You want to put it away and not see it. As I've thought back on it, I think they left me there because they wanted me to get an education. They knew they were handicapped because they didn't know English. My dad would go to work and do labor work, hard work, and when he looked up there would be an Anglo, usually the boss, usually not doing that much work and usually getting more pay, too. My parents wanted their kids to be educated because they wanted a better life for them.

I remember I ran away from boarding school when I was in third grade. It was March or February and there was no snow in

Kayenta so we kind of underestimated what was before us. The snow on Black Mesa was probably four feet high. A couple of us took off from the boarding school and went straight up the mountain. I heard some of the teachers, some of the aides and policemen came after us and they tracked us all the way to the mesa and then they gave up. They couldn't follow us up the mountain. Some went around the other way and then found they couldn't get up the mountain on the road either. My dad got word, somehow, that we were already up on the mountain. Somebody told his brother and he started sectioning up that way with his four-wheel and his horse.

We started walking up the mountain and got lost, so we kept running around trying to find the trail. We finally found a trail. As we started heading up the sun was getting real low in the sky. We had to hurry because it was getting very cold and the snow was deep. Our shoes were just regular school shoes and our feet were getting cold. We were running and we lost two of the guys. I guess they got tired and just stopped or something. They were my age and the other two that were still going were older than me. We stopped and looked back, and they were gone. We started yelling, but we didn't hear anything. We had to make a decision—shall we go back and look for them or shall we continue? Somebody said maybe they had headed back to the boarding school. Somehow we just felt that they were going to make it back.

We were heading to the valley on the ice and I got really tired. I kept feeling like going to sleep and every once in a while I would stop and kind of start falling asleep as I was standing. The other two boys were just barely going along and they, too, stopped. We all said, "Come on, we've got to get back," and gave each other encouragement. We kept going and we finally made it all the way back to the house. When we got there and they saw that there were only three of us, my Uncle Cecil backtracked and found one of the guys who was half frozen. Cecil thawed him out just like you do a little lamb when it is born in the snow. He saved him and went after the other one, but that one was already frozen.

My parents weren't mad at me when I first got home; they were just relieved. After a while they were mad, and asked me why I would do something like that. They didn't yell at me or punish me, they just spoke to me about it and drove me back to the school. There were a lot of complaints against the school and it changed a lot after that. They started letting us go home every weekend, and they let off a little bit on the punishment and haircuts. It was the haircut that had made us run away. That was the boarding school life, my first schooling experience.

Many things helped me get through school. I periodically think about Upward Bound and the great things we did together. I remember the campfires and getting together, drinking coffee and telling stories, getting to know one another. Learning where people were from and what kinds of plans they had for later, that kind of thing. When you hear somebody's story, it encourages you. When you hear somebody say, "I came from this type of family and I was raised this way and that's why I want to do this." That type of story motivates you and you want to do something. Maybe somebody has a real difficult life and you hear it and you hear them say, "That's why I want to improve the reservation, that's why I want to get this kind of an education." It reinforces what you want out of life. That is where I probably decided to go into engineering, going out camping with a lot of kids and hearing the same stories.

At the time, I was scared of college so I was set on following my brother's footsteps and signing up for the Marines. Fortunately, Southern Utah State College's head cross-country/track coach approached me after the Salt Lake City Marathon about running on the team. He offered me an athletic scholarship to go to school. This was what I wanted to do, so I accepted the offer and attended college.

Years later when I started my engineering program, my wife, Shirley, was behind me all the way. She helped me a lot. We used to study together. She should have gone into engineering too, she was good at math, and she used to help me with my calculus. She also gave me the freedom to study. She understood that I needed to study and she would always bring me coffee and whatever I needed. When I needed quiet, she would leave. It was just the little things she did. When I needed to be in the library, she would bring me a sandwich. Before tests she would always say, "You should be reading your book." She would outline everything that should be done. Sometimes I would stay up too long and she would tell me, "That's enough. You might be better if you have rest and then in the morning you might go jog or do something different and then go take the test." She was right. If I were by myself, I might've studied all night and by the next day I wouldn't know anything. Shirley did a lot of things that helped me.

There was also a professor at Northern Arizona University, Gene Leverage. I remember he was a good encourager. He never turned me away—he always answered my question and went even beyond it and always tried to help me to understand. He even asked me where I came from. He was interested in me. I really worked hard for him because of that. It seemed like that was important. If somebody has an interest in you, then you work for them. If you know somebody, then you work harder for them. And I got good grades in his class. I did very well. He's the one that wrote me a letter of recommendation to look for jobs. He was one of those that really influenced me.

There were others that made me know that they didn't really like me. For some reason they were trying to push me down. There's one professor that put me down when I asked a question and it was very discouraging. After I noticed that he wasn't going to answer my questions, I just went to class and would seek help someplace else.

I studied with a group. From the time I started at NAU, I studied with a group and I stayed with them all the way. We all graduated together. Two of them are also with ADOT now and two of the other guys work for soil conservation. We were a real cross-cultural group, one guy was Chinese, another guy was Anglo, two of us were Navajo.

I was also involved with AISES [American Indian Science and Engineering Society]. They had a setup where one guy was in an office and if you wanted some help you could go to him. They had engineering books donated from professors and other students that were free and available for your use. If you had a question that this guy couldn't answer, he could direct you to somebody else, to a tutor or something. All the upper classes were brothers to the lower ones. When we had a meeting we would all get to know each other and exchange phone numbers. Usually we tried to make friends with the freshmen, and the ones transferring in, to encourage them and help them with their classes because I heard one of the professors say that about 95 percent of the freshmen Indians were dropping out. When I was there we started that—helping the freshmen when they come in, exchanging phone numbers and having a get-together to get to know each other. We would tell them we were available if they needed help.

All of these things helped me graduate from college. I also think the way I was raised has a lot to do with it—not giving up on things. It was more physical back then, now it's more mental, but it works the same way. When you're doing something physical, in order to keep going it has to be up here in your thinking—so it works that way for school, too.

Today, retaining my language is one thing I hold on to. Every time I go to the reservation I speak Navajo just to keep in practice. I have a lot of interest in Navajo culture and always ask my parents about certain things. I want to keep in touch with the culture and I'm trying to teach my kids to do the same thing, but it's hard. Every generation we lose something and some day it might die out. I'm hoping not, but there's not much you can do about it unless there's some kind of education program. Even for me, I was raised completely the Navajo way, but then as I grew up I went away to boarding school and missed a lot. All that time I'm away from my parents and only come back during the summer and that's less time than my dad spent with his parents. My mom knows a lot of plants to use for medicine, and I don't know any of them. There's a lot, like the clan system, that's really complicated. I know something about all of this, but I miss out on a lot being away from home. If I had stayed home, I would have learned much more about Navajo culture.

READING KEE YAZZIE'S NARRATIVE

As with all reading, following Roland Barthes (1970/1974), Kee Yazzie's narrative is read intertextually, within existing understandings from multiple texts and within the existing ideologies and structures of feeling in this society. All readers will engage a different experience and leave with different interpretations, interpretations directly related to the understandings they bring to their reading. For the purposes of this chapter, here I offer multiple readings of the narrative, not to deconstruct from some privileged point of view the meanings Kee Yazzie assigns to his experiences, but rather to illuminate the varieties of meaning his narrative contributes to my understanding of Native American families and education.

I read to pursue the nexus of biography and society, the nexus where individuals construct themselves within the constraints of postmodern institutions (see Bertaux, 1981). Kee Yazzie's narrative affirms numerous onerous conditions that constrain his educational journey, conditions he must negotiate. I revisit the horrendous conditions of boarding schools designed to "civilize savages," a schooling experience his parents believe he needs to have to better negotiate the white world, but they are unable to explain to him where he is going or what he will encounter. Through Kee Yazzie's telling of his experience, I come to new understanding of the significance he attaches to the school's effort to "civilize" him with a haircut, a haircut that is so demeaning to his sense of Navajo heritage that as a young boy he risks his life by running away from school. I revisit the stereotypical images and expectations he must negotiate in the form of "signing up for the Marines" and "professors who were trying to push me down."

Kee Yazzie's narrative confirms the importance of positive interventions that facilitate his negotiation of constraining institutions: the intervention of his parents in their insistence that he return to the boarding school and be educated; the intervention of the Upward Bound program that allowed him to hear campfire stories from others who shared similar life conditions and similar aspirations to "improve the reservation"; the intervention of the track coach who offered him a scholarship; the intervention of the professor who respectfully answered his questions and wanted to know his story, where he came from; the interventions of his wife as she tutored him in calculus, encouraged him to develop healthy study habits, and provided emotional support in the form of "coffee and sandwiches" or quiet time; the intervention of his study group and the AISES program.

Reading Kee Yazzie's narrative from the vantage point of the cultural constructions of "at-risk" students, a marked contradiction emerges. It is clear that the risk or the "disadvantage" emerges from the institutions, not from Kee Yazzie. He consistently makes do by acting upon his everyday conditions. He is no victim of white cultural determinism. Rather, he takes up multiple positions as both student and researcher in the academic community. His research into the conditions for Native American students at NAU, that 95 percent of the freshman drop out, informs his work with AISES, his willingness to be a "brother" to the newer students.

Reading Kee Yazzie's narrative for understandings of family, I encounter family values of learning to be strong, to persist against overwhelming odds, by running in extremes of hot and cold weather. These are the values that may have saved his life when he survived the walk up the snowy mountain, the walk that killed his peer. It is the value of running that also opens the door to college through an athletic scholarship. I encounter family values that are tied more to community than to a nuclear family unit, as I hear his concern for "improving life on the reservation," improving the academic environment for other students, and retaining Navajo language and culture.

I am not trying to suggest here that Kee Yazzie is immune to the dominant popular cultural forms that circulate in this society. I am suggesting that along with those forms he has access to non-dominant cultural understandings from his Navajo heritage; and that these understandings inform his movement through problematic postmodern terrain.

I encounter similar learnings from promising family interactions within the narratives of the other co-investigators.

Cheryl Yazzie Singer (Navajo) tells of how her mother became directly involved in her education when she was in the sixth grade and her family moved to Tuba City, Arizona. Because she was more advanced than the other students, the school district wanted her to skip seventh and eighth grades and just go straight to high school. Cheryl Yazzie Singer relates:

> My mom said, "No. I want her to develop and I want her to go through junior high school to see how it feels. In the future she'll probably be wondering how junior high was or she'll be a lot younger than those in high school and she'll be pressured." My mom put up a fight with them. I think she made the right choice for me at that time because I really did need to go to junior high school. I learned a lot more and made a lot more friends. I don't think I would have been involved in as many activities if I had skipped those two years. It seemed like it prepared me for what was coming up in high school, where I was involved in student council and a lot of other organizations.

Another form of parental support is described by Tallethia Chischilly (Navajo). Her words about her mother's inspiration echo what many of the co-investigators relayed about their parents:

> My mother is so happy about my college degree. . . . She has always been willing to do everything she can to help put us through school, even though most of it was through grants and stuff. She'd call us and find some way to help if we were having a problem. She'd always come up and visit us and let us know that she was happy with what we were doing. She knew it was hard. Even if we failed, she never was ashamed

of what we were doing. . . . She was always there for us. We always knew she couldn't do a lot, as far as finances, but she'd write us letters. She kept us going.

Noreen Sakiestewa (Hopi) tells of the crucial involvement of parents in her sponsorship of the Indian Club during her first year as a teacher at Tuba City High School. When the principal refused to support the Indian Week activities that the club had organized, she moved the activities to the local community center. The parents expressed their concern to the school board members and the superintendent. The next year the principal was fired, and Noreen Sakiestewa received a promotion to chairperson of her department.

Not all of the co-investigators tell stories about positive family involvement in their education. Robert Nash (Navajo) relates that he was very rebellious as a child because his parents were never home: "Whenever they said something to me, I completely turned them off. Upward Bound gave me a new family to attach myself to." As he tells of his journey through college and his eventual employment as a teacher on the reservation, his story returns to his parents: "After I graduated from college and started raising a family, my parents changed. They stopped drinking and became what I wanted them to be—to be my parents."

The co-investigators provide numerous examples of family as a group of people, related by birth or simply by place, who are willing to share a common destiny and nurture each other in an ongoing manner. As Andrew Singer (Navajo) put it, "We have to wiggle our way through life." None of these narrators wiggled alone. They survived the constraints they encountered because people they encountered understood the oppressive landscape they were traversing, and people honored their feelings. Reflecting upon the difficulty of traversing the oppressive landscape of racism, James Baldwin and Nikki Giovanni (1973) explain that often "you have to . . . make so many difficult and dangerous choices that the one thing you're really trying to save is what you lose. And what you're trying to save is your ability to touch another human being or be touched by that person" (p. 86). These narrators maintain their ability to touch and be touched by another human being.

Reflecting upon the stories encountered in this borderland research, I return to the wisdom offered by Reuben Honahnie: "If you go in with the attitude, 'I'm different, you're different, I don't like you because of that,' nobody's going to make it, no matter what color you are. You're not going to make it anywhere." And reflecting upon encounters with what Keith Bitsuie terms "average Anglos," Reuben offers the following:

> Every once in a while we get visitors here from either really far back east or California who have never been away from the city. They will ask, "Are you an Indian? Can I take your picture?" Sometimes I get some outrageous questions like, "Where can we see some Indians?" They are expecting to see head-dresses and tipees. Fortunately, I don't get that very much any more. When it does happen, I explain to them that Indians are no different from you and me. They watch t.v., they play computer games, go to school, work and everything else.

Refusing essentialized notions of Native American identity, Reuben explains how his affirmation of either/and, sameness/difference is a consequence of his borderland travel:

> I'm not like a computer that swaps identity. When I go home, I'm just at home, it's not any different. At first I could see the difference when I just got out of high school because it was the first time I was exposed to people asking me questions about my culture. Things that I took for granted they found really interesting. Now I'm exposed [as a ranger for the National Park Service] to so many other cultures because people come from all over the world. I see them doing different things and I see such a variation that any variation is just minimal any more.

Following the work of Norman Denzin (1991), this chapter tells "tiny stories about the human condition, showing how these histories we live, the freedoms we gain and lose, are constrained by larger cultural narratives that work their interpretive ways behind our back" (p. 157).

These co-investigators narrate how they live this time in history into existence. They challenge institutional racism and attempt to fit their biographies to a historical social structure which has yet to learn how to accept Native Americans.

EPILOGUE

This is a story written from a city, Cleveland, that refuses to listen to Native Americans as they tell of the pain they are caused by the derogatory imaging of a racist red Sambo, Chief Wahoo, mascot for the Cleveland Indians baseball team. This is a story written with research supported by a university, the University of Illinois, that refuses to listen to Native Americans as they tell of the pain they are caused by the derogatory imaging of the Chief Illini mascot. This is a story that challenges the social construction "at risk" within a text that places the co-investigators at risk by appropriating their experiences, albeit with their consent. I traverse this problematic terrain with Paula Gunn Allen's (Laguna Pueblo) poetry (1990) and Native Americans who think "caring-sharing about the earth and each other a good thing . . . everybody is related to everybody in pain, in terror, in guilt, in blood, in shame, in disappearance that never quite manages to be disappeared, we never go away. . . . Because the only home is each other, they've occupied all the rest, colonized it; an idea about ourselves is all we own" (p 298-301).

NOTES

1. Originated as part of President Johnson's War on Poverty, Upward Bound Programs are charged with providing academic, social, and cultural activities to low-income, disadvantaged, first-generation students to develop the necessary skills for successful pursuit of postsecondary education. Upward Bound programs typically enroll students from ninth grade through high school graduation. Weekly tutoring and counseling meetings are offered during the academic year. Students usually attend an intensive six-week residential summer component that emphasizes academic skill development. Students live on a college campus during this time.

2. This biographical study has roots in the American traditions of slave narratives, western hero autobiographies, captivity narratives, and the life history tradition of qualitative research that includes Willard Waller's influential work, *The Sociology of Teaching*, published in 1932, and Howard Becker's work with Chicago schoolteachers in the 1950s. Today, biographical method is experiencing a revival across the work of feminists, new social historians, anthropologists, and scholars in post-positivist cultural studies and the symbolic interactionist tradition, and among educationists.

REFERENCES

Adams, D. W. (1979). Schooling the Hopi: Federal Indian policy writ small, 1887–1917. *Pacific Historical Review, 48*(3), 335–356.

Adams, D. W. (1988a). From bullets to boarding schools: The educational assault on the American Indian identity. In P. Weeks (Ed.), *The American Indian experience* (pp. 218–239). Arlington Heights, IL: Forum Press.

Adams, D.W. (1988b). Fundamental considerations: The deep meaning of Native American schooling, 1880–1900. *Harvard Educational Review, 58*(1), 1–28.

Adams, D.W. (Forthcoming). *Education for extinction: American Indians and the boarding school experience 1875–1928.*

Allen P. G. (1990). Some like Indians endure. In G. Anzaldua (Ed)., *Making face, making soul: Haciendo Caras* (pp. 298–301). San Francisco: Aunt Lute Foundation Books.

Anzaldua, G. (1987). *Borderlands la frontera: The new mestiza.* San Francisco: Aunt Lute Books.

Baldwin, J., Giovanni, N. (1973). *A dialogue.* Philadelphia: J.B. Lippincott.

Balsamo, A. (1990). Rethinking ethnography: A work for the feminist imagination. *Studies in Symbolic Interaction, 11*, 45–57.

Barthes, R. (1974). *S/Z* (R. Miller, Trans.). New York: Hill and Wang. (Original work published 1970).

Becker, H. (1951), *Role and career problems of the Chicago public school teacher* (Doctoral Dissertation, University of Chicago).

Bertaux, D. (Ed.) (1981). *Biography and society: The life history approach in the social sciences.* Beverly Hills: Sage.

Campbell, P. B. (1982). Racism and sexism in research. In H.E. Mitzel, J.H. Best, & W. Rabinowitz (Eds.), *The encyclopedia of educational research* (Vol. 3, pp. 1515–1520). New York: Macmillan.

Cook-Lynn, E. (1987). You may consider speaking about your art. In B. Swann & A. Krupat (Eds.), *I tell you now: Autobiographical essays by Native American writers* (pp. 57–63). Lincoln: University of Nebraska Press.

Deloria, V., Jr. (1978). The Indian student amid American inconsistencies. In T. Thompson (Ed.), *The schooling of Native America* (pp. 9–26). Washington, D.C.: American Association of Colleges for Teacher

Education in collaboration with The Teacher Corps, U.S. Office of Education.

Denzin, N. K. (1991). *Images of postmodern society: Social theory and contemporary cinema.* Newbury Park: Sage.

Denzin, N. K. (1992). *Symbolic interactionism and cultural studies: The politics of interpretation.* Cambridge: Blackwell.

Denzin, N.K., & Lincoln, Y.S. (1994). Introduction: Entering the field of qualitative research. In N.K. Denzin & Y.S. Lincoln (Eds.), *Handbook of Qualitative Research* (pp. 1–17). Thousand Oaks, CA: Sage Publications.

Dewey, J. (1897). *My pedagogical creed 9.* In M.S. Dworkin (Ed.), *Dewey on education: Selections* (pp. 19–42). New York: Teachers College Press.

Dorris, M.A. (1981). The grass still grow, the rivers still flow: Contemporary Native-Americans. *Daedalus, 110*(2), 43–69.

Dorris, M. (1991). Indians in aspic: Reflections on *Dances with Wolves. Winds of Change, 6*(2), 74–75.

Ellsworth, E. (1992). Teaching to support unassimilated difference. *Radical Teacher, 42,* 4–9.

Fine, M. (1991). *Framing dropouts: Notes on the politics of an urban public high school.* Albany, NY: State University of New York Press.

Fine, M. (1994). Working the hyphens: Reinventing self and other in qualitative research. In N.K. Denzin & Y.S. Lincoln (Eds.), *Handbook of Qualitative Research* (pp. 70–82). Thousand Oaks, CA: Sage.

Gordon, E. W., Miller, F., & Rollock, P. (1990). Coping with communicentric bias in knowledge production in the social sciences. *Educational Researcher, 19,*(3), 14–19.

Grossberg, L. (1988). Postmodernity and affect: All dressed up with no place to go. *Communication, 10,* 271–293.

hooks, b. (1989). *Talking back.* Boston: South End Press.

Horseman, R. (1981). *Race and manifest destiny: Origins of American racial Anglo Saxonism.* Cambridge, MA: Harvard University Press.

Lincoln, K. (1983). *Native American renaissance.* Berkeley: University of California Press.

Lugones, M. (1990). Playfulness, "world" travelling and loving perception. In G. Anzaldua (Ed.), *Making face, making soul: Haciendo Caras* (pp. 390–402). San Francisco: Aunt Lute Foundation Books.

Marx, K. (1994). From the eighteenth Brumaire of Louis Bonaparte. In E. Kamanka (Ed.), *The portable Karl Marx* (pp. 287–323). New York: Penguin Books. (Original work published 1852).

McDermott, R.P. (1987). The explanation of minority school failure again. *Anthropololgy & Education Quarterly, 18,* 361–364.

McKenney, T.L., & Hall, J. (1972). *The Indian tribes of North America— with biographical sketches and anecdotes of the principal chiefs* (Vols. 1–3). Totowa, NJ: Rowman & Littlefield. (Original work published in 1836).

Mills, C. W. (1959). *The sociological imagination.* New York: Oxford University Press.

Narayan, U. (1988). Working together across differences: Some considerations on emotions and political practice. *Hypatia, 3*(2), 31–47.

Popkewitz, T.S. (1992). Culture, pedagogy, and power: Issues in the production of values and colonization. In K. Weiler & C. Mitchell (Eds.), *What schools can do: Critical pedagogy and practice* (pp. 133–148). Albany: State University of New York Press.

Rose, D. (1990). *Living the ethnographic life.* Newbury Park, CA: Sage.

Ryan, W. (1971). *Blaming the victim.* New York: Random House.

Sadker, M.P., & Sadker, D.M. (1994). *Teachers, schools and society.* New York: McGraw-Hill, Inc.

Sanchez, C.L. (1984). Sex, class, and race intersections: Visions of women of color. In B. Brant (Ed.), *A gathering of spirit: A collection of North American women* (pp. 163–167). Ithaca, NY: Firebrand Books.

Senese, G.B. (1991). *Self-determination and the social education of Native Americans.* New York: Praeger.

Stanfield, J.H. (1985). The ethnocentric bias of social science knowledge production. In E.W. Gordon (Ed.), *Review of research in education, 12* (pp. 387–415). Washington, D.C.: American Educational Research Association.

Stanfield, J. H. (1994). Ethnic modeling in qualitative research. In N.K. Denzin & Y.S. Lincoln (Eds.), *Handbook of qualitative research* (pp. 175–188). Thousand Oaks, CA: Sage Publications.

Strickland, R. (1982) . White memory, red images, and contemporary Indian policy: A foreward. In R.W. Stedman, *Shadows of the Indian* (pp. ix–xiii). Norman: University of Oklahoma Press.

Tijerina, K.H., & Biemer, P.O. (1987–88). The dance of Indian higher education: One step forward, two steps back. *Educational Record,* 68(4)/69(1), 87–91.

Troyna, B., & Carrington, B. (1989). "Whose side are we on?" Ethical dilemmas in research on "race" and education. In R.G. Burgess (Ed.), *The ethics of educational research* (pp. 205–233). New York: Falmer Press.

Tuchman, B. (1981). *Practicing history: Selected essays.* New York: Alfred A. Knopf.

Vetter, B.M. (1992). *Professional women and minorities: A total human resource data compendium.* Washington, DC: Commission on Professionalism in Science and Technology.

Waller, W. (1961). *The sociology of teaching.* New York: Russell and Russell.

White, C. J. (1991). Experiencing Upward Bound: An interrogation of cultural landscapes. Doctoral Dissertation, University of Illinois, Champaign-Urbana.

III. Reconstructing Classrooms and Community Contexts

B. ROBERT TABACHNICK
MARIANNE N. BLOCH[1]

8

Learning in and out of School: Critical Perspectives on the Theory of Cultural Compatibility

This chapter focuses on ways in which constructions of "at risk" or "at promise" are developed. The chapter uses, as a base for exploration, our study of 23 young children from diverse cultural and linguistic backgrounds as these children entered into public school during their kindergarten year and moved into first and second grades. The reported research comes from a longitudinal study of young Hmong, Latino, and African American children in three schools in a midwestern city that we have described in greater detail elsewhere (Bloch & Tabachnick, in press; Bloch, Tabachnick, & Espinosa-Dulanto, 1994). Our data are from observations of children's activities at home and at school, from interviews with parents and children's teachers about children's progress, about their strengths and skills, and from an array of documents that speak to constructions or "regimes of truth" about children's competence in different contexts (Bloch, Cradle, Dean, Espinosa-Dulanto, & Tabachnick, in press; Foucault, 1980).

CULTURE AND THE CONCEPT OF
CULTURAL COMPATIBILITY

We began our study by examining the theory of cultural compatibility which suggests that patterns of behavior that are learned by minority culture groups in the United States are often seen by teachers to be dysfunctional or deficient, and are not recognized as useful even when they are potentially functional in existing classrooms. When changes are made in school practices to increase the similarity or compatibility of cultural behavior and value patterns in children's home and school "culture," gains in positive social behavior and academic achievement are reported (see for example, Heath, 1983; Vogt, Jordan, & Tharp, 1987; Tharp, 1989).

The theoretical framework of cultural compatibility theory, and most cross-cultural research, assumes that children from different cultural and linguistic backgrounds learn to behave competently in their natal cultural and linguistic contexts. It assumes that values and other normative beliefs and learning patterns are taught by parents and other community members and are learned by children, in ways that help them survive and succeed in their home and community settings. It assumes that children are not "at risk" because of the cultural or linguistic community into which they are born, but that they may be "at risk" because other contexts into which they go, such as school, may require or expect different cultural patterns and values than those that they have learned. This framework assumes that children's competencies may not be recognized as strengths, but as abnormalities, as behavior that doesn't fit the new cultural context(s) into which they go. Summarizing, in most interpretations of this theory, and in our own, there appear to be two major factors that influence the construction of children as more or less "at risk" for failure rather than competent and "at promise" for success. These are: the nature of the differences between cultural contexts and how well significant persons in the new context are prepared to recognize, accept, and incorporate culturally different behavior into such important social interactions as classroom practice.

The idea of culture is central to any discussion of cultural compatibility. Culture is most readily encountered as a visible surface reality that leads someone to say something like, "Toto, I don't think we're in Kansas anymore." Things may look different from one culture to another—business suits and dresses, T-shirts over blue jeans, long flowing caftans and long black gowns that veil head and face and body. Things may not look too different but the sounds may differ—different languages, different uses of language, a quiet meal or a noisy one. The noticeable cultural objects may be different from one culture to another—the forms of houses, eating utensils, agricultural implements, toiletries, vehicles and means of transportation, and education.

Less visible, but more significant, are the inner driving forces of culture. These are dispositions to view the world and judge or value its events in certain ways that are coherent within a culture but are not necessarily congruent to the worldviews of other cultures. There are dispositions for recognizing and making the meanings of events, for determining the truth-value of statements, for responding to anomalies, contradictions, and puzzlement. There are also patterns of social behavior and relations of power, social control, deference, resistance; among these institutionalized social forms are patterned responses to social class and gender divisions and patterned responses from within the perspectives of class and gender groups.

Acquiring the ways of thinking and acting of members of a culture group results, in our view, from a process of social interaction. Culture is transmitted directly at times, even didactically, but culture is also transmitted indirectly, as well as constructed by individuals and groups in different ways and under different circumstances, as people model, demonstrate, and benefit observably from culturally approved behavior and receive negative sanctions for behavior that is culturally "inappropriate" *within specific contexts and at different times.* Since the transmission and acquisition of culture are processes of social interaction, the various participants, including the cultural "newcomer," do more than transmit and reproduce forms of behavior and thought that preexisted the interactive processes of cultural transmission. Cultural forms are invented and produced in the process of transmission as well as preserved and reproduced in more or less modified form. Social mechanisms of welcome, acceptance, affiliation, or rejection and resistance are a part of the meanings of culture as the participants in cultural transmission (for example, parents or teach-

ers) encounter it. Infants and young children are cultural neo-
phytes, yet they participate in the creation of new forms of "culture."

By the time a child enters school, that child has a well-devel-
oped sense of culturally approved ways of acting and thinking.
There is still much to learn, however, especially in the broader
complex culture that is formed by continuing acculturative forces.
The bearers of somewhat different cultural backgrounds meet and
influence one another to create new cultural forms, including
forms of inclusion, exclusion, or accommodation.

It is not separate elements or examples of thought, behavior,
or objects that identify a culture but the existence of all its elements in subtle, mutually supportive interaction that creates and
recreates "culture" over time. How teachers understand, value,
and use the subtle aspects of their own culture influence how they
construct some children's actions as more "at risk" of failure than
"at promise" for success.

Cultural compatibility theories usually do not search for
compatibility between the whole complex, rich, multitextured fabric of one culture with another. More typically, they identify key
cultural elements from a child's home culture that are contradictory to that of the school in such a way as to interfere with a child's
using her/his abilities to become a valued and successful member
of both cultures. In addition, the contradictions may prevent a
child from creating a set of coherent cultural behaviors that vary
from situation to situation in patterned ways that the child understands, expects, and controls to her/his advantage (see, for example, Erickson,1987; Tharp, 1989).

A brief summary of critiques of cultural compatibility theories would include: 1) questions about how easily important home-
school cultural discontinuities can be discovered (e.g., Bloch &
Swadener, 1992; Tharp, 1989); 2) how well or poorly cultural patterns fit all members of a given cultural group, with a strong
emphasis on intragroup variability being an overlooked element in
most conceptions of cultural compatibility research and theory
(Trueba, 1988); 3) whether the concept of cultural compatibility,
which has been tested largely in homogeneous cultural contexts,
works in multicultural contexts (Bloch & Tabachnick, 1988;
Tharp, 1989); and 4) the conception that cultural compatibility
theories are weak conceptions of why children of color "fail" in
school, and that notions of social structure, including economic,
political, and ideological concerns are missing from the majority of

cultural compatibility types of research and theoretical expositions (e.g., Ogbu, 1987; Villegas, 1988).

Recent work by Singer (1988) argues that cultural compatibility theory never promised to "correct the world"; it only proposes minor alterations in classrooms to allow for different cultural competencies and to facilitate comfort and success of nondominant cultural and linguistic group children in school. Beginning in the 1970s, sociological studies representing critical, neo-Marxist, and postmodern perspectives supported the need to see children and their families as competent and "at promise" rather than "at risk." From this perspective, children were often seen to be active constructors of their own cultural histories and behavior; resistant to structural inequalities, while at the same time being acted upon by these inequalities (e.g., Willis, 1977; Erickson, 1987); powerful while also marginalized; and varying by complex intersecting elements, including race, class, ethnicity, language background and history, and gender, as well as "culture" (Apple & Weis, 1983).

Thus, the explanations as to why some children are perceived to be "at risk" rather than all children being perceived to be "at promise" within a particular social context are extremely complex. They range from explanations of teacher knowledge of discrete aspects of cultural behavior, values, and language to broader expositions on the relationships among culture, race, class, gender, and language and children's learning in and out of school. Postmodern analyses try to discount the potentiality of grand structural theories to provide all-encompassing explanations or solutions and return to an examination of the discourse of power and the marginalization of voices and events from stories that are told. In the following vignettes or stories that we tell from our study of young children and their families in three schools and their communities, we try to give voice to children's stories, while illustrating the difficulty of using one theoretical conception to explain the complexity of "at risk" discourse and the issues faced in helping all children achieve their promise.[2]

THE CONSTRUCTION OF SUCCESS RATHER THAN "AT-RISKNESS"

Success and failure are not merely in the behaviors of school children, as measured against an impersonal, "objective" (de-contextualized) set of standards. Classifications of "successful" or "failing" responses to school tasks depend on the ways teachers interpret the behavior. Teacher interpretations are likely to be influenced by their expectations, by tendencies to expect success or to anticipate failure.

Pablo was a five-year-old child at the beginning of our study. His family emigrated to the United States from Central America. His relatives came from a rural community, and they try to maintain traditional views of adult-child relationships. In interviews at their home, Pablo's mother's and grandmother's comments suggest that they believe that children need strict control in order to learn to obey and respect their elders and behave properly. The family's traditional values are supported and reinforced by their membership in a fundamentalist Protestant congregation. Pablo and a cousin stay with their grandmother after school since their parents are working. Pablo is strictly disciplined, and he is expected to show respect by asking his grandmother's permission to do anything different from what he has been permitted to do previously. He spends a lot of time indoors, watching TV, looking out the window at other kids playing, sometimes coloring with crayons on paper. Once in a while he and his cousin play together; more often they watch videotapes or TV together.

Pablo was one of the poorer performers in kindergarten, although he showed flashes of good achievement. His mother had insisted that he start kindergarten (he was of age), although his Head Start teachers had suggested that he wait a year. In first grade his academic performance at midyear was described as "very low." His regular teachers and the ESL teacher, all Euro-American in background, are both puzzled and frustrated by Pablo's frequent refusals to try to do the assigned work. His first-grade teacher comments:

> TEACHER: He has the ability to do it [assigned work].
> INTERVIEWER: Why do you think so?
> TEACHER: Because there have been times when he has been really focused and he does it, and he doesn't have a problem with it. And I think . . . I wonder if he is afraid to succeed.
> INTERVIEWER: Why?
> TEACHER: Why do I wonder that? Because he doesn't really take risks at all . . . even very comfortable ones, where today he did a nice job with his calendar and I gave him the class one and I said, "Would you like to fill out the numbers on here so that we can put it up on our class board?" "Oh, no,

uh-uh." Yet he could fill out the calendar he had for himself beautifully. (Interview, First-Grade Teacher, 2–1–91)

Later in the school year, in discussing Pablo's academic work, this teacher describes some instances of success:

They're math number sentences and we had the kids working on them and solving them in any way [that they can], and he . . . direct modeled it all and counted everything out, but he really stayed with it and worked really hard. He got about half-way through on one day and the next day I asked him to finish it, and he said, "No, I don't want to," and I said, "Let's think about it. Is it just because it's too hard?" "Oh, yeah, it's too hard." And I said,"But look what you've done here; I bet you could solve it," and then he sat down and he got . . . the majority of them correct. About a week later he was writing story problems [and his] story problems were just so gorgeous. . . . He was so much fun to work with on this day because at first he said, "No, I can't do it." In the beginning that's what he always [says]. . . . "No, I can't do it." You're not going to set him up to fail because . . . you're not going to get him to do it. And I say, "Oh, come on, yes, you can do it." . . . [and] he did do some gorgeous ones. This one was "Pablo had three rabbits, Eduardo gave me four more rabbits, then Eduardo gave me five rabbits, how many rabbits does Pablo have himself?" Then he came up with the answer [three plus four plus five] . . . So you can see he got a little bolder with the numbers because he started feeling like, "Oh, I can do this." (Interview, First-Grade Teacher, 6–5–91)

When Pablo doesn't complete school assigned tasks, the expectation that he can do these tasks successfully is so strong that his teachers explore the possibility that he only pretends to fail so as to avoid the burdens of success. (They expect that he would be expected to complete work and do it well consistently.)

Eduardo lives in the same subsidized housing complex as Pablo and attends the same school. His mother and father were born in a South Texas rural Latino community where they have a large extended family and a small farm. They come north in late winter or early spring for the canning factory season. Both parents work double shifts until the work runs out, usually as late as November or even December, when the whole family returns to

Texas until the next spring. If there were work enough they would stay, according to Eduardo's mother, but without work they return to the house and farm on which they can live at very little cost.

In first grade, Eduardo is a tall, large-framed six-and-a-half-year-old. In an interview at their home, Eduardo's mother refers proudly to how responsible he is, and she acknowledges that she doesn't think they could manage without his help. Eduardo began kindergarten speaking almost no English, but by mid-year he seems fluent in English. He made rather slow progress at letter recognition and recognizing written numerals, but his kindergarten teachers comment on his excellent storytelling ability. Early in the first-grade year, Eduardo takes his turn at Show and Tell to tell how his baby sister started to cry about 2 AM one morning. He jumped out of bed and picked her up so she wouldn't wake his parents. He carried her into the kitchen, warmed up her bottle. and fed her. Then he changed her diaper and put her down, and she fell right to sleep. His eyes are shining as he talks, and he smiles as he describes his sister drinking from the bottle and then falling asleep.

Eduardo is still having trouble with conventional school performance by the middle of first grade:

> TEACHER: And Eduardo, with his reading, he's below grade level because he didn't have any words in his sight word vocabulary, so he finds reading very hard to do, but he is so motivated. He puts his effort in there to learn these words, and I look at Eduardo, and I see him as a child where these things are going to click. His language . . . he can tell you anything you want to know. He reminds me of the kids that I call "alternative learners" where the language and cracking the codes for the reading and writing was just so hard, but yet if you sat down and talked to them you'd have a very sophisticated conversation. He is very sophisticated. He watches that Discovery Channel. He just soaks it up, and he can tell you facts like you wouldn't believe. (Interview, First-Grade Teacher, 2–1–91)

At the end of the school year, Eduardo's teacher feels that her confidence in him has been justified:

> I've noticed this all of a sudden change in him that's been coming about slowly, and then all of a sudden it really has

been made. And that is in his writing and . . . now he knows he can read somebody's words and pick up a few of the little books and the words really do make sense, and it's not just memorizing. . . . Now he's putting that onto the paper to write. . . . He's writing a book called *Spike's Trip to Hawaii* . . . and he came back to me, and he started kind of reading it, and his invented spelling was much better than I had seen it before. But to me what was really interesting [was that] here they had all these options and games and kids playing soccer and all these fun things, and he said, "Oh, no, I want to write." (Interview, First Grade Teacher, 6–5–91)

Examining the underlying values of these two families reveals important differences in what each family thinks are appropriate social relations between adults and children. Pablo's family is committed to strict adult controls to prevent children's impulsive behavior from leading them into antisocial acts. Children are expected to learn how to act properly by being told what to do and when to do it and by being punished for disobeying or disrespecting their adult mentors. Eduardo's family finds it easier to expect him to act responsibly on his own initiative. When he meets their expectation, they reward him with approval and extend his opportunities to act independently, but with the family's interests in mind. These two different sets of cultural values for families that are grouped within the same "Latino" category underscore the variety of ways of inventing and enacting cultural responses to "cultural discontinuity." In school, Pablo's learned dependent behavior frustrates his teacher while Eduardo's willingness to risk failure by trying to do the work as best he can receives an approving teacher response.

For both children, the prevailing question for their teachers seems to be "What can we do to get them to succeed, to achieve well?" rather than simply "Are they going to succeed or fail?" In the case of these two children, their teachers helped them to succeed in school by employing a variety of teaching strategies based on expectations that success was possible and by interpreting Pablo's and Eduardo's end-of-year classroom responses to be evidence of acceptable achievement.

For some children, the construction of success or failure seems to be in the balance, and it is not clear which way it will go. Mai is such a child. She was born in the United States, the oldest

of five children of a Hmong couple who entered the country with
refugee status. Mai's kindergarten teacher describes her behavior
in school as "very good. She is very attentive . . . well liked. Her
work is good. She's beginning to talk up more. She still is somewhat shy but she's doing well" (Interview, Kindergarten Teacher,
3–29–90). Mai's kindergarten teacher is concerned about Mai's shy-
ness, and she seems pleased and a little amused to report noticing
Mai giggling and being silly as she plays with several non-Hmong
girls in the playhouse.

During the summer between her kindergarten and first-grade
years, Mai is six years old and tells the following oral story (a
Hmong folk tale) (also see Johnson, 1985) to one of our research
assistants and to a group of about ten other children, who would
on occasion add their own voice to the folktale that Mai was
telling *in English*:

> MAI: "My, my um, my, my dad told me this: um a, tiger um
> she she killed a man that went to country and she came back
> and the um the she came and the tiger, she made like his dad
> . . . and, and . . . and his, and his, she want to marry the a um
> a daughter. So she ate all up the uh his family but not the
> daughter that she want to marry. GIRL interrupts storyteller
> with question: You tell a folktale? STORYTELLER-MAI): Uh-
> huh. . . .

Mai continues to tell the story, ending with the girl calling her
extended family to come protect her from the tiger.

> MAI: Then, then she his family, he they make, made a track
> [trap] and then, the dau . . . they are just kidding him, that the
> tiger can getting the daughter. The daughter went and, and
> went and said um "you can marry me now'."
> ANOTHER GIRL: I know that story. . . .
> MAI: The cat got uh cut [caught], then she, they they lived
> happily ever after.

In the middle of Mai's first-grade year, Mai's teacher is very
unhappy with her behavior and with Mai's apparent lack of academic progress:

> Well, we'll be sitting on the rug, and she'll be goofing around
> and giggling and laughing and poking and . . . where most of

the Hmong kids will sit there quietly and solemnly and look into their book, and ten bucks to a doughnut Mai will be doing something she's not supposed to be doing, and kind of bringing other kids down. . . . Robert [a male Hmong classmate of Mai's] talks a lot more in English, so you get a better idea of what his thought processes are and what his language [ability] actually is. But Mai, she refuses to talk. She has a real stubborn streak in her, and I don't know where language is a problem for her or she's just afraid to make a mistake, so thus we don't say anything, then they can't tell us that we're wrong. I don't . . . really know what her language is like because she kind of refuses to speak. . . . We read a lot of books . . . we do a lot of writing. You ask Mai to read the page, the first word might be "here" [and] she has no idea what it is. But we've read it ten times up to that point, and Mai has no idea what the first word is. And the other [Hmong] kids do, they notice the pattern . . . and she really isn't noticing it. It's a real decline. (Interview, First-Grade Teacher, 1–24–91)

In spite of her teacher's comments, Mai is sought out by other Hmong children for help in doing their work. There is no obvious indication on Mai's report card that she is doing poorly in any academic area. Mai's teacher seems to be uncertain about how to describe Mai's performance to her parents, and this may result from the teacher's uncertainty about whether the performance is the result of lack of ability, willful refusal to achieve, or a canny avoidance mechanism that prevents failure. If Mai's teachers accept her lack of progress as all they can expect from her, then there may be a "spiral down" leading to one or another special learning classification to explain and "respond" to Mai's poor achievement. If her teachers use her earlier good academic performance to project expectations of future successful achievement, that could lead to varying teaching strategies aimed at encouraging Mai to risk trying to accomplish assigned tasks and revealing what she can do so that there is the possibility for her teachers to interpret her academic performance as evidencing success.

Hoa was a child who entered into school with more knowledge of English than other Hmong children in our research study. His parents both spoke limited English and tried to speak English around the home with their children. They encouraged Hoa to speak English at home. When they were given a chance to offer advice about his next year's placement at the end of his kindergarten year, they asked that Hoa be placed in a classroom with fewer Hmong children (particularly boys). His parents had emigrated from Laos in the early 1980s, and his mother sold Hmong hand-embroidered cloth in markets while his father worked as a laborer. They lived in the same public housing area as many other Hmong people (including Mai and her family).

Hoa began kindergarten after one year of a bilingual Head Start program in which he had been with other Hmong children. From the beginning of kindergarten, he appeared happy and active, while at the same time remaining close to other Hmong children in the classroom for play. Like other Hmong children, he remained in the back of the class during large group, teacher-led activities, but raised his hand more in response to the teacher's questions (e.g., related to a book she was reading) than other Hmong children in the class. During the kindergarten year, Hoa remained active as a friend to Hmong and non-Hmong children, speaking Hmong to Hmong children and speaking increasing amounts of English with others. At the yearly kindergarten conference, his teacher described him as average to his mother, who attended all conferences. In the first-grade year, he was seen by his teachers to continue his good academic progress, although in first grade, his teacher claimed he was too noisy at times. Hoa remained at about the average level in his academic work. Hoa's teacher was able to involve his mother in an activity for children in which she demonstrated Hmong clothing on a large doll which she had dressed with handmade cloth. Hoa's mother and father were both able to volunteer at least once in Hoa's classroom because they felt comfortable with the English language spoken and with the teacher. Among the Hmong parents we visited, Hoa's mother, especially, was an exception in her ability to speak English and her willingness to work with her children's teachers. By the end of the first grade, Hoa's teacher suggested he was average to above average in most of his abilities and would have little trouble, in her opinion, succeeding in second grade.

Hoa's and Mai's cases illustrate intracultural variability as well as individual and gender differences among children. They also reflect the power and complexity of home-school collaborations to affect a child's actions being perceived as successful school behavior. While Hoa is different in many ways from other boys in our Hmong group of children, he represents the greater extroversion and verbal/physical activity levels of the boys we observed in contrast to the Hmong girls, who, according to cultural norms, were expected to be quieter and to interact less directly with adults. The fact that Hoa and his family were able, from the beginning of kindergarten, to be active in English helped Hoa to succeed in the school context and culture. Hoa could interact in social and academic ways within the broad Euro-American/English dominant language culture of the classroom. His parents encouraged bilingual development at home but also made strong efforts to have Hoa know English and be in contexts where Hoa's proficiency with English and knowledge of non-Hmong culture would be enhanced (e.g., by recommending a first-grade placement for Hoa in a classroom with fewer Hmong boys with whom he could play and speak Hmong). Hoa's parents and teachers encouraged the development toward cultural and language assimilation, at least within the school context, and this helped Hoa make a successful transition to the "American" school context and culture.

This successful transition, however, has negative aspects. First, many children and their parents who have less English background than Hoa and his family (e.g., Mai in our example above) were implicitly faulted for their knowledge of Hmong or lack of family/child knowledge of English. Second, the fact that assimilation in language and culture is expected for success has costs to the maintenance of children's primary language and their cultural background and history. These are costs to the children, their families, and communities, and to the broader heterogeneous American population in general. A richer perspective is portrayed, for example, in Moll's (1992) writing on "funds of cultural knowledge," where the resources of family language and competence are brought into the classroom. Although Hoa's family collaborated with Hoa's teachers and his school within the framework of the mainstream or dominant Euro-American culture of the school, through conferences and presentations in classrooms, the majority of other families (nine out of the ten we observed and interviewed) were unable to represent their children as well within this framework of social, school, and teacher expectations.

The case of Lorene, an African American girl from the third school we worked in, also represents a case of success, although Lorene was originally constructed by the school as "at risk" for failure in both kindergarten and the first half of first grade. Lorene seemed to be an outgoing, happy girl when we first met her in a preschool program during the summer before her kindergarten year. Lorene lived in the subsidized housing complex in which many of the low-income African American children attending Greendale School lived and in which the summer program took place. During that summer and the next (between kindergarten and first grade), we observed that Lorene loved to play physical games, was fairly well liked by other girls and boys, and was generally a happy child. She roamed from house to house where her friends lived, while at the same time behaving responsibly at home with her younger siblings. She was the third child in a family where both the father and mother had low-wage jobs; they had recently moved to this city from Chicago.

When Lorene got to kindergarten, early teacher assessments showed that she had little letter knowledge, and she was recommended to be in Chapter 1, a special "pull-out" program where intensive, small group work emphasized letter identification. Lorene left her classroom for Chapter 1 work with four or five other children, all African American children who lived close to her. The pull-out program occurred in the beginning of the morning when other children had rich whole language instruction with the teacher. The Chapter 1 children returned to the classroom at the same time that the whole language period was over for the day.

Lorene was involved in various activities during kindergarten, but at first she had some problems with other children. Lorene sulked when she didn't get her own way or attention from the teacher. She also was a big child for her age, and physically dominated, or appeared to dominate, some of the outdoor activities that she did with the other girls (e.g., jumping rope). At one point in her kindergarten year, Lorene was recommended for special assessment because "she was so slow going from one place to another and bumped into things often"; her teacher thought she might have a physical problem. The fact that she had few academic skills worried the teacher, who also often smiled and "reinforced" Lorene with hugs when she was close to her. The assessment of Lorene's "physical problem" in being slow and bumping into things did not result in specialized placement, though the kindergarten teacher remained concerned about Lorene throughout her year and was concerned about how she would fare in regular first grade.

When Lorene went to first grade, she remained in Chapter 1 and was assessed as having relatively low academic skills as an entering first-grader. In her first-grade class, she was placed in the lowest reading group, composed entirely of African American children, some of whom had been with Lorene in kindergarten and in her Chapter 1 classroom. Lorene remained a relatively happy child, although she still was shy with other girls in her classroom and found that her size appeared to frighten some children away from playing outdoor games with her. One of her African American friends teased her about her family in front of other girls, getting great satisfaction out of building herself up while encouraging other Euro-American and African American girls to make fun of Lorene and make her cry or leave a game.

Mid-first-grade assessments of Lorene by the teacher expressed concern for Lorene's academic and social progress. However, assessments by Reading Recovery teachers showed that Lorene qualified for this specialized one-on-one tutorial program that the school offered to some of the first-graders. With tutoring through this program, Lorene's reading skills began to get better during the second half of first grade. She began to gain self-confidence in reading and in writing and began to enjoy both as she could engage in the process of reading and writing with greater public and private success. At the end of the year, her first-grade teacher suggested that Lorene was a changed girl who smiled much more and initiated additional reading, writing, and math work problems and tasks that earlier in the year she had left incomplete or unstarted. She was assessed by the first-grade teacher as "below average, but getting better" (also see Bloch, Tabachnick, & Espinosa-Dulanto, 1994).

The case of Lorene takes the form of a success story, largely because of the late first-grade intervention through the tutorial program; in effect, at least by the end of first grade, Lorene had been saved from further constructions of her as "at risk." Lorene's participation in school characterizes many of the complex issues facing children who are constructed as "at risk for school failure." The activity and responsible behavior she displayed within her home/community context, both of which seem to be representative of culturally valued behavioral patterns for African American children (see, for example, Ladson-Billings, 1992a,1992b), were not competencies that served her well within the school context. In the first case—high activity orientation—she was faulted for low attention span in kindergarten; at the same time, she was being referred for "slowness" in moving from one activity to another. Her independence and energy when she moved freely from household to household in summertimes or her energy in outdoor games at home were largely unknown within the school context; the richness of her verbal play in games and songs at home—although in a different form than those of the Hmong folktales told by Mai—was also unknown. What was recognized was that she had few entering preacademic letter, word, and number concepts or skills as these were defined by school personnel, and she was perceived by her teacher to be "at risk" for school failure.

The intervention of the special tutorial program pulled Lorene out of what appeared to be a downward spiral in first grade. Teacher expectations began to change as teachers saw that she could learn and participate more actively in school-expected academic tasks. According to teacher accounts, Lorene's low perception of her own abilities was raised, and she took a new interest in her work. While Reading Recovery is appropriately criticized by Arnold and Swadener (1993) as a program that includes the discourse of "at risk" in its label, in this case we saw the program pushing one child into the potential "success" category. However, the processes that brought Lorene to the point where she needed to be "saved" by Reading Recovery are the most problematic. These issues are further exemplified in the story of Tyrone below.

Tyrone is the last child we want to describe, and his story is the hardest one to tell. Not only was this young African American boy immediately constructed as "at risk" upon his entry into public school, but his was not a success story in the end.

Tyrone was a child who was perceived by his teachers to have few academic skills as he entered into the same kindergarten classroom as Lorene. He was active and happy at home, where he was the oldest child of a single, full-time working mother who had two other younger children. Tyrone was considered to be responsible enough to care for his younger brother and new baby sister when she was born during his kindergarten year. He was also responsible and independent enough as a six-year-old to travel by bus alone to visit grandparents in a neighboring city one hour distant from the study site. He was a sweet boy who always greeted us with affection and, over the years, appeared to look forward to the attention we gave him when we were in his classroom.

Tyrone was in a special needs early childhood education program during his preschool years. His placement was enabled by a diagnosis of language delay and the judged need for "at risk" placement. He was assessed by the prekindergarten screener to have little preacademic knowledge of letter or number concepts or skills. He was placed in the same Chapter 1 pull-out program that Lorene

was in and that also took place during the major language arts period of the day in his kindergarten classroom. During first grade, he
continued to be in the Chapter 1 program and was in the lowest
reading group (with Lorene and several other African American
children). Unlike Lorene, he was considered too weak in first grade
to be eligible for the school's Reading Recovery program, which
required certain skills and knowledge for entry. By the end of first
grade, Tyrone was considered for special education referral, but he
was moved on to the second grade where an experienced second-
grade teacher thought she could help him (for a related story, see
Taylor, 1991).

Tyrone's skills for school may have been low upon entry into
the public school, and they may have remained low despite careful
instruction. However, in Tyrone's case, he was also faulted in the
classroom for constant interruptions of other children and for
moving about the classroom instead of working by himself. In the
first grade, Tyrone could not engage in the majority of classroom
interactions that required some letter knowledge or knowledge of
words or numbers. He learned some preliminary reading skills in
the Chapter 1 class and in his reading group, but he was always
behind the other children, and he appeared to suffer from every
other child's recognition that he could not do the work or keep up
with them. In addition, as he couldn't enter into instruction easily,
he had little to do; he moved around in his seat, appeared restless,
sometimes bothered other children, and quite frequently was sent
out of the room to the hallway, to a corner for a "time-out," or,
more and more regularly as the year progressed, to the principal's
office. Although anyone who has taught understands that there are
children who have problems learning in any class, the
teaching/learning context for Tyrone, the cultural belief system of
the school toward children's skills and rates of "progress," led to
Tyrone's downward spiral from entry into kindergarten through
the end of our intensive observations in first grade. Teacher expectations about Tyrone, the organization of intervention services
(pull-out programs, Reading Recovery for children with certain
skill levels), disciplinary methods (hallway/principal's office,
thereby missing more instruction), school cultural expectations,
belief systems about African Americans (particularly active boys
who don't demonstrate the skills teachers expect or want to see),
and the generalized perception that remediation through specialized services was the primary way to help some "low skill" chil-

dren, led to Tyrone's continuing characterization as someone without any promise of success.

There were other African American males who benefitted from a different and more "promising" characterization than the one constructed for Tyrone. Their stories were different because of a variety of factors, including different responses by the children that represented greater readiness to conform or recognition of evidence of conventional academic ability. Some of the less-conforming children had more powerful parent advocates who were unwilling to accept negative school characterizations and who continued to support their child's image of himself as a competent person. As a result of several such factors, some African American male children persisted in trying to achieve school success and, in their cases, teachers began to see them as potentially successful (Bloch, Cradle, Dean, Espinosa-Dulanto, & Tabachnick, in press; Bloch, Tabachnick & Espinosa-Dulanto, 1994).

CONCLUSION

We began our longitudinal study with the expectation that we would examine the theory of cultural compatibility within the context of schools that had heterogeneous ethnic and linguistic communities (Bloch & Tabachnick, 1988). As our study progressed, the complexities, possibilities, and remaining problems with this theoretical framework became clearer.

As Singer (1988) suggests, cultural compatibility theory is a limited response in its identification of elements of cultural norms, values, language or behavioral patterns that might be recognized and included in school cultural and instructional practices. Consistent with this perspective, we have focused some of our attention in this chapter on the idea that children's language and cultural behavior, taught to them at home, have value, represent competence, and might be recognized more and honored in current school cultural practices and belief systems. If making these small adjustments in the practice of teachers makes school life more bearable for children, then there is merit to discovering patterns that can be adjusted to make home-school "culture" more compatible for children. However, cultural compatibility as an idea has the potential to be more than this. In contrast to the alienating results of some teaching practices, it can aim to create a new vision of schooling, of how teachers think and act toward nonmainstream children. Underlying its elements is the aim to give all people and groups, rather than simply some, access to power and to feelings of acceptance and worth in the contexts in which they work and learn.

Our data also have supported the idea that factors related to the construction of children as successes, possible successes, or "at risk for failure" are more complex than inclusion of certain values or behavior in school repertoires of acceptable behavior. Along with others (e.g., Bloch & Swadener, 1992; Cazden, 1990; Erickson, 1987; Ogbu, 1987; Trueba, 1988; and Villegas, 1988), we suggest that there is difficulty determining which features of "culture" are significant and should be changed in schools, particularly in multicultural school contexts (Tharp, 1989). We suggest, with others (e.g., Bloch & Swadener, 1992; Cazden, 1990; Trueba, 1988), that there is a great deal of variability within groups and that cultural compatibility theory is often used in such a way as to overlook this variability, supporting stereotypes that work to the disadvantage of some groups. We suggest that the definition of "culture" itself is problematic. Culture is not a static concept but is a dynamic process, being formed by its carriers as well as received from cultural transmitters. Culture is, therefore, always in need of discovery rather than being describable for all members of a group in advance of knowing any specific individual members and the particular sociocultural contexts in which they enact their cultural identities or behavior. This perspective does not deny shared group outlooks, worldviews, rules for behavior, values, or recognition by insiders and outsiders of membership and affiliation with the group. But it does avoid decontextualizing membership in a culture or the meaning of culture for individuals within and across particular contexts.

Our data also support those who suggest that macrostructural factors—social, political, economic—are powerful and, as yet, not included as factors in the cultural compatibility framework. These factors influence continuing perceptions that some children, by virtue of family background, first language, or skin color, will be automatically "at risk of school failure," while other children, different from them in these characteristics, or mirroring to a greater extent behavior/skills/attitudes of the dominant culture, will be considered competent and promising. These factors, interrelated as they are in ideological discourse, relate to who is likely to succeed and who is likely to have more difficulty succeeding in and out of school. They relate to whose voices are heard and whose are marginalized in educational and social discourse. They relate to what is perceived and expected of children about whom very little may be known by educators outside of the school context (see Fine & Weis 1993).

A new theoretical framework is needed that incorporates powerful elements of cultural compatibility theory but that goes beyond these. For example, such a theoretical framework would honor knowledge from multiple sources, language, community, and cultural backgrounds (see, for example, Moll, 1992); it would not force a model of cultural and linguistic assimilation, thereby losing the wealth of cultural/language practices and traditions that communities can offer to each other. At the same time, a new theory is needed that recognizes the range and variety of differences within groups and across gender and class and that responds to the dynamic qualities of culture as expressed in multiple contexts. Such a theory would aim to explain how access to power can be distributed more equitably through socially constructed meanings for children's behavior that follow from discourse and expectations of promise and success.

NOTES

1. We gratefully acknowledge the Spencer Foundation for their generous support of the research project from which come data reported in this paper. We also acknowledge the invaluable work of graduate assistants who worked on this project over its three-year duration: Miryam Espinosa-Dulanto, Jay Hammond Cradle, Carolyn Dean, and Seehwa Cho. Finally, without the support and collaboration from families, children, school teachers, and staff, we would not have been able to explore the issues presented in this paper; we are particularly indebted to them for continuing to work with us on these issues. All names are changed to protect the rights of individuals and institutions participating in the research.

2. The context of this study as well as research methods have been described in Bloch, Tabachnick, and Espinosa-Dulanto (1994). It is important to note here that the study took place in one midwestern city where the majority of teachers and children in all schools were of Euro-American descent. Compared to the rest of the district in which this study took place, the three schools studied had large percentages (over one-third) of children of color. Interviews in schools were done by the project directors and the authors of this paper, who are both Euro-American. Project assistants were African American, Peruvian, Korean, Hmong, and Euro-American and spoke the primary language of families during interviews and observations with families and children at home.

REFERENCES

Apple, M. W., & Weis, L. (1983). Ideology and practice in schooling: A political and conceptual introduction. In M. W. Apple & L. Weis (Eds.), *Ideology and practice in schooling*. Philadelphia: Temple University Press.

Arnold, M. S., & Swadener, B. B. (1993). Savage inequalities and the discourse of risk: What of the White children who have so much green grass? *The Review of Education, 15*, 261–272.

Bloch, M., Cradle, J., Dean, C., Espinosa-Dulanto, M., & Tabachnick, B. R (in press). Young children and the construction of school success and failure. In K. Borman (Ed.), Families, communities, and schools: Contexts for literacy learning. New York: Teachers College Press.

Bloch, M., & Swadener, B. B. (1992). Relationships among home, community and school: Multicultural considerations and research issues in early childhood. In C. Grant (Ed.), *Research and multicultural education: From margins to the mainstream.* (pp. 165–183). Philadelphia: Falmer Press.

Bloch, M., & Tabachnick, B. R. (1988). *Increasing the school achievement of low-income minority children through improved home-school-university collaboration.* Proposal Funded by the Spencer Foundation. Madison, Wisconsin: Wisconsin Center for Education Research.

Bloch, M., & Tabachniclc, B. R. (in press). Rhetoric or reality: Improving parent involvement as school reform. In K. Borman & N. Greenman (Eds.), *Changing schools: Recapturing the past or inventing the future?* Albany, State University of New York Press.

Bloch, M., Tabachnick, B. R, & Espinosa-Dulanto, M. (1994). Teacher perspectives on the strengths and achievements of young children as these relate to ethnicity, language, gender, and class. In B. Mallory & R. New (Eds.), *Diversity and developmentally appropriate practice: Challenges for early childhood education* (pp. 223–249). New York: Teachers College Press.

Cazden, C. B. (1990). Differential treatment in New Zealand: Reflections on research in minority education. *Teaching and Teacher Education, 6*(4), 291–303.

Erickson, F. (1987). Transformation and school success: The politics and culture of educational achievement. *Anthropology and Education Quarterly, 18*(4), 335–56.

Fine, M., & Weis, L. (Eds.). (1993). *Beyond silenced voices: Class race and gender in United States schools.* Albany, State University of New York Press.

Foucault, M. (1980). Truth and knowledge. In C. Gordon (Ed.), *Power/knowledge: selected interviews and other writings 1972–1977 by Michel Foucault.* New York: Pantheon Books.

Heath, S. B. (1983). *Ways with words: Language, life and work in communities and classrooms.* New York: Cambridge University Press.

Johnson, C. (1985). *Dab neeg hmoob (Myths, legends and folk tales from the Hmong of Laos).* St. Paul: Linguistics Department, Macalester College.

Ladson-Billings, G. (1992a). Culturally relevant teaching The key to making multicultural education work. In C. Grant (Ed.), *Research and multicultural education* (pp. 106–121). Philadelphia, Falmer Press.

Ladson-Billings, G. (1992b). Reading between the lines and beyond the pages: A culturally relevant approach to literacy teaching. *Theory into Practice, 31*(4), 312–320.

Mallory, B., & New R. (1994). *Diversity and developmentally appropriate practice: Challenges for Early Childhood Education,* NY: Teachers College Press.

Moll, L. (1992). Bilingual classroom studies and community analysis: Some recent trends. *Educational Researcher,* pp. 20–24.

Ogbu, J. (1987). Variability in minority school performance: A problem in search of an explanation. *Anthropology and Education Quarterly, 18,* 313–334.

Singer, E. (1988). *What is cultural congruence, and why are they saying such terrible things about it?* Occasional Paper No. 120. East Lansing, Michigan: The Institute for Research on Teaching, Michigan State University.

Taylor, D. (1991). *Learning denied.* Portsmouth, NH: Heinemann.

Tharp, R. (1989). Psychocultural variables and constants: Effects on teaching and learning in schools. *American Psychologist,* pp. 349–359.

Trueba, H. (1988). Culturally-based explanations of minority students' academic achievement. *Anthropology and Education Quarterly, 19*(3), 270–287.

Villegas, A. M. (1988). School failures and cultural mismatch: Another view. *Urban Review, 20,* 253–265.

Vogt, L., Jordan, C., & Tharp, R (1987). Explaining school failure, producing school success: Two cases. *Anthropology and Education Quarterly, 18,* 277–286.

Willis, P. (1977). *Learning to labour.* London: Routledge Press.

MARY E. HAUSER
CYNTHIA THOMPSON

9

Creating a Classroom Culture of Promise: Lessons from a First Grade

The scene on the TV screen showed an overview of the classroom . . . children in pairs, small groups, individually . . . at desks, on the floor, at the work tables. They appeared to be reading . . . children in pairs, small groups, individually . . . but the noise level was high . . . and not everyone was staying in one place. . . .

We were watching a video made earlier in the year of Paula's first grade classroom. "Is this SST [sustained silent reading]?" We weren't sure . . . it wasn't very silent.

Paula laughingly replied, "What am I going to do? They read with whomever they want to. I'm not going to make it silent. I always have to write in my plans for substitutes, 'This is silent reading time, but don't expect it to be silent.'"

We watched the screen for another minute or two as the picture moved from group to group of children and then back to a whole class shot. "I really have to say," Paula commented, "I place a high value on having these kids work together."

In our work together over the last three years, we have been considering the collaboration that Paula values. How is it constructed? What does it look like? Why is it important for the students she teaches? This chapter is designed to explore the ways in which the atmosphere of collaboration that Paula creates in her classroom puts her students at promise for school success. We will look at how Paula uses collaboration to achieve what she considers to be the most important outcomes for her students: socialization in a multicultural context, growth in communication, and student development of a strong sense of their own ability to function effectively (self-esteem).

Paula's goals for her students are consistent with those articulated by Au and Kawakami (1991), Cummins (1986), Ferdman (1990), Gibson (1984), Hornberger (1990), and Kagan (1986). They, and a host of other researchers concerned with the education of linguistic and cultural minorities in the United States, work in classrooms that are similar to Paula's culturally diverse group of students who have limited knowledge of English. Their research indicates that students who do not have English as a first language and who come from cultures that are at variance with American "mainstream" culture, the standard for school success, need to be in settings where the activities of the classroom empower them to develop a strong sense of identity as well as to learn the "rules" of the dominant culture. As an illustration, Hornberger's (1990) research describes situations in which successful Cambodian students operate in a learning environment that allows them to draw on their own linguistic and cultural backgrounds even though the class is taught in English. Gibson's (1984) work and that of Ferdman (1990) point to the importance of a strong self-concept for students of every cultural group in a culturally diverse learning environment. Ferdman argues that, to the extent that learning forces a child to become disconnected from what is personally significant, his or her ability to construct a positive and coherent cultural identity will be weakened.

Learning activities in which teachers draw on the background experience and knowledge of students, in which students are encouraged to assume greater control over their own learning, and in which oral and written language is used for collaboration all legitimize the students' knowledge and communicate respect for them as persons. While this description seems applicable to all good teachers, we felt that Hornberger's (1990) analysis fit this classroom as well as the ones she studied. She observed that "although good teaching in these classrooms may look a lot like good teaching anywhere, it actually reflects sensitivity to a wide range of factors unique to these classrooms" (p. 213).

THE SCHOOL SETTING

Paula teaches in the Bankton School District, in a small city adjacent to a large metropolitan area in California. In the last five years the community has received a large influx of refugees from Laos, Cambodia, and Russia, necessitating the reopening of Brand School in the 1988–89 school year. We have been working with the school and with Paula since its second year, the year that she came to Brand. During this time, the school population has ranged from 322 to 360, and 44 to 46 per cent of the students are limited- or non-English-speaking.

Her first-grade class is designed as an enriched language environment for students who are classified as NEP or LEP (non-English-proficient or limited-English-proficient) on the Ideal Language Proficiency Test. During the three years we have worked together, she has taught students who speak Hmong, Lao, Khmer, Russian, Mien, and Spanish. Her class size averages twenty-eight. Three of that total were native English speakers who were placed in this room because it was determined that they were in need of the kind of classroom environment she creates. Paula commented to us that because these students were good language models for the other students, their placement in the class was actually more mutually beneficial than had been anticipated.

There is one other first grade at Brand and it contains all of the native English speakers and an occasional refugee student whose English level is considered high enough to be able to cope with the more advanced language demands and the more traditional organization of the class. There is little, if any, sharing of activities between the two classes.

THE STUDENTS

By all yardsticks that could possibly be used to measure "risk," the majority of the students at the school and all of the students in Paula's class would be considered to be "at risk." The school has qualified as a Chapter 1[1] school for the last three years. A high percentage of families in her class receive AFDC funds and other kinds of public assistance. Her students do not have English as a primary language; some families are religious refugees from Russia, but most families are political refugees from Laos and Cambodia. It is difficult for the parents to participate fully in their children's education because of language and cultural barriers and limited experience with schooling themselves. The practice in Laos and Cambodia was for parents and teachers to have separate spheres of influence over the children, therefore parents are not accustomed to interacting with the school personnel. Lao, Hmong, and Cambodian parents had limited opportunities to go to school in their homelands, since most came from small villages in the mountains of their countries.

But Paula focused on her students' strengths. Her words speak for themselves:

> I don't look at their past. Well, I do and I don't. I look at what I have in front of me. I know that there are a lot of things out there that are affecting their lives and you do have to think about that, but I also think that these are kids who love coming to school and they are ready to receive anything. I look at it as no one has any problem receiving information and processing it just because they are so-called "mountain people."
>
> I think my students have potential, motivation. They're not turned off to anything. They have motivation from themselves and from the group. They have determination and will. They haven't been handed everything on the proverbial silver platter. Everything we do is new and great . . . every book, every piece of art.

How Paula developed this viewpoint about her students has been considered in an earlier report (Hauser, 1991). How she implements this philosophy, that is, the nature of the classroom events and interactions that allow the students to function at promise, is the focus of this chapter. The quote above serves as an action philosophy for Paula, a living theory, so to speak. It is the driving force of everything that she does in her classroom. From her thoughts and from her actions in the classroom we can learn about teaching children at promise. The words of Schubert & Ayers (1992) are relevant: "Teachers can be the richest and most useful source of knowledge about teaching; those who hope to understand teaching must turn at some point to teachers themselves" (p. v).

THE CLASSROOM

Collaboration

Since collaboration is important to Paula, we will look first at how it is structured in this classroom. Kagan (1986) describes collaborative classrooms as active environments involving movement, interaction, and a variety of roles for students. He discusses the idea that the role of the teacher shifts from director to consultant. The following vignette from the daily math period will provide a context to demonstrate how these ideas are enacted.

> Mathematics is generally taught in four rotating groups. The primary language aide, Mr. V, does a small group activity, often a math game related to skills being taught. Paula works with another small group to teach the first grade math concepts and to monitor their progress in math workbooks. One group copies number sequences or does about twenty computation problems from the blackboard, and one group uses math manipulatives on the rug or works in pairs at the computer. This mix of activities allows children to learn using a variety of modalities. The groups rotate about every twenty minutes.
>
> However, on this day, Paula has a special addition fact math worksheet on an insect theme. The students are to match a number printed on the thorax of an insect with an equivalent set of addends printed on an abdomen by cutting and pasting the parts. She introduces this to the group as a whole and then dismisses them to do the worksheet independently. Students choose a variety of work settings. Five boys and one girl work at a table in the front of the room. R——, the only girl whose home language is Russian, is quiet during this period. The boys around her chatter constantly. The Russian-speaking boy is in this group and exchanges a few words in Russian with R——. Four girls work together at the corner of a cluster of desks. One speaks Hmong at home, one speaks Lao, one speaks English, and one Mien. The language of this group is English as they converse and jointly arrive at answers. Two boys sit across from one another at a cluster of desks. They work independently and talk about the worksheet and a variety of topics, including what they will play at recess. One boy sits alone to complete the paper. At another table, one girl also sits alone. Three boys are working together at the end of a table cluster. This group grows to six boys as three return from a short session of primary language instruction in Lao. Two boys sit at the other end of the table cluster, on the margin of this group. Of the eight, six boys are very productive even though they engage in conversations that are tangential to the worksheet. Some conversation takes place in English and some in home languages. Two of the boys seem to find it difficult to

focus on the task. They take longer to get the answers on their paper. Two boys in this group have English as their home language, two have Spanish, three have Lao and one, Hmong. They are talking about friends and cousins . . . how big they were, how many they had.

B: Hey K——, where's 15 at [one of the numbers needed to be matched to a combination]?

N: Hey K——, what's this one?

E: EL——, he be my friend, I could give a ticket to him. (Tickets are accumulated and used periodically to buy things from the classroom treasure box).

T: (approaching the group) Who needs help?

E: Me!

T: No way! (moving on to another group)

N: J—— my friend, I like to go to his house play games.

R: I could go there, too.

N: You live too far.

K: I could ride my bike to your apartment.

K: What's your phone number?

E: What's 9+9, EL?

EL: 9+9 is 18, man.

As this group of boys finishes their worksheets, they disperse. They hand their papers to Paula and then independently begin another activity. Most of them go to a kidney-shaped table to do their workbooks. Their conversations continue, this time focusing on who has completed more pages in the math book.

During this time Paula walks around the room receiving papers as students finish. She is also consulted for some number facts: G: "What's 8+7?" Paula: "Put 8 in your brain and add on. Start with the big number." The primary language aide, Mr. V, also circulates and helps children. He works in Hmong with a "new" boy who has the least amount of English in the class. He also goes to E., a child who has trouble with math, using English to help him.

The activity pattern described is typical of what is seen in Paula's classroom. Children collaborate with one another for the most part in groups that they choose. They complete their work in the context of personal conversations about a variety of topics.

These groups almost always include students from more than one home language background. Before T came to offer assistance to the group of boys, he had turned in his paper and asked Paula if he could help. After rejecting E, he did help another child. Often, Paula reported, the children will spontaneously go to aid others. "I never taught them that. It just happened. It has been true of the last three classes."

As the children work in these self-chosen groupings, they are not restricted in the amount or subject matter of their conversation and combine task-oriented talk with topics not at all related to the work at hand. They help one another, correct one another. They learn about one another as they converse informally. Vocabulary is developed as well as the skills of conversation: turn taking, introducing topics, responding to topics. Paula had this to say about the "visiting" that goes on: "I never stop those side conversations, if possible. They are learning how to get along with one another in those situations. I want them to have awareness of one another's personal and cultural similarities and differences. It is an opportunity to develop and strengthen friendships." Another time she made this comment: "I hope the kids develop enough self-esteem that they won't have to get involved in gangs. That's why I like them interacting with each other. That [interaction] will help them with problems later on with different groups of kids."

While it may appear that students are operating in a chaotic environment, in reality Paula has an authoritative style of management supporting the informality. She uses her voice as a management tool: directing, encouraging, supporting, approving/disapproving through variations in her tone. She has no formal management program.

In summarizing her thoughts about collaboration, we have further evidence of a teacher's personal theory in action:

> The goal is collaboration and what comes from that. Everything comes from that. There are so many things going on in the room in the course of the day. They learn more from each other than they do from me. Self-esteem, to me, is recognizing everyone as an individual and part of the group . . . working together. Everyone is important. Socialization kind of goes with the self-esteem . . . to believe in yourself you have to be able to work with others and to respect others. I really feel that if they are going to function, they have to have this . . . they are going to have to feel good about themselves. . . . English comes

with all of this . . . we are always working with the English. . . . Basic skills are always in the back of my mind. Basic skills are always my intent, but not my priority.

She then made a comparison to other teachers who are so worried about their annual test scores. "I say, yes, but can your kids work, can they think, can they function?"

Autonomy

We can also look at the math vignette for evidence of the autonomy that children are encouraged to develop. Autonomy is a component of the sense of self that Paula considers important. The students can work where they want in the classroom and can choose their co-workers. For the most part they can choose their materials: colored pencils, crayons, markers, and so on. They can work at their own pace. They are encouraged to move independently from one activity to another. In all of the transitions I observed during the mathematics period, Paula spoke only occasionally to individual students. Usually it was, "Freeze [the signal for quiet attention]! I need the blues group, greens go to Mr. V, and purples to the rug. Be sure to clean up the blocks for the next group. Melt and move!"

On another day, the class was going outdoors to collect some of the insects they had been studying. This activity allows us to see the students act autonomously in a more informal setting.

Students walk out (with partners) to the grassy area beyond the playground. They do not seem to stay in partners because they each have their own collecting equipment (a clear plastic cup and a kid-sized magnifying glass). Some kids have more sophisticated bug cages, but no one seems to see this as a problem. They move freely about the grass. Paula gives no directions about where they are to look for insects except to give permission to go to the tree at the far end of the grassy area. Most students come to show her their finds. She responds to each child, it seems. She is interested, enthusiastic, excited about their finds. Everyone is expected to participate. But if they don't come up with a bug, there is no penalty or disparaging remark. She doesn't seem to be monitoring the class as a whole while she focuses on the discoveries of the individual children. She has a cup to collect ladybugs to take home for her rose bushes and many children give her the ladybugs they find. She seems to have no expectation for "off task" behavior. When students share their finds, she asks questions about size, shape, body parts, and so on. She is the focus of their finds for the most part. They really want to share what they find with her. When it is time to go in, she asks a child to call those farthest away and then doesn't monitor the result. They all come in.

Observations on this experience that were written at the time it occurred indicate that she is very much in charge and gives procedural directions to the group but allows for a lot of individual autonomy in carrying out the task. She interacts with each child in turn as they come to her. Sometimes it is only validation. Sometimes it is a question. She doesn't seem to favor any children over others.

Communication

Improvement of communication is another goal of Paula's. She includes learning/improving English vocabulary and grammar as well as the pragmatics of communication. The following excerpt from a language arts lesson is illustrative. The students were seated on the floor in front of a chart rack. The teacher was seated on a small chair beside the rack. (In this transcript, T=teacher, S=a student who spoke without being called on specifically, and other letters refer to specific students who were addressed.)

> T: These are the rules. We just raise our hands. We don't say, "I know, I know." Think, think hard of all the things you can do in the summer. I'll try to call on everyone.
> S: I play.
> T: (speaks and writes) I can play.
> T: O——, what can you do?
> O: Can swim
> T: Who can swim? Its B——'s [turn]. I want her to say it.
> B: I can swim.
> T: That really is fun, I agree.
> S: Pick apple in the tree. My mom she drives the car.
> T: (speaks and writes) My mom can drive the car to the apple trees.
> T: And besides, it's nice and cool where the trees are. You can sit.
> S: My dad drives the car to pick strawberries.
> T: What else can you pick besides strawberries?

T: Y——?

Y: My brother drives the car pick cherries.

T: Mmm, you have my favorite fruits, strawberries and cherries.

T: How many go to pick strawberries? (hands go up) Do you eat them when you pick them? Are they sweet and juicy? Mmm (a chorus of voices responds in agreement.)

T: M——?

M: My brother, I go to the zoo.

T: Oh, that's really fun. To see what?

S: I go to the zoo to see the animals play.

T: N——, where do you go?

N: I go to the park.

T: How many people go to the park? (Many hands go up.) Do you eat lunch at the park?

S: Everyone go to the park.

T: I go to the park, too.

S: I went to school.

T. Of course, everyone goes to summer school. (writes:) I go to summer school.

S: I see the butterfly.
(T writes and comments.)

The lesson proceeded with more of the same kind of interaction.

Paula used the experiences of the children to develop the topic rather than tell them what the appropriate responses were. She modified their utterances in such a way that the grammatically incomplete responses were not considered inadequate. She focused on the content rather than on the form. For example, she turns "I play" into "I can play"; she writes "My mom can drive the car to the apple trees" after a child volunteers "Pick apple in the tree. My mom she drives the car." She reacted to the comments by the children and related them to her own experience as well as to others the children had. While this lesson was going on, she did not discourage small side conversations in English or in other home languages as long as they were not disruptive. The transcription, unfortunately, cannot reflect this situation. All of these language teaching techniques build confidence in the children's ability to communicate. The verbal and nonverbal messages transmitted to the children in this interaction were ones of validation of themselves and of their ideas. She rejected no ideas and communicated that she really liked what they had to say.

Paula's focus on developing communication skills not only focused on learning English, as mentioned above, but also on valuing the student's home language. The fact that her students came with no English is not considered a disabling factor. Rather, she viewed these students as potential bilingual speakers, definitely a viewpoint of promise. Evidence for this was observed one day when students were learning about the life cycle of a butterfly. She had presented the lesson and they had each been given a worksheet with pictures to cut out and organize into the sequence of the life cycle. As usual, students were working at a variety of places in the classroom and in a variety of groups. There was a lot of conversation going on related to completing the assignment as well as about other topics of interest to the students. Paula was circulating among the students. "How do you say butterfly in Hmong?" she asked one. The student gave a reply and then Paula asked for the word for caterpillar. Soon she had a group of students around her, volunteering words in Hmong, Lao, Khmer, and Russian. This exchange was not without conflict, however, because the students did not always agree on the words their classmates used. She encouraged students who did not know the vocabulary in their home language to go home and ask their parents and report back the next day.

Later on, we commented to Paula how that exchange with the students had demonstrated that she did value these students as potential bilingual speakers. "Do you know what happened to that?" she laughed. "It generated a period of intense home language vocabulary comparison. They told me the names of many items in the classroom in their home language. I was inundated with requests: 'Do you know what window is in Hmong?' 'I can tell you chair in Lao.' It is wonderful to see, but I feel so guilty, because I don't remember the words. A child will say a word and then I will repeat it, but I don't remember it one minute later. I feel so bad about that." As a fluent Spanish speaker, Paula, of course, knows that a second language is not acquired in such an incidental way. But she wishes that she could show more connections to the students by understanding a bit of their language.

Collegiality

A situation in Paula's classroom that also contributes to the atmosphere of promise is the nature of her interaction with the two primary language tutors, Mr. V and Ms. D. Mr. V is Hmong and also speaks, reads, and writes Lao. Ms. D is Cambodian, and, while she does not write Khmer, is able to speak and read it. Of Mr. V who spends the majority of the morning in the classroom, Paula has this to say: "He is like another teacher. I don't know what I would do without him." Her interactions with him are that of one colleague with another. She doesn't interfere in his management problems if he has them, and she encourages his autonomous behavior as well. She is impressed with the ideas he comes up with to implement a lesson and reports that he has different ways of explaining things— math procedures, for example, that help to accommodate the variety of learning styles in the classroom. She feels that they complement one another in working with the students. She completely trusts his judgment. The students, of course, observe their collegial relationship. Mr V feels the students also trust him. He related a conversation he had with Lao and Hmong students about the use of a "delicate subject," profanity, that indicated trust. He felt the students needed to use their home language in order to express themselves satisfactorily. Ms. D spends one and a half hours a day in the classroom and so Paula directs her time more. It is an important period, since it is the only opportunity for the Khmer speaking students to have home language instruction.

SUMMARY

Paula's goals of promise for her students—socialization skills, growth in communication ability, and development of a strong sense of self—have been illustrated by drawing on examples from her interactions with students and from the organization of her classroom. We have documented situations in which, within the context of the first-grade curriculum, socialization occurs, examples of how children are encouraged to behave autonomously, and ways in which students' ability to communicate is fostered. The vignettes attest to Paula as a skilled enabler of learning. They demonstrate how she values the experiential, language, and cultural backgrounds that the students bring to her classroom. An additional condition, the professional relationship that she has with the primary language tutors in her classroom and its possible positive effect on the students' cultural identity, has also been described.

Will these students become citizens who can work, think, and function, as Paula expects? That outcome cannot be guaranteed. There are many experiences ahead of these first-graders that will also affect the kind of adults they become. As this volume indicates, the situation is complex. What we do know, however, is that what Paula is doing to value and empower these students is consistent with what the literature indicates is significant for the success of students who come to school from linguistic and cultural minorities. Within her realm of influence, Paula is diligently working to ensure that the students develop a good sense of self, possibly one of the best tools for them to use in dealing with the experiences of the years ahead. It is her hope, and ours as well, that with this strong, sound, nurturing beginning their educational experiences will continue to be positive and stimulating, facilitating promise rather than risk.

NOTE

1. Chapter 1 is a federally funded program designed to support educationally disadvantaged students in the areas of reading, math, and language arts. Students who score below the 36th percentile on a standardized test of reading or math qualify for funding to receive extra help. Schools in which more than 75 percent of the students receive free or reduced lunches can apply for a schoolwide Chapter 1 Project, which allows the school to use funds for the entire student body instead of just for the qualifying students. Funds can be used for hiring specialists and aides, purchasing health services, equipment, and instructional materials, and compensating staff inservice.

REFERENCES

Au, K., & Kawakami, A. (1991). Culture and ownership: Schooling of minority students. *Childhood Education, 68,* 280–284.

Cummins, J. (1986). Empowering minority students: A framework for intervention. *Harvard Educational Review, 56,* 18–36.

Ferdman, B. (1990). Literacy and cultural identity. *Harvard Educational Review, 60*(2), 181–204.

Gibson, M. (1984). Approaches to multicultural education in the U.S.: some concepts and assumptions. *Anthropology and Education Quarterly, 15*(1), 54–62.

Hauser, M. (1991, November). *Cultural conflict in teacher development: A case study.* Paper presented at the American Anthropological Association, Chicago.

Hornberger, N. (1990). Creating successful learning contexts for bilingual literacy. *Teachers College Record, 92*(2), 213–229.

Kagan, S. (1986). Cooperative learning and sociocultural factors in schooling. In Bilingual Office of Cal. Dept. of Ed. (Ed.), *Beyond language: Social and cultural factors in schooling language minority students* (pp. 231–298). Sacramento CA: Bilingual Education Office, California State Department of Education.

Schubert, W., & Ayers, W. (1992). *Teacher lore: Learning from our own experience.* White Plains, NY: Longman.

JOYCE S. WALDOCH

10

Student Success:
A Matter of
Compatibility and
Expectations

The terms "at risk" and "regular education initiative" have flooded educational journals. The consensus of most of these writings is that there is something wrong with the learner that makes his or her classroom participation less than adequate. Costly new programs have been developed to address these problem learners. In this article, I will describe a program in which I am working, in an elementary school, that merges a special education class with an "at risk" regular education class, builds on students' strengths, requires no extra funding, and has been created within the existing school structure.

The project, called the Rainbow Room, was developed at Schulte Elementary School in Racine, Wisconsin. A portion of the school day was restructured to provide disinterested learners with a variety of teaching styles, hands-on activities, and opportunities to develop more positive views of themselves in relation to their peers. The program is presented here in the hope that it will trigger the development of other programs that use existing resources within schools to encourage students "at risk" to become active learners and confident risk-takers in the school environment.

RATIONALE

Most students enter school full of excitement and ready for new experiences. As some students proceed through their early years in school, this excitement begins to diminish. By the time they reach fourth or fifth grade they have become frustrated and turned off by the prospect of the years ahead of them that will be spent in an academic setting. They have not found successes in school and do not expect that it will get any better for them in the future. A poor self-concept regarding their school success develops, and some question their ability to ever succeed at anything. The defenses that these students have built up around themselves make it almost impossible for them to make progress within the projected school goals for all students. It becomes necessary to look for new approaches to use with these students in order for them to value their own importance as human beings who can make useful contributions in any situation.

Failure in the academic environment and low self-esteem lead to behavior problems in the classroom that result in excess referrals for gray-area students who do not qualify for special education placement. Those students typically are not eligible for special education placement—not classified as having a cognitive disability (CD) because they are not low enough, and not classified as having learning disabilities (LD) because they are not high enough with a profile of strengths and weaknesses. These are the students who frequently come from poverty who have not fit into the slot in the regular classroom, but for whom no alternative program has been available. Many of the students placed in special education pull-out programs demonstrate escalation of unacceptable behaviors when placed in a mainstream class where they do not feel acceptance from their peers. The result for students who do not fit the mold is often seen in their frequent absences from school, which further separate them from the day-to-day interactions with peers. In *Multicultural Teaching*, Tiedt and Tiedt (1986) expressed the belief that children have the right to value themselves for whatever they are and whatever they do. They need to gain acceptance from their peers and teachers as they go through their school years. Glasser (1987) noted that students who do poorly in school say to themselves that they can't work in a place where there is no sense of personal importance. Glasser found that even poor students describe a "good student," as "having a positive attitude."

Teachers' lounges often reflect the frustration among colleagues in reaching students turned off to learning. They can also be places where colleagues work together to solve a problem. Often this results in a referral for an M-team (multidisciplinary team) evaluation, and the student is labeled and placed in a special education class. Now the student is in the hands of the special education teacher, to be fixed in some way and be transformed into a well-behaved (i.e,. quiet) student who does not interfere with the normal classroom routine. Those of us in special education feel the failure when our students do not interact with other students and become the class clowns in the mainstreamed settings. But it was in listening to the frustration expressed by my colleagues when students did not meet the criteria for special education placement, combined with my own frustration in working with a non-mainstreamed group of students who were completely isolated and ignored by their peers and who, when mainstreamed into art or music, were placed in isolation so that they caused no discipline problems for the teachers, that the idea of combining efforts to achieve student success began. Special education cannot take into the fold the millions of non-exceptional learners "at risk," nor would it be appropriate to do so. What special education can and should do is become part of the collaboration team that builds a professional solution (Greer, 1991).

DEVELOPMENT AND CRITERIA

In attending the Wisconsin Education Association Convention in Milwaukee five years ago, I saw a presentation by the Beloit School District in which a regular education teacher and special education teacher worked as a team in a classroom of gray-area students. In discussing the presentation with my colleagues, one of the intermediate staff, Jackie Hood, showed an interest. In spring of that year, Hood and I were able to view a similar program for "at risk" students in the Whitnall School District. The enthusiasm of the teachers led us to develop a proposal that would accommodate

Schulte Elementary, blend with the philosophy of Racine Unified in avoiding ability grouping, and reflect no added cost to the district.

Our objectives were to increase self-esteem, teach compensation techniques to aid school success, improve school attendance, reduce off-task behaviors in the classroom, and integrate the special education students into the school population. Students would be instructed in the core curriculum, and all of the district curriculum would be covered. Regular education students would be instructed at grade level and special education students would meet their Individual Education Plan (I.E.P) goals, [as designed under the guidelines of the M-team evaluation.] Students would develop self-confidence,which would allow them to take a risk and try.

The student makeup of the Rainbow Room would consist of one special education class with seventeen intermediate self-contained LD students and fifteen regular fifth-grade students who were selected on the basis of attendance, parent referral, teacher observation, and achievement who were labeled "at risk." These were students with poor self-esteem and lack of motivation in an academic situation who displayed inappropriate behaviors in the classroom setting and did not qualify for special education. Staff consisted of an intermediate regular education teacher, a special education teacher with LD/ED certification, and a special education teaching assistant. In addition, we were also able to add the speech and language pathologist for one hour each day. This gave us a teacher:pupil ratio of 1 to 8 during that hour, and we used this opportunity to work on a variety of showy projects which caught the attention and interest of the other students.

TECHNIQUES TO ACHIEVE CLASSROOM SUCCESS

The Rainbow Room began very slowly. During the first three weeks of the school year, both classes were instructed in cooperative learning techniques, which would be the major tool used in the combined classroom. Students who have low self-esteem and lack social skills generally increase their achievement and improve in psychological health when placed in small, heterogeneous cooperative groups and assigned special roles (Augustine, Gruber, & Hanson 1990). In addition, each classroom was instructed in the meaning of "learning disability." We used a unit I developed with a primary and middle school LD teacher. It included a video describing the frustration of an intermediate student whose learning disability had not been identified and the steps taken in remediation and compensation to achieve success; also included were worksheets to examine strengths and self-concept, cooperative learning projects to exemplify compensation skills and work with learning strengths, and filmstrips to reinforce the positive qualities in all students.

The students began to view their learning disability as a *small* part of their learning repertoire. They needed to develop techniques to accomplish tasks in another way, but they all had learning strengths and could contribute much to any classroom if they took the risk. It was imperative that *both* groups of students knew that they *all* possessed strengths and weaknesses in their classroom skills and that by using their strengths, all of them could be of value to other class members.

Initially, the two groups worked together for one hour each morning. We began with group guidance activities that emphasized cooperation. We developed a unit to increase awareness in our different cultures and accomplishments. We cooked stone soup and made cooperation sundaes. We made a mile of footprints on the hallway ceiling to support students in their campaign to achieve their book report goal: "Give them a book and they'll read a mile." We also began to approach cooperative math activities using pumpkins to estimate and then measure number of seeds, circumference, and weight and progressed to small group science projects that were prepared for the district science fair. Every effort was made to build an "I can" attitude in each student. Learning began to be viewed by the students in a new way. No longer was their stress associated with individuals competing for grades. That competition had already proven to be ineffective for them. Rather, learning was seen as a process of collaboration in which students had a valuable role in helping each other learn what they needed to know (Claxton, 1990). Students were pleased to bring positive comments home, and we carefully looked for as many positive reinforcements as possible. This also proved to create more successful parent involvement, since when we needed to contact parents about a problem we found them much more willing to help after a firm, positive groundwork had been laid.

INTEGRATION OF GIFTED AND TALENTED PROJECTS

During the second semester, the Rainbow Room began to more specifically incorporate and focus on thinking skills. Since Schulte had been one of four schools chosen to pilot a gifted and talented emphasis, which recognized that students may be talented in one area and have a deficit in another, all teachers, including special education teachers, were instructed in teaching techniques to encourage creativity, leadership, and talent, as well as the thinking skills curriculum.

Self-confidence as a learner is more than just a store of knowledge. It is knowing how to listen, how to question what you do not know, and how to attend to new ideas and question why (Wiggins, 1989). Of course, there are always those unkind remarks in any teachers' lounge about wasting effort on the low-achieving students whose time would be better spent in mastering academic skills or (even worse) unkind snickers about the type of projects the LD classes would come up with. In all of this, our principal was very emphatic about *all* classes participating and showed a particular pride in the achievements of our students.

Those very remarks, both positive and negative, were the fuel that the Rainbow staff needed to fire us up. We began to teach the students to brainstorm, not only ideas they knew, but those they wanted to know and, at the completion of a project or unit, those they had learned. This technique seemed to give them a confidence as well as an active ownership in their learning

Our school theme for the first year was "Up Up and Away," and the classrooms were encouraged to study and experiment with various aspects of flight. We developed a unit on insects in which the students listed insects they wanted to know more about, then chose an insect to study and a partner from the other class to work with. Students began to select partners with skills that could compensate for their weaker areas. Each group listed five questions that they wanted to answer about each insect and then headed for the library. It was expected that 100 percent of the students would complete a research project. Many of the regular education students initially said they would just take an F, but this was not an option. The LD group were sure they could accomplish the research project, since they had done an endangered species project last year. The regular education students were encouraged to help them read and the research began. About halfway through the written projects, we invited a team of entomologists from Johnson Wax to give an insect demonstration. The students were very eager to participate and surprised the entomologists with their knowledge and excellent questions.

When the written reports were completed, the results were outstanding. Many of the students in the regular education class expressed shock that they were able to complete a long written assignment, but the LD students reminded them, "We told you so!" Far too often students who are low in self-esteem do not believe they can complete a project satisfactorily and so they opt to take a failing grade that further reinforces the belief that they cannot succeed. It takes little more effort on the part of the teacher to guide them through a difficult assignment and point with pride to an accomplishment that increases their self-esteem than it does to deal with the behavioral overtones of a student who has just shut down.

After the completion of the written projects, each team of students designed an insect kite to accompany their written work and be displayed at the district science fair. This became an excellent motivational tool that developed predicting, observation, and questioning skills. Some groups chose to construct traditional kites, some to construct elaborate three-dimensional insect kites, and others set up the overhead projector and copied transparencies onto large paper and constructed free-form kites. All were especially proud of their display and delighted when the kites were moved from the fair and selected to hang in our own intermediate learning center. "Self-confidence evolves from success at a complex task that is viewed as valuable by the students and their peers" (Pogrow, 1988).

We continued to teach thinking skills to the students through various direct instruction methods. Many of the students in our program did not know when they knew and when they did not know, and few were able to verbalize what they did not understand. We taught a cycle of metacognitive processes, described by Miles (1990) as a three-stage spiral of *awareness* of what they were doing, whether they were concentrating or whether they were lost, then *assessment* of that behavior to the setting, and finally the *self-management* skills to decide on an action to change inappropriate behaviors. Pogrow (1988) suggests that many students identified as "at risk" do not know how to generalize, nor do they use ideas to develop understanding because understanding conversations has never been consistently modeled for them by the adults at home or at school.

Many of our loner students began to stop by the Rainbow Room for long chats during the lunch hour with the Rainbow staff and, as the semester progressed, these same students stopped for shorter periods of time *but* comments from other faculty members noted that they also saw the students interacting more with peers and other faculty members. Whether the reason for this change was increased self-esteem or better communication skills is uncertain and would be even more difficult to prove, but positive changes were taking place and many students began to express an anticipation of future projects. It should be noted that thinking activities cannot be occasional or haphazard if they are to be of value. It takes two or three months of daily exposure to thinking activities (Pogrow, 1988) before these students catch on to what understanding is and well over a year before they will begin to habitually apply those thinking skills.

The second "Up Up and Away" project was "bubble science." This time we assigned students to groups of four and assigned each student a role (recorder, encourager, praiser, or checker) that corresponded to his or her academic strength. (In later projects, after students felt more secure, we have assigned students a role that corresponded to a weakness; for example, students who seldom had a kind word for others were assigned the role of praiser.) Several students who had been the most difficult to motivate, whose off-task behavior influenced others, became the leaders of this activity, and our bubble unit became very popular.

Using water in cups and straws we made scientific observations about surface tension and by adding dish detergent we made further observations about surface tension, and density. To our surprise, one group of students discovered that the soap bubble solution worked well in cleaning desks that had resisted the cleaning solution provided by our custodian. They were quick to present her with a bottle of their new product and were eager to demonstrate its effectiveness. As a final lesson, we studied the atmospheric conditions that were most compatible to bubble making.

As in other projects, leaders began to surface. One student had a lot of emotional problems associated with the dramatic murder of her father several years before that had attracted much media attention. She was absent frequently and was self-involved during most classes. We began to notice that she became very animated and happy when working on a project with our students with the most severe learning disabilities. She often began to assume the role of class organizer and was very creative in inventing new ways for students to accomplish a task while compensating for their severe deficits. One day she appeared at my classroom door with an armful of giant bubble makers, a pail, and detergent. We had been promising to take the students outside to experiment making giant eight-foot bubbles but had never gotten around to bringing the needed supplies. Now, she informed me, there was no excuse not to go. She had convinced a friend of the family to sell the giant bubble makers at cost to faculty and interested students. When she found that the price was too high for some of the more interested students, she brought in smaller versions for less than half the price. Her classmates were delighted, our bubbles a huge success, and this student glowed with excitement and enthusiasm the rest of the year.

Our excitement with our projects was not always shared by our peers. In fact, for a time we seemed to be moving farther away from our peers, and tension was obvious. We were attempting a type of change that made many teachers uncomfortable. Perhaps some of our peers even felt that we were attempting one-up-manship with so many showy projects; however, we knew our students were changing. Boys who never participated were waving hands, eager to be included in activities; students like Jon, who had never participated, were coming to us with suggestions for new projects, and Joe, a previous non-reader, volunteered to read aloud in class. We were told by the students that our class was fun and exciting, and it convinced us that the change in our teaching style made a positive difference.

We are currently beginning our fifth year and our relationship with our peers has strengthened. Perhaps we were the ones who had changed in the way we dealt with others, perhaps we were searching for approval from our peers, but as we felt success, our confidence grew. In this way we were no different from our students. The more we believed in ourselves and our students, the more supportive our colleagues became.

Our remedial reading teacher approached us with a project that appeared to be an impossible undertaking: making hot air balloons. The students were divided into six teams, each with an adult supervisor. Each group had to decide on a color scheme and design and then construct an eight-foot tissue paper balloon. Sheets of tissue paper were glued together in eight-foot sheets; the sheets were then cut to shape at each end and glued together. The tops were secured with yarn, and a wire circle was attached to the bottom of each balloon to allow the hot air to enter the balloon

I knew the project was a success when I saw my most severely disabled student cutting the strips of tissue paper very carefully with the regular education team teacher nodding approval. The look on this student's face said it all and made all the extra physical work of this class worthwhile. This student had always been an observer, never a participant, in anything but verbal activities and because of Pervasive Developmental Disorder was very shaky and highly emotional. She is probably the last student that a teacher would hand a pair of scissors when the success of a rather expensive project was at stake. Mrs. Hood had given her the confidence and assurance to believe in her ability, and the other students in the group treated her as any other classmate. It was a giant step toward the carefully controlled mainstreaming that we had envisioned at the beginning of our project.

On the launch day, many members of the Schulte staff volunteered their help and support. Our initial launch was a success, so we decided to invite all of Schulte to view another launch day. Our students were the stars of the school for several hours, and they were able to handle it with maturity and self-confidence. The newspaper photographer appeared the next day when damp weather prevented a successful launch, but the students handled their disappointment well. They began to brainstorm on the effect of moisture and air pressure, and a unit on weather was begun.

In the next years we "hitchhiked" on various school themes. We began to include full group reading activities using a whole language approach. This was risk-taking at its highest for some of my non-readers, and several firmly refused. Only after a closed door class meeting did they agree to give it a cautious try. We used a charade game to teach vocabulary and used choral reading and story mapping in a unit carefully designed to emphasize student success. Both classes eagerly looked forward to trying it again. Five of my "non-mainstreamable" students were mainstreamed into Mrs. Hood's fourth-grade math class, and they succeeded. Ability grouping may be harmful to some remediation students who tend to learn more in programs for more advanced classes (Peterson, 1989).

The students felt better about themselves, and it showed. The Rainbow Room developed a newspaper staff and printed a school newspaper on a bimonthly basis. Our most popular entry was an advice column called Sunnyside. We also designed several all school surveys which we used to collect important marketing data. We worked with an electrical engineering student from the University of Wisconsin-Milwaukee to design a display for the science fair. In addition, many of our students joined the afterschool science club and met with area scientists to plan science fair entries. (Our class entered sixteen cooperative projects in the science fair that year, and several of our groups won awards.)

Journal writing was an important part of the program, and we encouraged students to write by allowing them to bring in their own tapes to listen to during this time. Students told of the stress of illness and alcoholism in their homes, of parents who had several jobs to make ends meet and the loneliness they felt, of critical illness or the death of a grandparent, of problems that occurred in the past and scared them at night, of how much they would miss the program and how frightened they were of middle school.

Through these projects we saw leaders emerge, students cooperate for a common goal, giftedness emerge (one of the Rainbow students received the highest score on the district science test), attendance increase, off-task behaviors lessen, self-esteem increase, and an understanding of the talents that each of the students possessed emerge. Students with learning disabilities were developing friendships with regular education students, and the playground reflected this integration. In addition, students in the self-contained LD room were divided into two groups of eight and fully mainstreamed without special education support staff in music and physical education. The result was very successful.

STUDENT SUCCESSES

The students who had gained the most were the students with learning disabilities. It appears that a two-year program with emphasis on developing a working rapport between parent and teacher, as well as learning techniques that result in carefully structured sucesses for students in the first year, would be beneficial. The two-year intermediate program for the LD students allowed them to enter their fifth-grade year with cooperative learning skills firmly in place, knowledge of learning styles and techniques that allowed them to use their strengths and compensate for weaknesses, and the confidence that comes with pride in past achievements. The defensive barriers had been removed during the fourth-grade year, and the students soared in their accomplishments during the fifth-grade year. Many of the parents expressed their delight in accomplishments they had never expected. In addition, a strong parent-teacher rapport was established during the fourth-grade year which was imperative to the success of the students in the fifth-grade year. One student entered the LD class in fifth grade and by the time his defensive attitudes were broken down and a working relationship was developed between home and school, the school year was over.

It is hoped that the success of this program may encourage other teachers to consider a team approach in meeting students' needs. It is not necessary to lower our expectations for students. Even "at risk" and special education students can meet those expectations in an atmosphere where the adults around them believe in the ability of the students to learn and the ability of themselves to teach. Students who are in a program that teaches new thinking and learning skills and emphasizes the strengths they possess have an excellent starting point to become active learners. To be exposed to possible teaching strategies to encourage teaching success, our team attended seminars, student assistant workshops, multicultural education workshops and updates, science workshops, gifted and talented workshops, and cooperative learning workshops. These groups also provided us with the peer support and encouragement we needed to continue to change and improve our program.

We were given approval to include the fourth-grade regular education students from the 1990–91 school year for an additional year, and students requested a video project to begin with video book commercials instead of book reports and ending with a documentary about the Rainbow Room. When students take responsibility for their learning, we have taken a giant step in promoting motivational equality in the classroom (Alderman, 1990). The video book reports were a great success. In addition, we began to incorporate more controlled collaboration throughout the school day by working with Mrs. Hood's fourth-grade language, social studies, and guidance classes in the afternoon. The door between classes was open for a greater portion of the day, but there were times when lt was necessary to close the door and add extra guidance or direct instruction steps to help the students with severe learning disabilities better generalize concepts necessary to continue.

Our future plans include expanding the collaboration to include several different groups of fourth- and fifth-graders during the school day, which will allow more integration for our "self-contained" classroom. Although students considered "at risk" will still be targeted, these students will be included in a more heterogeneous population that reflects our other intermediate classrooms, thus avoiding the possibility of creating and labeling still another group of "dysfunctional" students within our building.

The Rainbow Room has changed and been redesigned each year in an attempt to better meet the needs of the students during a particular school year. More student planning has been encouraged and the classroom has become a laboratory for students to explore thinking and the process of learning rather than a system of delivery of facts and concepts within a curricular area. Change has been most evident in the exceptional education students. The reason may be that the focus here had already centered around an Individualized Educational Plan that focused on individual learners within a group instructional setting rather than a delivery system that hit only the middle-of-the-road student and missed the opportunity to challenge students whose educational needs were different from the majority of their classmates. It is hoped that a more heterogeneous grouping will provide an opportunity for data collection that will be valuable for the future of the project.

One thing is certain. Although the delivery system for the students in our district with the most severe learning disabilities had once been in a fully self-contained special classroom, we have slowly achieved a setting that does not include a student or two in a "mainstreamed" class where they are isolated and unhappy without positive peer interaction. Rather, we have achieved a carefully controlled group mainstreaming in which social interaction mainstreaming has been achieved and mutual understanding, support, and learning takes place.

> Mainstreaming means that children who need special supports are receiving good special education while they enjoy the personal and social advantages of life in regular school classes with all the other neighborhood youngsters of their age. It also means that good regular and special education go on at the same time, complementing each other. Further, it means that the regular teacher coordinates pupil activities with colleagues made up of special educators, aides, the school principal, and other specialists. With parents, these professionals make up a team whose central concern is to provide top-flight instruction for all children. (Reynolds & Birch, 1988, p. 8)

It is our hope that the continued collaboration will provide us with students who are "at promise," who manage and take responsibility for their learning and who contribute valuable insight into our efforts to change our classrooms to meet future challenges.

REFERENCES

Alderman, M.K. (1990). Motivation for at-risk students. *Educational Leadership, 48*(1), 27–30.

Augustine, D.K., Gruber, K.D., & Hanson, L.R. (1990). Cooperation works. *Educational Leadership*, 47 (4), 4–7.

Claxton, C. S. (1990). Learning styles, minority students, and effective education. *Journal of Developmental Education,14*, (1), 6–8.

Glasser,W. (1987, May). The key to improving schools: An interview with William Glasser. *Phi Delta Kappan*, 656–662.

Greer, J. V. (1991, March/ April). At-risk students in the fast lanes: Let them through. *Exceptional Children*, 390–391.

Miles, C. (1990). The fourth "r": Teaching more or teaching better? *Journal of Developmental Education,14 (2)*, 34.

Peterson, J. M. (1989). Remediation is no remedy. *Educational Leadership*, 46 (6), 24–25.

Pogrow, S. (1988, April). Teaching thinking to at-risk elementary students. *Educational Leadership* 79–86.

Reynolds, M.C., & Birch, J.W. (1988). *Adaptive mainstreaming*. New York: Longman.

Tiedt, P.L., & Tiedt, I.M. (1986). *Multicultural teaching*. Boston: Allyn and Bacon.

Wiggins, G. (1989). The futility of trying to teach everything of importance. *Educational Leadership, 47* (3), 44–48, 57–59.

LISA LEIFIELD
TINA MURRAY

11

Advocating
for Aric:
Strategies for
Full Inclusion

LISA: This chapter presents the at-promise perspective through a description of Tina Murray's advocacy efforts on behalf of her son, Aric, to attend a regular education classroom in his neighborhood school rather than a special education classroom in a school outside his neighborhood. Tina and I first met at the Family and Child Learning Center, an early intervention program. Tina was the Parent Coordinator at the Center and I was completing an assistantship for my doctoral program in Special Education at Kent State University. Besides coordinating parent activities at the early intervention center, Tina has been actively involved in advocacy networks for children with disabilities. She has made presentations at national and state conferences on family-centered care for young children with disabilities, parent-professional collaboration, inclusive schools, and strategies she has utilized to maintain an educational placement for Aric congruent with her belief system.

TINA: Aric is eleven years old and has cerebral palsy. He attended a regular education classroom in our neighborhood elementary school from kindergarten to third grade. By attending a regular education classroom, Aric is advocating—for himself and for others—for understanding, equality, and normalcy. Currently, we are advocating for the school district to make the middle school, close to our home, accessible so that Aric can attend school with the same children he has gone to school with since kindergarten.

Aric even testified before the United States Senate Subcommittee on Disabilities in March of 1991 on the importance of early intervention for young children with disabilities. Aric will speak to college students, to children at other grade schools, and at conferences to educate people on the abilities of individuals with disabilities. Lisa and I have also had the opportunity to talk with graduate students in regular education classes on inclusion for children with disabilities.

LISA: A central focus of our discussions with graduate students is expectations regarding children with disabilities and their families. We feel it is important for students to examine their expectations because, historically, according to Turnbull and Turnbull (1991), there has been a set of beliefs that "wrongly taught":

1) Children with disabilities are burdens and can make no overall positive contributions;
2) Families and children should have few expectations and be realistic about their lives and grateful for only a few privileges and limited rights and opportunities;
3) Families and children should have few choices because they have few abilities, including the ability to choose;
4) Families and children "are disabled" and inherently without strength, their disabilities being their chief attributes; and
5) Families and children with disabilities should accept second-class citizenship, because that is all they can deserve or can earn. (p.3)

Our discussions challenge students to think about their expectations regarding children and families, to identify the basis of their expectations, and to become aware of the outcomes of their expectations for children and families. We want students to move beyond a focus on the student's disability to a focus on the whole child and his/her connectedness to family, school, neighborhood, and community. This view provides a panoramic view of the child in context rather than a focus on the disability in isolation.

TINA: A focus on the disability in isolation is a "pieces-parts perspective." Parents of children with disabilities frequently put their own lives on hold. Everyone is breaking their child into pieces—"Oh, his legs need this. Oh, his eyes need this." Parents and teachers can begin to view the child as a "pieces-parts." They can lose sight of the child as a whole being. At some point families and teachers need to come to a decision about how they will view the child. We made the decision early on. From the time Aric was born we saw him as a child at promise. Webster's dictionary (1984) defines promise as "ground for expectations usually of success, improvement, or excellence." We saw a full and happy future for Aric. A lot of people will tell you I was looking through rose-colored glasses. I prefer to think I saw Aric's promise.

LISA: An at-promise perspective does not ask teachers to look at children through rose-colored glasses. Rather, it asks people to expect children to have unique capabilities and make their own contributions to both their families and their classmates, a community of learners.

This chapter provides an overview of the discussions we have had with graduate students in regular education classes regarding Tina's at promise expectations for Aric, expectations which guide her advocacy efforts. Since belief systems often direct action, the chapter begins with "Philosophy," Tina's beliefs regarding education. In this section, Tina discusses an alternative view to the perspective that children with disabilities should be educated separately from typically developing children. This view is called "inclusion." In contrast to integration or mainstreaming, inclusion emphasizes the need for children to begin and continue their education in the regular classroom rather than return to the mainstream via a placement (Stainback & Stainback, 1991). Inclusion has been described as a

> value that is manifested in the way we plan, promote, and conceptualize the education and development of young children. The underlying supposition in inclusive programs is that all children will be based in the classroom they would attend if they did not have a disability. Teachers, students, parents, and administrators (in fact all stakeholders) define the school and

classroom culture as including children with diverse backgrounds, abilities, and contributions. (Salisbury, 1991, p. 147)

Since inclusion is not the norm for children with disabilities, it is important for families to find individuals who support their vision. In the section entitled "Early Intervention," Tina describes her search for and experiences with the Family and Child Learning Center, an early intervention program where people shared her perspective. Her positive experiences with this program, which utilized an enablement model of helping, provided initial impetus for an empowerment philosophy which would guide her future actions in advocating for Aric's full inclusion in his neighborhood school. Specifically, Tina provides examples of how professionals utilized behaviors consistent with an enablement model of helping, including providing assistance congruent with family priorities, allowing the locus of decision making to lie with the family, and being positive and proactive (Dunst, Trivette, & Deal, 1988).

Tina's perception of Aric as a child of promise was given new meaning through early intervention and guides her vision of him for the future. Tina discusses how the staff at the early intervention center helped her "gel the vision of Aric." In the section "The Future," Tina discusses how having a vision is central to meeting future goals.

Tina's view of Aric both now and in the future reflects what is known as the normalization principle. Nijre (1985) refers to normalization as "making available to all persons with disabilities patterns of life and conditions of everyday living which are as close as possible to . . . regular circumstances and ways of life of society" (p. 67). It is this vision of Aric participating in all aspects of life, both now and in the future, that propelled Tina to continue her advocacy despite challenges to her perspective from the school system. In the section "Advocacy Strategies," Tina relates how her expectations for Aric were operationalized in action steps to secure a regular education placement which she felt was most likely to nurture his individuality, promote his capabilities, affirm his connectedness to his peers and neighborhood, and essentially prepare him for life. Tina explains how she used federal legislation—the Individuals with Disabilities Act (IDEA)—in advocating for Aric's inclusion in the regular education classroom. Initially, Tina utilized the "least-restrictive environment" provision of the law to advocate for Aric's full inclusion in a regular classroom placement. The least restrictive provision of the law means that, "to the maximum extent appropriate, students with disabilities should be educated with children who do not have disabilities" (Strickland & Turnbull, 1990, p.20). More recently, Tina has utilized the Americans with Disabilities Act to advocate that the school district make the local system accessible so that Aric can attend school with the same children he has gone to school with from kindergarten through third grade.

The section on advocacy efforts is followed by one on "Teacher Support." In this section, Tina provides examples of strategies to promote inclusion.

In addition to education goals, socialization is an important outcome of attending school. Subsequently, besides instructional inclusion, social inclusion must be a reality. In the section on "Friendship," Tina discusses how children's actions reflect an at promise perspective in their ability to see beyond the disability. Social inclusion provides children with the opportunity to learn about social norms and expectations (York et al., 1990) as well as to develop friendships. Turnbull & Turnbull (1991) illustrate the importance of friendships by referring to them as the "real social security safety net." (p. 4). In Aric's case, while adults have debated the merits of full inclusion, children have remained a source of steady support. It is this vision of Aric's being involved with other children which is a source of strength for Tina and is one of the things that sustains her when her perspective of Aric as a child of promise is challenged. In her discussion on "Coping Strategies," Tina explains other coping strategies she has utilized to deal with challenges from the school district.

Finally, Tina responds to teachers' reactions to her presentations. She presents the ways she has addressed some of the attitudinal and structural challenges to inclusion. Tina raises issues identified in the literature regarding teacher preparation, specifically the need for restructuring of education programs to prepare all teachers to be able to teach all children (Lilly, 1989). Tina also discusses how attitudinal barriers, including fear and the tendency to view children in terms of single attributes rather than holistically, can interfere with an at promise perspective.

PHILOSOPHY

Think back to when you were little and really wanted to be invited to a party. Mainstreaming is like inviting you to the party. Only this isn't a party—this is life.

Aric is our son. Like his sister, Rachel, he is a child of promise. When it comes to my children, I want them both treated equally. I don't ever want Aric excluded in a special education classroom.

The reason we have gone through all the therapies, the reason we have at times almost gone broke, is born out of our belief in Aric's promise. Only an equal education in a regular classroom setting is acceptable. We won't settle for anything less, because he isn't anything less.

We did not want Aric based in a special education classroom and then integrated into other classes for some subjects—the more typical placement in our school district. We wanted an inclusive placement. This means we wanted him based in and able to receive supportive services within a regular education classroom with children he would be with if he did not have a disability. Aric will not be bused to a school halfway around town just because "children like him" traditionally go to those schools. Since kindergarten Aric has been in a regular education classroom rather than a special education class.

Aric's father and I have chosen to advocate for inclusion because we don't believe in segregation. The best way to describe the difference between mainstreaming and inclusion is to ask you to think back to when you were a child and really wanted to be invited to a party. Mainstreaming is like inviting you to the party. Only this isn't a party—this is life.

When children are in segregated classrooms they miss out on activities that go on in school at large. They miss out on school sales, school assemblies, and class pictures. You learn from these things. You learn responsibility, motivation, and a sense of belonging.

Inclusion is a radical idea. It's like the Beatles. It takes a while for it to catch on. In a world where physical prowess and beauty are valued, it's easy to see why some people don't get it. It's not in the mainstream. When I was growing up I never saw a child with a disability. Most of the people my age, in their thirties, never saw a child with a disability when they were in school. We never saw these children, so we learned to devalue them. Now these people I grew up with are teaching school.

If you ask people our age to close their eyes and visualize a classroom, what do you think they would see? They might see a community where children learn, play, and help each other, perhaps children with visual impairments or children in wheelchairs working side by side with children without disabilities. But it is more likely they would visualize a classroom of thirty-two typically developing children with their hands folded on their desks.

Why is it that people my age are more likely to visualize such a classroom? Perhaps because of stereotypes. When people hear the words "cerebral palsy" they have preconceived ideas, and they see every person the same way. Segregation is born out of preconceived ideas. People use their preconceived ideas to make placement decisions. All the children with vision impairments need to go to this classroom, all the children with mental retardation go to this room. Segregation on the basis of race, religion, disability, or gender is wrong. Our children will not grow up in a better world, into a world where people are accepted for who they are, if we continue this segregation.

When Aric's sister was twelve, in her yearbook they had pictures of all the classes. Under the picture of the children in the learning disabilities classroom it says "LD Class." Why don't they just put little neon lights around those children that say "I have a learning disability"? Aric will never have to deal with that. It will never be an issue. He has always been part of a regular class.

When children are segregated, not only do the segregated children lose, but the typically developing children also lose. The children in Aric's classroom are learning to respect and value difference. The children are learning that not everyone gets up and runs around, not everyone uses a pencil to write. Rather, there are some children who use a wheelchair to get around and a computer to write. That's okay. They are seeing by example that Aric is a person of value and that there is value in his life. They have already begun to learn that just because he's in a wheelchair doesn't mean he can't go to school. Just because he's in a wheelchair doesn't mean he can't think. The children see all the times he raises his hand to answer a question other kids didn't know. He is educating the teachers as well as the children.

LISA: Despite Aric's cerebral palsy, Tina expected that Aric would reach out and respond to others, explore and learn, and play and have fun. These, of course, are typical outcomes families have for their children, and the expectation was that typical outcomes would be met in typical settings. Tina found a place early on that shared her view of Aric as a child of promise and focused on family-determined outcomes.

EARLY INTERVENTION

*It was like they looked inside our heads and saw
a vision for the future and made that a reality.*

My initial experience with having other people view Aric as a child of promise was at the early intervention program. We walked into this program, and a teacher met us at the door. She grabbed Aric out of my arms and said, "What a beautiful little boy you have. I mean, look at the potential in his eyes." She could have hung him from the ceiling by his thumbs, I wouldn't have cared. This was an individual who wasn't afraid to take him from me. She wasn't afraid of him. She said they saw potential, in him. She told us they would be able to take him to his fullest potential, and they wanted to work with us.

In addition to viewing him as a little boy instead of just a child with a diagnosis of cerebral palsy, they said they would welcome our ideas. The speech therapist and the physical therapist wanted to come to the house to see how we played with and managed Aric at home. It just blew our minds. All the way home I kept thinking, "This is where I want him to go, this is what I want to do." Paul, my husband, is the real sensible one; we balance each other out. He said, "Tina, do you realize this is a thirty-minute drive four days a week, every day? You've got Rachel. You have got to get up there." I didn't care. It could have been two hours away, and I wouldn't have cared.

These people had given us such an up feeling. It was like they looked inside our heads, and they could see that we had a vision for his future, and they wanted to make that a reality. They were giving us things we could do to make our dreams come true for Aric. Nobody was telling us it was ever going to be, you know, an easy road to haul. Nobody said that. They kept saying it would be a lot of work, a lot of therapies, but they could see the future for him.

Up until that point it was just like Paul and I and my family were the only ones that could see this vision. It was like all these people were thinking, "Oh those poor people, what are they going to do when reality sinks in?" At the early intervention program we had people that were willing to work on his vision and that was exciting. There were no ifs, ands, or buts. This was the program for him.

Once he was in the early intervention program, the attitudes that the staff had when we first met them were put into action. The staff shared the vision and then implemented teaching strategies to make the vision a reality. The messages communicated to me at the early intervention program were that Aric was capable, and that he could learn and play with the other children. The message communicated to me was "You are a good mom."

The staff were very systematic about their approach and had an expectation for success. Everything worked on was approached with the vision for his future. It was not in a hurry-up let's-fix-it kind of way, but as "We know this kid is going to succeed, so let's see what we can to do to support that." They knew he was going to go into a regular kindergarten class, so they focused on prekindergarten skills. They also focused on mobility with his chair, so he could get through the building. They emphasized speech therapy, so he would not have any trouble being understood. This all started in the fall of 1985, a full year before he made the transition to kindergarten.

The staff at the early intervention program listened to our priorities for Aric and utilized our ideas in implementing programming for Aric. For example, one of our goals for Aric was, and still is, that Aric will walk. The staff sat down with us and explained the steps involved in obtaining that outcome. I'm not sure they always agreed with us, but there was always staff movement toward reaching that goal. We went to the store and bought a toy car we thought the staff could adapt for Aric. Sure enough, the staff took off with our idea, adapted the car, and taught Aric how to activate it so he could be independently mobile. This led to Aric's learning how to use an electric wheelchair. At the same time they continued to work on walking.

It was at the early intervention program we had our ideas validated that Aric could indeed be part of a group of other children. At the early intervention program we were never taught to view our child as someone who needed a special place. When it came time to begin planning for Aric to leave the early intervention program, we planned for him to go to the local elementary school. Aric had always been in a total inclusionary setting within our home and within our community. We couldn't see taking a child that lives at home in a regular setting and then for six hours a day putting him away in a separate room. If he was going to be in an integrated society, it didn't make sense to have him be in a segregated school setting.

The staff at the early intervention center knew we wanted Aric to attend a regular kindergarten class. No one came to us and said "You are out of your minds." Instead, they matched services with what we wanted. They said "Okay, this is what you want to accomplish, and this is how you can do it." We had support. They gave us ideas to get him into the setting. They never took control out of our hands, and we always did the steps ourselves. They were there as a resource and support. The staff at the early intervention center helped me to gel the vision. But it didn't take the Family and Child Learning Center to show me promise; I could see that when he was born.

LISA: It was at the early intervention center that Tina's vision of Aric as a child of promise—capable of success—was affirmed. Tina was empowered when staff matched services with her priorities and implemented intervention strategies congruent with her vision for Aric.

Tina has a life-span perspective of Aric. When he was very young, Tina's goals were typical of other parents of young children—that he would learn, play, and have fun with other children. Similarly, when he is older, she sees typical outcomes—independence, relationships, employment. In the following section, Tina discusses how her vision of the future for Aric directs present actions.

THE FUTURE

*In order to help someone succeed, you have to
have that vision for the future.*

Our decision to have Aric placed in a regular classroom was based on our vision for Aric's future. In order to help someone succeed, you have to have that vision for the future. I fully expect Aric to go to college, have a good job, and get married. So, above and beyond anything else, Aric's placement in a regular classroom setting is preparing him for our vision for his life. If you want to give him the best possible chance, keeping him in the mainstream is important.

Our initial experience in utilizing the future as a way of planning intervention was at the early intervention program. The staff focused on skills they knew would be critical for him to have to function in the regular kindergarten classroom: prekindergarten skills, mobility, communication.

To plan for the future you take one step at a time. Our next step is to get him into the regular classroom at the middle school in our neighborhood, then the junior high, then the high school. After high school, I fully expect Aric to go to college. A college education has almost become a necessity for success. It seems people with disabilities need to prove they are ten times more capable than others. If you ask Aric, he'll tell you he's going to be a cowboy or a truck driver. I never tell him he can't do these things. Why stifle his creativity?

He's always been allowed to explore and let his own personality grow. I question if that would have happened in a segregated setting. Being in a regular classroom has helped his self-confidence. This is a child who walks into a Senate subcommittee and just drives right up and has no qualms about speaking to a group of United States senators.

If Aric were in a segregated setting for the majority of his childhood and early adult life, I don't think he would be able to deal with society, because he never would have been in the society at large. It's important for Aric to learn the educational curriculum, but it is also important for him to learn the ways of the world.

I hope someday he marries and has children. He likes children very much. Paul and I look forward to the day we will be in the house again by ourselves. That may sound selfish, but we do. That's the normal life cycle. You have children, they go to school, they leave, and then they bring their children back to visit you. We love them more than anything in the whole world, but we also want them to have lives of their own. We will support them in whatever they choose to do.

LISA: Tina's vision for Aric affirms his connectedness to others, promotes independence rather than dependence, focuses on possibilities rather than limitations, and validates his individuality rather than focusing on categorical labels and attendant prescriptions. Tina believes that affirmation of connectedness, nurturing of individuality, and reinforcement of capabilities would be most likely in a regular classroom placement. In the following section, Tina discusses how she advocated for a regular classroom placement, which she saw as central to meeting future outcomes.

ADVOCACY STRATEGIES

It's like they keep trying to pound it into our
heads that eventually they are going to succeed
in putting him into their system.

In contrast to the early intervention program, the public school system was not in agreement with our position to place Aric in a regular education classroom. I initiated everything myself when it came time to begin planning for Aric's enrollment in the public school. I called someone down at the special education department and explained I wanted him to go to a regular school. I had done a little bit of homework. I knew there were four schools that were all on one floor. They suggested I go see the school where they typically send children with physical disabilities. I went to visit the school because I wanted to be able to say I did so and also be able to share my thoughts and perceptions.

In addition to visiting the school they wanted me to see, I also visited the school I wanted Aric to attend. I didn't ask for permission to call the principal, I just called. In my initial contact with him I said, "You know, I'd like to come in and meet with you. I have a child that I am hoping will be able to come into your school." I explained cerebral palsy to the principal. He was very nice and didn't see a problem with Aric's attending his school.

We had Aric's initial I.E.P. meeting in August, right before school started. An Individualized Education Plan (I.E.P.) is a plan that every child with a disability must have. The educational and therapeutic goals for your child are identified on the plan. It is a document binding among you, the teachers, the therapists, and the special education department. During annual meetings each person presents a report on the past year and the concerns for the future.

Aric's initial I.E.P. meeting went pretty well. It was agreed Aric would begin school in a regular kindergarten. It was my impression the district agreed because they thought the placement would fail. However, Aric did not fail. At Aric's I.E.P. meeting the following year, they again suggested Aric attend the special school. So again I went and visited the school and said "Absolutely not." He had never been segregated, and I wasn't about to start. It was at this time we really had to start justifying that the regular classroom was the best placement for him.

From the very first I.E.P. meeting that we had, they made a point of telling us he would go to the special junior high school. From kindergarten they've been telling us this. We have proceeded to tell them every year that no, he will not go to the specialized school; they can adapt. It's kind of like they keep trying to pound it into our heads that eventually they are going to succeed in putting him into their system. It's like they are waiting for us to fall into their system.

Particularly during the beginning of his third-grade year, the school district personnel began reminding us that when he hit fourth grade, he would have to go to another school because our neighborhood middle school is not on one floor.

It's all very simple to me: You just adapt the next environment. I gave the school district information at the beginning of the year on how to make structural adaptations to the building for children with disabilities. However, at Aric's I.E.P. meeting at the end of this school year, the district recommended Aric attend the school for children with physical disabilities. We have proceeded with our request to have Aric attend our neighborhood middle school with his classmates. We have met with great opposition from the school district and have had to obtain an attorney.

Our vision of Aric as an at-promise child has not changed. We don't want him ping-ponged all over the city to go to school where children with disabilities go. It's not natural. How can children establish friendships when they are always coming and going.? He has established friendships—why should he have to give those up?

Over the years I have been informed about Aric's rights. I have always felt that arming myself with as much information as possible would put me at ease. I didn't go to college, as have all the people in Aric's I.E.P. meetings. At all times I remember that, even though I didn't go to college, *no one* knows my child as well as I do. All the tests in the world cannot tell you what a parent can. I have always tried to be treated like an equal in the meetings, and I feel better equipped if I have the knowledge base.

I have utilized several strategies to become aware of Aric's rights, including going to conferences, reading the *Blue Book*, which is Ohio's handbook on the rules and regulations governing special education, and talking with other parents and professionals. This knowledge helped me when the school district presented me with their decision of a segregated setting for Aric. I knew Aric's rights and argued for the least restrictive environment. One of the things I ask of people working with Aric is to see him as a child, a whole child. Yes, he has cerebral palsy—that is part of him—but he is a child first. Sometimes people want to attribute behavior to his disability. For example, when I would go to pick up Aric in kindergarten his teacher would sometimes tell me he misbehaved. But the problem, as explained to me, seemed like typical behavior the other six-year-old boys were doing. Because of his disability, sometimes people don't know what to do with him. You need to look past his wheelchair. There's a little boy in there who can be just as ornery and mischievous as other children his age. Why is that surprising?

Why does that present a problem? I discipline him at home, but I scream for joy inside because he is doing what he should be doing.

I have had to be prepared to hear negative comments about Aric and be able to respond. For example, in a letter at the end of his first-grade year his teacher stated, "Aric has been unable to progress well in this setting as much of our work involves visual and motor skills, reading, writing, cutting and coloring. Aric is very limited in those areas." There was no mention of his strengths. I responded by telling her about Aric's capabilities. He can take tests orally, can work on the computer, and does not need to know how to color or cut.

When I sit alone and think of our experiences with the school district so far, I become frustrated. Why is it that I, as a mom, can see so easily the perfect situation for my son? Why should I have to negotiate his right to go to our neighborhood school? Why does it seem that the administrators who chose to be in this field not only seem to lose sight of the objective, but can spout more rules and regulations as to why every suggestion we bring up just can't be done that way?

This whole struggle over inclusion and accessibility raises many issues. What happens to children when buildings and recreational facilities aren't accessible? What happens to children when friendships are not facilitated in naturally occurring ways? What are the ways that school districts can work with families to resolve differences without ripping families apart?

Finally, as a parent I know what is best for my child. I have been self-confident in my knowledge of Aric. As a parent I come with a gut instinct. I know what he can handle and what he can't handle. People have argued with me that the goals I have for Aric are my goals and not goals of his choosing. They are right. When children are little we make choices for them. As they become older and can make decisions, we release some of the dreams we made and join them in theirs. This is one of the exciting parts of parenting.

LISA: In contrast to situations which collided with an at-promise perspective, Tina also experienced situations which reinforced an at-promise perspective. In the following section, Tina provides examples of how some individuals nurtured this perspective by providing opportunities for success, promoting full classroom membership, and maintaining high expectations.

TEACHER SUPPORT

There was a belief. There was no question he
was part of the class.

Aric's second-grade teacher turned out to be the most wonderful teacher we could have had. First and foremost she liked all the
children equally. She would hug all the kids when she came in. Aric
got his hug every day—that was just her sense of being.

She also tried to make him a full member of the class. In her
classroom all the students had responsibilities. Aric was given
responsibilities just like the other children. He was always given his
turn on the jobs whatever the jobs for the day were. Granted he
couldn't wipe off the board, but he could go down with the bucket to
the janitor's room and get the water and bring it down. So whatever
the jobs were he got to participate.

What really stood out about Aric's second-grade teacher was
her problem-solving attitude. She knew that because of his fine
motor problems he couldn't take tests manually, by writing down
the answers. She simply made the adaptation and gave him the test
orally. Everything the other kids did, Aric did. For example, when it
was time for the children in the class to submit articles for the
young authors' contest, she made sure Aric submitted one. She simply had Aric dictate the story to me. There was no question. Aric
was part of that class.

Aric just loved his second-grade teacher because she treated
him as an individual. One day, when Aric was in third grade, he was
working on walking with his physical therapist. They were walking
down the hall, and he started to go into her room. His former teacher
saw him and invited him in. She stated, "Come on in, Aric. I want
everyone to see how well you are walking. " So, in the room he goes,
and the PT just beamed. Aric stood up real straight and started walking around, because he knows she cares about him.

She was also very sensitive to Aric's cues. For example, Aric
isn't able to really raise his hand up high, so she was very in tune to
how high he could raise it. She took the time and trouble to realize
how high he could raise his hand. So, when he raised his hand, she
would call on him. In addition to being concerned about Aric's academic and social progresss, she also considered his physical comfort. He is real thin and gets chilled easily. She would make sure he
was on the opposite side of the room from the window. She took

extra time and was very patient. She would sit by his desk when all the children were doing their work and help all the children with what they need to know.

Aric had a student teacher, and she came in with a zillion ideas. She was so fired up to find a way for him to participate in what the other kids were doing. She would make things so he could hold a pencil better. She would bring him an audio tape in conjunction with what they were learning to reinforce whatever concepts they were learning. When we had our conference, she provided us with resources she had gone out and dug up. She didn't know I already had all this information.

Aric's music teacher also had high expectations for him. One day after school she told me, "One of these days, I'm going to be listening, and this kid is going to break into song." She believed he would do it. She did not discount his ability to do it, if given enough opportunities to express himself. What a positive person. She was able to look beyond the disability and see the child within. She has a vision for him.

I have also had positive experiences with professional staff who have worked to develop collaborative relationships. One of the ways professionals can develop collaborative relationships is by respecting my expertise as a parent. For example, Aric's physical therapist respects the knowledge I've gained over the years. She says, "Tell me what you want. I know that you know this, and I will respect whatever your opinion is in this." I would then say what I wanted to work on. I told her what the goals were for him, and those are what we are working on. As Aric gets older, he will be able to articulate what he wants and needs to work on.

Aric's speech therapist also engaged in collaborative behavior. She was always in our corner. Even though she would hear other people say what he couldn't do, she would say, "Yes, but he can do this." She would always interject a positive, even when she had concerns early on. Her comments impacted on me as well as other people. I always left on a positive note, and she helped other people to see his capabilities.

LISA: Tina valued high expectations and the welcoming behaviors exhibited by some individuals. However, equally important to Tina have been the opportunities for Aric to participate in typical activities with his peers. in the following section, Tina describes Aric's experiences with his peers.

FRIENDSHIPS

The children see the child—not the wheelchair
that surrounds him.

Among the most valuable experiences for Aric in the regular classroom are the friendships he is developing. Basic skills are important but so are genuine friendships. When you have friends you have the world. To help the children understand Aric's disability when Aric started kindergarten, I provided an inservice for his class. We took Aric out of his chair and let everybody ride around in it. We took in pictures of him in the neonatal unit, so they could see that he was very tiny. I took one of Rachel's baby dolls that was about the same width and length that he was, so they could see how tiny he was. I just really geared down for the kids. I sat on the floor, passed the picture around, and let them ask questions so they would understand.

Aric has many friends. Like other ten-year-old boys, he likes to tease, to keep secrets, to tell jokes. No one forced anybody to be a friend with Aric. Certain people gravitated more towards him than other people. He has best friends, and he has friends. It's always been a situation where kids have invited him to birthday parties, and then we reciprocated by inviting them. I think this is much more normal than forcing kids into a position where they wouldn't feel comfortable saying no. Friendship can't be bought or tutored; it has to mutually grow, and it has.

When I see Aric outside playing with the other children, I see him at promise. The kids come and knock on the door for Aric to come out and ride bikes. Instead of riding a bike he uses his powered wheelchair. When he's riding with the other kids, he learns skills and a sense of belonging.

Not only does Aric have the opportunity to develop friendships with children in the regular class, he also learns what is expected. He learns what is acceptable and what is not. Children learn some of this at home, but the majority of learning how to take turns occurs in schools. You have to, with twenty other kids. You learn give-and-take and how to get along with other kids, how to handle it if someone takes your book—basic survival skills. He will come home some days and he'll say, "Oh, I don't like whoever it is," and I'll ask what happened. He'll tell me some normal little thing like any other kid, "Oh so-and-so said this, so I called him a jerk." I'll ask him, "Why did you call him a jerk," and he'll tell me. It's normal kid stuff. The teachers have never intervened. They let the children resolve it on their own.

What is interesting to me is the difference between the professional expectations of Aric and children's expectations of Aric. Professionals tend to expect the worst, while children see him for himself. They see the kid—not the wheelchair that surrounds him. I've traveled around the country, and one of the first things that professionals voice is that children are cruel. They are not cruel. Aric has been in a regular classroom for years and not once have the children been cruel.

The children have looked out for Aric. I remember being in his first-grade classroom for a Halloween party. All of the kids were dressed up, and the teacher asked the kids to raise their hands, and they would be chosen to get up and walk around the circle, so everyone could see their costumes. I had Aric sitting between my legs, and he was watching the kids go around. He was just having the greatest time. Well, he kept raising his hand, you know, just ever so slightly. You would hear the kids in the class call out, "Aric raised his hand, Aric raised his hand," but the teacher never once called on him. Whenever she would glance over and see his hand was raised, she would just gaze right over him, like he was invisible. It was funny, because the kids were so in tune to him, and they knew him so well.

For the most part, parents of children without disabilities have been very supportive. However, I sometimes get the impression some parents are unsure of what to do. You want to protect your children, all parents do. You want to protect them from all of the not-so-perfect things in the world. I don't know how to say it, but people with disabilities are one of those things. It's like, if you don't get involved, it could never happen to you. Actually, by maintaining negative expectations, parents are actually preventing children from the opportunities to know Aric and to benefit from being his friend. I remember a mother of a child in Aric's first-grade class telling me about a conversation she and her husband were having about Aric. Her son interrupted the conversation by stating, "What's the big deal? His legs just don't work."

LISA: The visual image of Aric participating with his peers is so strong that it is one of the coping strategies Tina utilizes when faced with challenges from the school district. In the next section, Tina discusses additional coping strategies she has utilized.

COPING STRATEGIES

*To know that he is happy is worth whatever it
takes to keep him happy, just as any parent
would want to keep any child happy.*

There has been an enormous amount of energy expended to keep Aric in a regular education setting. Just prior to his I.E.P. meetings, I think of nothing else. It takes me a whole month to gear up mentally and physically. There should not be a question of a child's going to school with his friends in his neighborhood.

There have been many different coping strategies I have used throughout the past eight years The strategy I use depends on the situation and where I am with my life. Anyone who knows me will tell you that one of the main strategies I use is humor. Working with the schools, that can be a pretty easy thing to do.

What sustains me through the moments when someone tells me the things that Aric can't do is to picture his smiling face. I picture everything he can do. I picture him playing with the other children. For all of the things he physically can't do, there are a hundred more things he doesn't have to physically do. I could never let him down. To know he is happy is worth whatever it takes to keep him happy, just as any parent would want to keep any child happy.

My husband, Paul, and my daughter, Rachel, are tremendous sources of support. Paul is there to listen to me, discuss issues with, debate with, laugh with, and just to give me a hug when he can read the stress in my body. Rachel is like my own personal cheerleader. She is always there to tell me she thinks what I am doing is right.

There have been some professionals who have inspired us. Pip Campbell, who was the director of the Family Child Learning Center at the time Aric was a preschooler, always believed in him and what I was doing. She was someone I respected and who made me feel I was doing the right thing. She's one person who inspires us to keep going and to keep him in a regular setting. Bonnie Strickland, who was the director of early childhood education at the center and a nationally recognized expert on the I. E. P. has also provided us invaluable information on the I.E.P. process.

I think by educating Aric in a regular education classroom and keeping him in the community we can start educating people. You can't imagine or put any type of a price on what he is doing. Aric has the right to be included in his school, neighborhood, and community. Aric will succeed with or without the support of the school. He has his family, his friends, his community, and some teachers and therapists. For every person who does not share the vision, there is one who does.

LISA: As we discussed in the beginning of the chapter, Tina and I have made presentations to undergraduate and graduate education students on inclusion. In these presentations Tina provides strategies for putting at promise expectations into practice, including being open-minded, utilizing problem-solving strategies, emphasizing strengths, and utilizing individual contributions. In this final section, Tina responds to students' statements in reaction to her presentations.

TEACHER PREPARATION

STUDENT: *We need to get beyond seeing just the disability and see the child as a whole person, student, child, sibling—something we often don't do.*

TINA: Take the opportunity to visit the child in his or her natural surroundings. Look at how the child gets in, out of, and around the house. Identify what activities the child does at home that you can incorporate into the classroom. For example, some of the things Aric does at home he could do at school. At home Aric carries the laundry basket on the back of the cart. At school he could take the attendance cards down to the office. Look at how the family has problem-solved at home so their child could accomplish a task.

STUDENT: Perhaps one day fears will vanish and teachers will be more open to individual differences.

TINA. Fear can interfere with adoption of an at-promise view of children. Be aware of your fears. If someone told me I was going to have a child with a disability I would be scared too. Fear is the thing that will stop anything. It will stop a bull in its path. I understand other people's fears and empathize and appreciate it. Ask questions, if it will help you to get over your fears.

STUDENT: This is something we don't get. We don't get it until we are out there. This is a perspective we *need* access to.

TINA: There are several things you can do to better prepare yourself for teaching children with disabilities. Take some special education classes. Do some volunteer hours. Request that your student-teaching experience is in an inclusive setting. Spend time with special education teachers. Suggest to your regular education professors that they team teach with a special education professor, or suggest to your regular education professor to take field trips to inclusive settings. Read information written by parents. Interview parents. Go on home visits with special education teachers. Offer to do respite care—what better way to get to know a child.

The best way for students to have access to this information is for colleges of education to combine special education and regular education departments. The special education curriculum and the regular education curriculum should be merged. If the intent of the law is for children with disabilities to be educated in the least restrictive environment, then it doesn't make sense to perpetuate two separate curricula. It's just perpetuating the fear.

We have had Public Law 99–142, now called the Individuals with Disabilities Act, for twenty years, and there are still separate departments of special education and regular education. Education majors need to know how to educate all children, not just separate groups of children. Everybody needs to be taught to teach every child. How many times have you heard teachers say, "I never learned how to deal with these kids." Everyone should have to take a certain amount of credit hours. People need the experience early on. It's not something teachers should do their senior year. It should be required early on. It's important to decide if this is what you want and if not—time to get out.

STUDENT: Teachers can't deal with the small differences in children, let alone deal with children with disabilities.

TINA: Classrooms need to focus more on the individual needs of each child. If teachers can't meet the needs of typically developing children, how can they accommodate the needs of children with disabilities? What can you do to meet the individual needs of each child? If a child needs additional help in reading, offer a tape recording of a book that he or she can listen to with headphones during a down time. Offer extra credit to an older child from another grade to tutor a younger child. Some children need to be able to help the teacher within the room to build self-esteem.

The way schools are set up today they don't foster creativity. If a child creatively finds the answer to a problem, and it's not done a certain way, then it is wrong. We need to teach creativity so that children can be problem solvers. Give children the materials and let them have a time set aside in which they can create and develop an idea. Give them no boundaries for solving the problem, and they will find the way to accomplish the goal. Support them in their ideas and praise them for whatever the solution is.

STUDENT: The lack of limitation she places on her son has probably contributed to his present progress. She does not dwell on his weaknesses, but appears to emphasize his strengths.

TINA: I don't believe that children should ever be taught limitations as far as their creativity, possibilities for the future, or life experiences go. To teach limitation is to teach defeat. There is always a way to support success.

When you set limits on a child, any child, you have set a limit to his or her ability. If you can be content to watch and listen and support you open an unlimited amount of ability. Children will take on just about any tasks presented to them given the chance. But if you preface an opportunity with words or body language (which children are very adept at reading) that indicates an outcome of failure, you have already sealed the outcome of the task.

For instance, given Aric's fine motor abilities, the thought that he would ever be able to open a door seemed beyond the realm of possibility. But we felt he should be given the opportunity to try and discover on his own whether he could accomplish this task. What we did was to provide an opportunity by installing a doorknob that he could possibly learn to use. Little did we know that within a few months he had problem-solved the situation on his own, and one day I found him outside laughing and laughing because he had figured out a way to do it.

I perceive the reason young people decide to become teachers is because they want children to succeed and they want children to reach the very best potential they can possibly get to. I think for the first few years teachers have this enthusiasm, then they get into problems, and they become real discouraged. Somewhere along the way the vision they have for their profession gets muddled. All I want teachers to realize is that I want them to give him the best experience.

LISA: The students' reactions to Tina's presentation are reflective of both the potential for teachers to adopt an at-promise perspective as well as the need for continuing education. Through this chapter and continuing presentations, Tina is able to demonstrate how a parent's at-promise perspective and subsequent actions can alter traditional educational structures.

Tina was successful in securing and maintaining a regular education placement for Aric at a school close to their home from kindergarten through third grade. At the beginning of Aric's fourth-grade school year he was unable to move with his peers to the middle school because it was not accessible. At that time, Tina secured a regular education placement for Aric at a private school of her choice. Tina felt this was preferable to the school district's option of sending Aric to a school further from home where many children with disabilities attend. Tina's preference remains a regular education placement close to home to enable Aric to remain with his friends. At the time this chapter was going to press Aric's fifth-grade placement remained uncertain. With legal assistance, Tina continues to advocate for Aric.

It remains important for prospective teachers, current teachers, administrators, and therapists to continue to examine their expectations regarding children with disabilities because, as Lipsky & Gartner state (1989), "Educational restructuring begins with the way children are viewed. It is a question of how they are valued and what is expected of them" (p.256).

REFERENCES

Dunst, C. J., Trivette, C. M., & Deal, A. (1988). *Enabling and empowering families: Principles and guidelines for practice.* Cambridge, MA: Brookline Books.

Lilly, M.S. (1989). Teacher Preparation In D.K. Lipsky & A. Gartner (Eds.). *Beyond separate education: quality education for all.* (pp. 143–158). Baltimore: Paul Brookes.

Lipsky, D. K., & Gartner, A. (1989). Building the future. In D. K. Lipsky & A. Gartner (Eds.), *Beyond separate education quality education for all* (pp. 255–286). Baltimore: Paul Brookes.

Nijre, B. (1985). The basis and logic of the normalization principle. *Australia and New Zealand Journal of Developmental disabilities,* 11 (2), 65–68.

Salisbury, C. (1991). Mainstreaming during the early childhood years, *Exceptional Children,* 58(2)146–155.

Stainback, S. & Stainback, W. (Eds.) (1992). *Curriculum considerations in inclusive classrooms facilitating learning for all students.* Baltimore: Paul Brookes.

Stainback, S., Stainback, W., & Jackson, H. J. (1992). Toward inclusive classroom. In S. Stainback & W. Stainback (Eds), *Curriculum considerations in inclusive classrooms facilitating learning for all students.* (pp. 3–17). Baltimore: Paul Brookes.

Strickland, B., & Turnbull A. (1990). *Developing and implementing individualized education programs.* Columbus: Merrill.

Turnbull, R., & Turnbull A. (1991). Including all children. *Children Today*, *20*(3), 3–5.

York, J., Vandercook T., Caugher, E., & Heise-Neff, C. (1990, May). Regular class integration beyond socialization. *TASH Newsletter*, p.3.

VALERIE POLAKOW

Epilogue

Naming and Blaming:
Beyond a
Pedagogy of
the Poor

. . . but schoolteacher beat him anyway to
show him that definitions belonged to the
definers—not the defined.
    —*Toni Morrison,* Beloved

  In whose space does the discourse of risk belong? And who is at risk? Them? Us? All? Who belongs in the gray zone between normality and abnormality, health and pathology? Or, put a little differently, upon whose contested terrain does the at-risk child walk? As Swadener and Lubeck argue in their introduction to this book, the term "at risk" has become a buzzword, and their intent as editors of the volume has been to present "an analysis and interrogation of the rhetoric of risk as it relates to the persistent social stratification in U. S. society and the ways in which it uses a medical *language of pathology* to label persons based on their race, first language, class, family structure, geographic location, and gender as 'at risk for failure.'" It is clear that the construction of an at-risk language serves to maintain stratification and the segregation of "difference" among children in our schools, forming part of an all-encompassing web of privilege and power *at risk* of unraveling if the politics of distribution and the poverty discourse were to be reframed.

Hence, as we confront the "savage inequalities" that scar the landscape of daily life, and as we witness the increasing destitution and homelessness to which millions of our fellow citizens have been consigned to live, we need to begin unpacking the multiple and insidious ways in which public policy has served to construct and maintain poverty, while simultaneously making its victims bear responsibility for such state-constructed poverty. As we listen to the current "welfare talk" from the Clinton Administration ("Welfare is not a way of life," "Two years and off—put them back to work") and to the conservative discourse by legislator Newt Gringrich and columnists George Will and Charles Murray ("The poverty of conduct," "Put their babies in orphanages," "Don't reward immorality"), I begin to wonder, with Codi in *Animal Dreams*, whether "the great American disease" of forgetfulness (Kingsolver, 1990, p. 316) has, in fact, become our Plague. And it is Tarrou who pointedly warns that "it is up to us, so far as possible, not to join forces with the pestilences" (Camus, 1972, p. 236).

The pestilences are everywhere in the Other America—in the 52,000 families that were homeless on any given night in 1992; in the 14.6 million children currently living in poverty; in an average AFDC grant which keeps poor mothers and their children at 41 percent of the poverty line, thereby assuring their economic inability to survive as a single-parent family unit (Children's Defense Fund,1993; National Law Center on Homelessness and Poverty, 1993). They, living out there in the spaces beyond, in the unnamed landscapes of public forgetfulness, are consigned to placelessness in the Other America. The discourse of democracy has succeeded in constructing myths that muffle the voices of poor women and their children as they stand on the margins, dispossessed citizens of the Other America, in which poverty is viewed as theirs, not ours. Fifty-nine percent of poor children live in female-headed families, and many of the families subsist on incomes less than one half of the federal poverty line (Children's Defense Fund, 1992).

To be poor, female, a mother, and a person of color is to live at the jagged intersection of a gendered, racist, and corrosive capitalist "democracy"—where it has become frighteningly clear that at the turn of the twentieth century, the United States has become one of the most dangerous democracies for poor women and their children to live. As both the feminization and the "infantilization" of poverty continue to rise, images of "generational welfare" and the "culture of poverty" are recycled through the media, lending an aura of naturalistic fatalism to *their* lives. But poverty in a wealthy industrialized society such as ours can hardly be seen as a product of national scarcity and dwindling resources; rather, it is a product of acquisition, of the politics and priorities of distribution. It has been made by public policy and it can be unmade by public policy.

How logical then, once we have produced poverty, to begin to manage it, and in cost-effective ways. Poverty talk, as with the construction of at-risk talk, is always about *them*—their pathology, their failures, their violence, their unmanageability. As they get closer, ways must be found to regulate and contain them. Their children constitute the growing threat that places comfortable indifference and unmitigated privilege at risk. It becomes necessary then, to name them, to constitute them, to research them, and—as with the *New York Times* Neediest Cases Fund—to display them, to show charity to them, to help those who prove that they are, indeed, the deserving poor. But as Michael Katz (1989) points out in *The Undeserving Poor*, "When Americans talk about poverty, some things remain unsaid. Mainstream discourse about poverty, whether liberal or conservative, largely stays silent about politics, power, and equality" (p. 7). This discourse of poverty as a private affair—whose causes are rooted in failed individuals, failed families, failed mothers, failed groups, and a failed work ethic, rather than a failed and diminishing public economy and histories of class, race, and gender discrimination—returns us to the nineteenth-century dilemma of the role of the state. This dilemma, discussed in *Broken Promises*, crystalized around the question of "whether poverty should be considered a public problem requiring expanded state involvement, or a private and individual problem for which the state should accept minimal responsibility" (Grubb & Lazerson, 1988, p. 197). Not much has changed in our public sensibilities from the religious justifications of the 1800s pointing to the depravity of the undeserving poor, to current right-wing commentaries on family breakdown and the decline of the moral values of the poor. And when definitions belong to the definers, not the defined, poverty continues to be produced as *theirs*, not ours— requiring a minimum of state responsibility.

What are the consequences for the education of children, when poverty is reconfigured as a private affair? First, *if* public

money is to be spent, it should always be *less*, rather than *more*—
part of the leftovers doled out from otherwise expansive budgets.
Second, poor families should have *poor* children, whose lives
should be less than those of other children, maintaining their second-class status. Both Chapter 1 Compensatory Education programs and Head Start offer ample testimony to the diminished
educational entitlements provided for poor children. They are
deserving of public money only if investment in their lives has
clear economic payoffs. Recent federal studies of Chapter 1 programs yield predictable outcomes: Programs organized for children
of poverty have met with little overall success, as they provide the
minimum amount of the least expensive instruction allowed
under federal and state guidelines (Knapp & Turnbull, 1990;
Allington, 1990). Few children who need intensive help actually
receive it; even fewer have any opportunities for access. Head Start
is another example of eulogized rhetoric and minimal success in
terms of access, actually serving 36 percent of income-eligible children part of the day, four times a week (Children's Defense Fund,
1994). Poor children are cheap. They matter instrumentally, not
existentially. Hence it is not surprising that they are ill-served by
the "savage inequalities" of public education. To be poor, at the
present time, is also to fall prey to a diminishing public economy
and a public education system under siege.

As we examine the multiple burdens of poverty that assault
children, whose lives and futures are placed at risk because of their
homelessness, their family stress, and the dailiness of destitution,
we also need to explore how children experience their school lives.
How do they encounter their classroom worlds? Are they consigned to the other childhood by virtue of their at-risk designation?
In my own ethnographic studies of young children in poverty, I
have observed a pervasive pedagogy of the poor, in which children
at risk are frequently constructed as impaired. In such cases, classrooms may become landscapes of condemnation, contributing to
the making of early educational failure.

Consider the following observation of four-year-old Duke, the
child of a single mother, who is struggling to survive on meager
AFDC payments while she works part time at minimum wage.
Duke attends a state-funded at-risk-four-year-old program each
morning.

> During story time about Sylvester, a donkey who discovers
> the powers of a magic pebble, Duke feels in his pocket and

excitedly exclaims, "See I have one too—maybe it can make magic like Sylvester," and he begins to rub the pebble and say, "biggledy boo." "Sit down and hush," says Mrs. Roby sternly, and a new student teacher is instructed to hold Duke on her lap, as he is now jumping up and down, saying, "see, see, it's magic" to the other children who have moved out of the circle and are trying to touch the pebble. As Duke continues to disrupt story time, he is given another warning and then sent to the time-out chair at the far end of the room. He is now defiant and begins to shout, "Nooo, leave me alone, you fucker," as he kicks the student teacher screaming, "gimme, gimme," and he tries to snatch his magic pebble back which has been taken away from him. Duke is removed screaming from the classroom, and Mrs. Roby later tells me, "I've had it up to here with him, he comes from one of the housing projects, his mother's on welfare and he'll end up in prison or on drugs like his older brother. I don't know what kindergarten teacher here is going to take him—we'll have to get him referred to developmental and special ed. . . . (Polakow, 1993, p. 111)

Duke, a lively, verbal four-year-old, is clearly a deviant child within Mrs. Roby's well-ordered and regulated classroom. He constantly sought recognition but rarely received positive acknowledgment. His excitement about his pebble could perhaps have been incorporated into the story time in a more flexible classroom, but clearly a rigid teacher agenda did not allow for that. When I later inquired about the possibility of recognizing Duke's contributions, even if they were out of order, I was told, "*These kids* have to learn to follow classroom rules—Duke's one of the really disruptive ones." As an "out of order" child, Duke, like many of his similarly labeled at-risk classmates, created a daily disruption in the routines of regulation and compliance, and his behaviors were marked for constant surveillance. Yet the same set of behaviors in a "normal" preschool, exhibited perhaps by a lively child of professional parents, a child similarly entranced by the magical possibilities of Sylvester's pebble, might be seen as early signs of a gifted imagination, to be cultivated through dramatic play and special times for storytelling. Hence, simple nuances in naming and framing construct early futures and embed targeted children in a web from which there are few exits.

An at-risk label is a ticket to a host of easy assumptions, not only about a four-year-old's imaginative engagement with a story, but about his lifeworld, his family, his past, and his future. The armory of at-risk labels, which ironically gain many poor children access to early childhood preschool programs from which they would otherwise be excluded, also contains proliferating weapons of future educational exclusion. In this case, Duke will be referred out of regular kindergarten into developmental kindergarten, effectively launching him, at four years old, on his tracked school career. Nether Duke nor his many brothers and sisters who share his at-risk "bloodline" are well served by a pedagogy of the poor. What happens inside classrooms does matter to children; it shapes their self-perceptions and the meanings they attribute to their daily school lives. Early tracking, scapegoating, sorting and sifting, and marginalizing, are not isolated experiences—rather, they are part of the pattern of neglect, of humiliation, and of disenfranchisement experienced by thousands of our children who are the targeted recipients of a pedagogy for the poor.

The language of pathology, therefore, constructs another world of otherness—of definers and the defined; of programs and outcomes and assessments; of technologies and methodologies of risk; of cost-benefit analyses related to funding and maintenance; of risk factor remediation. In short, the risk industry rests heavily on the poverty industry, which Funiciello claims has become "a veritable fifth estate" (1993, p. xvii) in which countless middle-class people in the human service professions have built their careers as the direct beneficiaries of poverty. So too, as we trace the formation of deficit images actively perpetuated in the college classrooms of teacher training institutions, disseminated through educational institutes and research associations such as the American Educational Research Association, and funded by major grant organizations, we see that diagnosis and remediation are the essential ingredients of a proliferating deficit/pathology business, nuanced by color and class codes.

In *Children and Families "at Promise": Deconstructing the Discourse of Risk*, we have seen how deconstructing the at-risk label is inextricably linked to a critical analysis of pervasive poverty and exclusionary and discriminatory educational practices within our society, and that unpacking embedded privilege reveals a discourse that frames oppression as compassion and remediation as entitlements. Many myths have been decoded in these chapters and the in vivo at-promise narratives present a countertext of possibility and action. It is also clear, in reading the accounts in this book of successful classrooms, that when classrooms do become landscapes of promise, they offer children a place where their self-hood *matters*, where they do find acceptance and possibility, and where they can become meaningmakers within their lifeworld of school. It is important to read about struggles that lead to empowerment and to successful advocacy, for resilient voices are critical to hear within the at-risk wasteland. After all, it is not adjustment to otherness that we must advocate; for it is Gertie, in *The Dollmaker*, whose failed struggle teaches us the full horrors of adjustment:

> "Adjust?" Gertie strode ahead, turned and looked at the woman.
> "Yes," Mrs. Whittle said, walking past her. "That is the most important thing, to learn to live with others, to get along, to adapt one's self to one's surroundings."
> "You teach them that here?" Gertie asked in a low voice, looking about the ugly hall.
> "Of course. It is for children—especially children like yours—the most important thing—to learn to adjust."
> (Arnow, 1954, p. 335)

Once again we return to the definers and the defined and how to challenge "schoolteacher," in *Beloved*, in *The Dollmaker*, and in countless classrooms in which children are violated; for schoolteachers do not live above their culture, neither do legislators nor academics. Many are complicit and part of the pervasive injustices of the society in which they live and work. But definitions must be reconstructed in order to make possible a different language of entitlements, a different way of seeing, so that, in "a pushing back of the horizons of silence" (Greene, 1988, p.130), we begin to name and to confront the raveled web of injustice.

REFERENCES

Allington, R. (1990). Effective literacy instruction for at-risk children. In M. S. Knapp & B. Turnbull (Eds.), *Better schooling for the children of poverty* (Vol.1). Washington: D.C.: U.S. Department of Education.

Arnow, H. (1954). *The dollmaker*, New York: Avon.

Camus, A. (1972). *The plague*, New York: Vintage.

Children's Defense Fund. (1992). *The state of America's children. 1992.* Washington, D.C.: Author.

Children's Defense Fund. (1993). Child poverty hits record levels. *CDF Reports* Vol. 14(12), 11, November.

Children's Defense Fund. (1994). *The state of America's children. 1994.* Washington, D.C.: Author.

Funiciello, T. (1993). *The tyranny of kindness: Dismantling the welfare system to end poverty in America.* New York: Atlantic Monthly Press.

Greene, M. (1988). *The dialectic of freedom.* New York: Teacher's College Press.

Grubb, N., & Lazerson, M. (1988). *Broken promises,* (2d ed.) Chicago: University of Chicago Press.

Katz, M. (1989). *The undeserving poor.* New York: Pantheon.

Kingsolver, B. (1990). *Animal dreams.* New York: HarperCollins.

Knapp, M. S., & Turnbull, B. (Eds.). (1990). *Better schooling for the children of poverty* (Vol.1). Washington, D.C.: U.S. Dept. of Education.

Morrison, T. 1987). *Beloved.* New York: Alfred A. Knopf.

National Law Center on Homelessness and Poverty. (1993). *No way out.* Washington, D.C.: Author.

Polakow, V. (1993). *Lives on the edge: Single mothers and their children in the other America.* Chicago: University of Chicago Press.

Contributors

Beth Blue Swadener is Associate Professor of Teaching, Leadership, and Curriculum Studies, Early Childhood Education, at Kent State University. Her interests and writing focus on social policy, antibias and inclusive early education, and preprimary education in African nations. Previous publications include *Reconceptualizing the Early Childhood Curriculum: Beginning the Dialogue* (with Shirley Kessler), and she is active in unlearning oppression work and collaborative work with teachers in urban schools. She was recently awarded a Fulbright African Regional Research grant to study family involvement in early childhood education in Kenya and Tanzania.

Sally Lubeck is Assistant Professor in Educational Studies, School of Education, at the University of Michigan. She has published on issues of race, class, and gender and on policy issues related to maternal employment, families, child care, and schooling. Her book, *Sandbox Society: Early Education in Black and White America—A Comparative Ethnography*, received *Choice Magazine's* Outstanding Academic Book Award in 1987.

Mary Smith Arnold is Assistant Professor of Family and Community Counseling in the Counseling and Human Development Program at Kent State University. Her research has focused on multicultural training practices for counselors and the dynamics of success in African American families. She is a member of the Institute for Education that is Multicultural at Kent State and frequently co-facilitates "Unlearning Oppression" workshops with her colleague Beth Blue Swadener.

Marianne N. Bloch is Professor of Early Childhood Education in the departments of Curriculum and Instruction and Child and Family Studies at the University of Wisconsin-Madison. She has written numerous articles and chapters related to the history of early education, critical curriculum theory and its implications for early childhood education, home-school relations across cultural groups, and edited (with Anthony Pelligrini) *The Ecological Context of Play.* She has conducted studies in gender socialization and early education in West Africa. and on child care policy in Eastern Europe.

Donelda A. Cook is a Counseling Psychologist. She currently holds an administrative position as Director of the Counseling Center at Loyola College in Baltimore, Maryland. Her research has focused on the life experiences of African-American mothers and families.

Michelle Fine is Professor of Psychology at City University of New York Graduate Center and Senior Consultant at the Philadelphia Schools Collaborative. Her recent publications include *Beyond Silenced Voices: Class. Race and Gender in American Schools* (co-edited with Lois Weis), *Disruptive Voices: The Transgressive Possibilities of Feminist Research,* and *Framing Dropouts: Notes on the Politics of an Urban High School.*

Mary Hauser taught in a variety of early childhood and special education classrooms before she received her Ph.D. from the University of California, Santa Barbara. She is currently an Assistant Professor, teaching curriculum, early childhood education, and multicultural education in the Education department at Carroll College in Waukesha, Wisconsin. In her graduate course dealing with children "at promise," she continues to develop with local teachers the ideas begun in her classroom research.

Lisa Leifield is a Ph.D. candidate in Special Education and Early Childhood Education at Kent State University, completing dissertation resource on the dynamics of parent-professional negotiation in the Individualized Education Plan (IEP) process. She is currently the Project Coordinator for the Northeastern Early Intervention Faculty training Institute at the Center for Research in Human Development and Education at Temple University.

Tina Murray is a parent who has worked for several years as a family advocate through the Family Child Learning Center, a family-centered early intervention program in Tallmadge, Ohio. She frequently lectures, with her son Aric, to special education and early childhood classes on full inclusion and the benefits of inclusive community in classrooms. She has also worked with a family support program for parents of young children with disabilities.

Valerie Polakow is Associate Professor of Teacher Education at Eastern Michigan University and teaches in the Early Childhood and Educational Psychology programs. She is the author of *The Erosion of Childhood* and *Lives on the Edge: Single Mothers and*

Their Children in the Other America as well as numerous other publications dealing with women and children in poverty, critical pedagogy, interpretive qualitative research, and social policy.

Elizabeth Quintero is Associate Professor of Early Childhood/Elementary Education at the University of Minnesota Duluth. Her teaching, research, and service revolve around her interests in early education, family contexts of diverse cultural groups, and biliteracy development. She designed and implemented as director for five years a bilingual, family literacy project in El Paso, Texas. Currently, she is providing technical assistance to a Head Start program in Duluth that is implementing a family literacy program for Hmong and Laotian families.

Mary Kay Rummel is Assistant Professor of Reading/Language Arts/Children's Literature at the University of Minnesota, Duluth. She has a Ph.D. from the University of Minnesota and her professional publications are in the field of writing. Her poetry has been published in many literary journals and her collection of poetry won a Minnesota Voices Award and was published in 1990 by New Rivers Press. She worked for many years in the Minnesota Writers in the Schools Program.

Christine E. Sleeter is Professor of Education at the University of Wisconsin-Parkside. She has published widely in the area of multicultural education, focusing on staff development for school change and teacher education. She is author of *Keepers of the American Dream*, Editor of *Empowerment Through Multicultural Education*, and co-author of *After the School Bell Rings, Making Choices for Multicultural Education*, and *Turning on Learning.*

B. Robert Tabachnick is Professor of Curriculum and Instruction and Educational Policy Studies at the University of Wisconsin-Madison. He is author or co-author of books about the teaching of elementary social studies and educational reform in the U.S. and abroad. He has written extensively on his research on teacher socialization and student teaching and about cultural resources that children from various culture communities bring with them to school. In addition, he has directed projects in several countries in Africa and in Indonesia.

Cynthia Thompson received her teaching credential from California State University Long Beach and her bilingual certificate from University of Southern California. She has had more than ten years of experience teaching in bilingual and multicultural classrooms. She is also a trainer for the State of California who helps prepare teachers for the language development certificate. In 1993 she was named her school district's Teacher of the Year.

Joyce Waldoch has been a teacher in Racine Unified Public Schools and Milwaukee Public Schools for 17 years. She has undergraduate and graduate degrees from University of Wisconsin-Milwaukee in Exceptional Education and has done post-graduate work in the Multicultural Studies program of the University of Wisconsin-Parkside.

Carolyne J. White is a feminist scholar employed as an Assistant Professor at Cleveland State University, where she teaches sociology of education and qualitative research methods, and a Visiting Professor at The Cleveland Institute of Art, where she teaches postmodern social theory and cinema. Her research focuses upon how individuals negotiate the constraints of postmodern institutions.

Index

A

absenteeism, and dropping out, 82
acculturation (assimilation), 31–32, 84, 199
ADA (Americans with Disabilities Act), 242
Adams, D. W., 166
affluence, effect on children, 37–38
African Americans: cultural compatibility study of, 199–204; and dropping out of school, 79, 82, 90, 91n. 2; history of education for, 30; in medical model of "risk," 24–25. *See also* families, African American; mothers, low-income African American
Alderman, M. K., 235
Allen, Paula Gunn, 180
Allington, R., 266
alternative schools, and dropping out, 83–84
American Council on Education, 60, 92n. 2
American Indian Science and Engineering Society (AISES), 174, 176
Americans with Disabilities Act (ADA), 242
analogy, categories of, 106
Anzaldua, Gloria, 164
Apple, M. W., 85, 191

Arnold, Mary Smith: chapter by, 9, 143–62; other works cited, 2, 4, 6, 19, 20, 21, 38, 146, 147, 202
Arnow, H., 269
assessment (screening), in medical model of "risk," 22–23
assimilation, cultural, 31–32, 84, 199
"at promise" view: applied to African American families, 157; applied to non-/limited-English-proficient students, 220; in case study of child with disability, 238, 240, 245–46, 247, 251–53; in cultural compatibility theory, 188, 191; general basis for, 42, 269
"at risk" label: alternative models for, 32–36; applied to African American families, 146, 157; applied to Native Americans, 176; applied to non-/limited-English-proficient students, 212; child psychology/early education models for, 29–32; children's response to, 34–35; child welfare model for, 25–29; and class stratification, 3, 20–21, 26–28; in cultural compatibility theory, 188, 191, 205; deficit models for, 2, 3, 18, 19, 25, 27, 28–29, 268; definitions of, ix, 17–18, 54, 71n. 2, 263; vs. "disadvantaged," 71n. 2;

and dropping out of school, 88–91; family/community issues in reconstruction of, 35, 37–39; historical and contextual background of, 21–32; and individual attributes, x, 18; and institutional responsibility, x, 3, 18, 31, 32–34; insurance industry metaphor for, 20; issues addressed in present work, x, 5–6; and low income, 2–3; medical/public health model for, 2, 3, 18, 22–25; number of children included in, 18, 53–54; and political oppression, ix–x; privileged class interests in, 5–6, 19–20, 264, 268; reconstruction issues, 36–41, 269; risk factors described, 56–60; school issues in reconstruction of, 32–34, 36, 39–40; social construction summarized, 1–3, 17–18, 263–64; and writing by children, 98
Atwood, M., 114
Au, K., 211
Augustine, D. K., 227
Austin, R., 120, 125
autonomy, teaching strategies for developing, 217–18
awareness/assessment/self-management process, 230
Ayers, W., 213

B

Bakhtin, M. M., 8
Baldwin, James, 178
Balsamo, A., 169
Bankton School District, 212–22
Bardige, B., 156–57
Barthes, Roland, 175
Bauer, G., 61, 64
Becker, Howard, 180n. 2
Belle, D., 119, 126, 128
Beller, A., 59
Beloit School District, 226

Belsey, Catherine, 88, 89
Bernanos, George, 21
Bertaux, D., 175
Biedler, F. M., 4
Biemer, P. O., 167
Billingsley, Andrew, 120, 127, 135, 145, 155, 156, 157
Birch, J. W., 236
Bitsuie, Keith, 164, 179
Black Families in White America (Billingsley), 155
Blackwell, P., 25
blame. *See* deficit models; individual responsibility; institutional deficiency models; institutional responsibility; victim blaming
Bloch, Marianne N.: chapter by, 9–10, 187–209; other works cited, 31, 104, 187, 188, 190, 201, 204, 205, 206n. 2
Blumer, H., 104
Bowles, S., 85
Boyd-Franklin, N., 119, 120, 127, 135, 147
brainstorming technique, 229
Brand School, 212–22
Brazelton screening approach, 23
Bremner, R. H., 26, 31
"Bridefare" program, 35, 69
Buell, M. J., 25
Bumpass, L., 59
Burchell, G., 20
Bureau of Labor Statistics, 58
Bureau of the Census, 58, 59, 60, 63, 91n. 2
Burns, M. S., 25
Bush, George Herbert Walker, 67, 143

C

Caldwell, B. M., 31
Calkins, L., 103, 106
Cambodian students, 212–13, 220
Campbell, Bebe Moore, 36

Campbell, P. B., 167
Campbell, Pip, 256
Camus, A., 264
capitalism, 64, 71n. 4
Cardenas, B., 33
Cardenas, J. A., 33
caring ethic in education, 41
Carrington, B., 167
Carter, K., 8
Castell, R., 3, 20
Catalyst: Voices of Chicago School Reform, 34, 36
Cazden, C. B., 205
Center for Responsive Education, 92n. 3
Chapter I reading instruction, 200, 202–3, 212, 222n. 1, 266
Cheatham, H. E., 147, 156
Chicago schools, 34, 36, 86
child psychology, "risk" models from, 29–32
Children's Defense Fund, 18, 57, 58–59, 60, 67, 264, 266
children's needs, family focus on, 61–62, 64–65
children's rights, 3
childsaving, 25–26
child welfare model, 25–29
Chischilly, Tallethia, 164, 177–78
Chodorow, N., 56
Chung, S., 59
Civil Rights movement, ix
Clark, Joe, 82
Clark, R. M., 119, 132, 136, 145
class stratification: and "at risk" label, 3, 20–21, 26–28; and dropping out of school, 82, 83, 86; in Head Start, 70. *See also* underclass
Claxton, C. S., 228
Cleveland Indians baseball team, 180
Clinton, William Jefferson, administration of, 264
"Cloud Love" (poem by student), 113

cocaine addiction, in medical model of "risk," 24–25
collaborative (cooperative) learning: with non-/limited-English-proficient students, 210–11, 213–17; in Rainbow Room project, 227–28, 235
Commission on Civil Rights, 149–50
Committee for Economic Development, Research and Policy Commmittee, 67, 80
communication, teaching strategies for improving, 218–20
Community Programs in the Arts and Sciences (COMPAS) Dialogue program, 99–100
compatibilities, theory of, 33. *See also* cultural compatibility
compulsory education, minimum age of exit from, 77–78, 83
Comte, Auguste, 52
conservatism: and child welfare model of "risk," 27; political views on families, 53, 60–63, 64, 67
Cook, Donelda A.: chapter by, 8–9, 118–42; other works cited, 122, 128
Cooper, M. M., 103
Copeland, E. J., 119
Costner, Kevin, 165–66
Council of Chief State School Officers, 18, 54, 83–84, 91n. 1
Cradle, J., 188, 204
Cravens, Hamilton, 25–26
critical theory, applied to children's writing, 101–3, 104
Crull, P., 84
Cuban, L., 21, 29–30, 54
cultural compatibility: case studies of, 192–204; theory of, 33, 188–91, 204–6
culture, definition of, 189–90, 205
Cummins, J., 211

cutural deficit model, 28–29. *See also* deficit models

D

Dances with Wolves (motion picture), 165–66
Dash, Julie, 40
Dass, R., 146
Davies, D., 37
Deal, A., 241
Dean, C., 188, 204
Defert, D., 20
deficit models, 2, 3, 18, 19, 25, 27, 28–29, 268
Delgado-Gaitan, C., 33, 39
Deloria, Vine, 167–68
Denzin, Norman K., 169, 179
Department of Labor, 90
Designs for Change, 92n. 3
detail, in children's writing, 104, 108, 110
Dewey, John, 163
diagnostic approach to "risk," 24
Dialogue program, 99–100
disabilities. *See* inclusion, for children with disabilities; learning disabilities
disability screening, in medical model of "risk," 22–23
disadvantage, vs. "risk," 71n. 2
discipline in families: in African American families, 152; in Hispanic families, 192, 195
discipline in schools, and dropping out, 82–83
distribution of resources, 2, 265–66
domesticity, myth of, 56
Dorris, M. A., 166
Dorris, Michael, 165
Dorsey-Gaines, C., 39, 145
Dreikurs behavior modification schemes, 68
driver's license penalty programs, 35

dropping out of school: among African Americans, 79, 82, 90, 91n. 2; and "at risk" label, 88–91; and class stratification, 82, 83, 86; Finn/Rogers debate on, 77–78, 91–92n. 2; among Hispanics, 79, 82, 91n. 2; among Native Americans, 167; and poverty, 58, 90; public controversies on solutions, 78–84, 89; statistics on, 78–79, 91n. 2; subjugated/silenced controversies on, 84–88, 89–90; West Virginia prevention programs, 35, 78; among Whites, 82, 90, 91n. 2
drug addiction, in medical model of "risk," 24–25
drug treatment facilities, 129
DuBois, W. E. B., 17
Dukes, J., 147
Dunham, R. M., 120
Dunst, C. J., 241
Dykstra, B., 104, 106, 108, 113

E

early childhood education: in case study of child with disability, 245–47; and dropping out of school, 80; "risk" models from field of, 29–32
Early Periodic Screening, Diagnosis, and Treatment program, 22
"Early Prevention of School Failure" assessment, 23
Economic Status of Black Women, The (United States Commission on Civil Rights), 149–50
Edelman, M., 58, 60
Edelman, M. W., 38, 145
Eduardo (study subject), 193–95
education, and poverty, 265–66. *See also headings beginning with* school; parent involvement with schools

Eisenstein, Z., 85
Elbow, P., 98, 104
Elkind, D., 38
Ellsworth, E., 6
Ellsworth, Elizabeth, 169
Ellwood, D., 59, 65–66, 70
El Paso (Texas) literacy project, 100–1
employment of mothers, 60, 61, 66, 71n. 5, 126, 149
English as a second language students. *See* non-/limited-English-proficient students
Epstein, J., 86
equal opportunities, and dropping out, 85, 90
Erickson, F., 190, 191, 205
Espinosa-Dulanto, M., 187, 188, 201, 204, 206n. 2
ethics of caring, in education, 41
ethnic groups: conservative view of, 63; and dropping out of school, 82, 83, 90, 91n. 2; and empowerment through writing, 105; in institutional deficiency models for "risk," 33; liberal view of, 66; statistics on, 59–60. *See also* cultural compatibility; racism; *specific groups*
Ewald, F., 20
expulsion from school, and dropping out, 82

F

failure and success. See success and failure
families, African American: Arnold's study of, 147–59; cultural compatibility study of, 199–204; involvement with children's education, 122, 128, 129–31, 135–37, 153–54, 204; poverty and, 145, 146–47; public criticism of, 143–44, 155; and racism, 155; religious activities,

154–55; social support within, 151–52; strengths of, 146, 156. *See also* mothers, low-income African American
families, Hispanic, 192, 195
families, Native American, 176–78
family: in "at risk" label reconstruction issues, 35, 37–39; political views on, 60–67; popular depiction of breakdown of, 50–52; public policy on, 67–71
Family Development Act (New Jersey), 68
family literacy projects, 99–101
fantasy analogy, in children's writing, 106, 109–11
feminist theory, applied to children's writing, 103, 104, 105
Ferdman, B., 211
Ferguson, A., 71n. 4
Fine, Michelle: chapters by, 7–9, 76–94, 118–42; other works cited, 3, 5, 6, 8, 19, 41, 81, 82, 83, 86, 88, 91n. 1, 122, 128, 167, 168, 206
Finn, Chester, 77–78, 91–92n. 2
Folbre, N., 71n. 4
Foley, E., 84
Ford, D. Y., 3, 4
Foucault, Michel Paul, 89, 188
Francis-Okongwu, A., 126
Franklin, J. H., 144
Freire, Paolo, 101
Fu, V. R., 120, 132, 133
Funiciello, T., 11, 268

G

Garfinkel, I., 59, 65
Garlington, J., 122
Garrett, P., 3, 17, 18, 19, 30, 31, 54–55, 70, 71nn. 3 and 5
Gartner, A., 260
GEDs, and dropping out, 79–80, 87–88, 91–92n. 2, 92n. 4
gender roles, in African American families, 152

generalization, by "at risk" students, 230
Gessell Developmental Readiness Screening Assessment, 23
Gibbs, J. T., 118, 119
Gibson, M., 211
gifted and talented projects, 228–34
Gilkes, Cheryl Townsend, 131
Gilligan, C., 105
Gintis, H., 85
Giovanni, Nikki, 178
Giroux, H., 102–3
Glasser, W., 226
Goldberg, M. L., ix
Goodman, L., 126
Gordon, E. W., 31, 167
Gordon, W. J., 106
Gorman, P., 146
Governor's Task Force on Education, 27
Graue, M. E., 23
Graves, D. H., 103
Greene, B. A., 124, 132
Greene, K., 103, 105
Greene, Maxine, 6, 97, 104, 107, 109, 269
Greer, J. V., 226
Gringrich, Newt, 264
Grossberg, Larry, 170
Grotberg, E. H., 26
Grubb, N., 54, 64, 67–68, 265
Gruber, K. D., 227

H

Haas, L., 70
Hall, J., 168
Halpern, R., 120, 132
Hanson, L. R., 227
Harris, J. J., III, 3, 4
Hartmann, B., 59, 71n. 4
Hauser, Mary E.: chapter by, 10, 210–23; other works cited, 213
Head Start, 18, 22, 67, 70, 266
Heath, S. B., 188

Hewlett, Sylvia Ann, 38
High School and Beyond data set, 91n. 2
Hill, Robert, 127, 135, 145, 146, 150, 153, 157
Hispanic students: cultural compatibility study of, 192–95; and dropping out of school, 79, 82, 91n. 2
Hmong students: in collaborative first grade classroom, 213, 220, 221; cultural compatibility study of, 195–99, 213, 220, 221
Hoa (study subject), 197–99
home, as site of strength and resistance, ix, x. *See also headings beginning with* families; mothers
Home Advantage (Lareaux), 39
Honahnie, Reuben, 164, 168–69, 178–79
Hood, Jackie, 226
hooks, bell, ix, x, 21, 32
Hornberger, N., 211
Horseman, Reginald, 167
Huttman, E., 119, 123, 132

I

"I am a red fox" (poem by student), 112
IDEA (Individuals with Disabilities Act), 241–42, 258
illness, effect on low-income African-American mothers, 126–27
immigration policy, 63
immunization metaphor, 22
inclusion for children with disabilities, case study: advocacy strategies, 241–42, 248–52, 256–60; early intervention, 246–47; future planning, 247–48; philosophy, 242–44; socialization, 242, 254–55; teacher support, 242, 252–53

inclusion for children with disabilities, description of, 240–41. *See also* mainstreaming
income: and GEDs, 92n. 2; as risk factor, 2. *See also* poverty
Indiana programs for dropout prevention, 35
individual responsibility: conservative view of, 62; in construction of "at risk" label, x, 18; and criticism of African American mothers, 120; in deficit models, 2, 3, 18, 19, 25, 27, 28–29, 268; and dropping out of school, 81, 82–83, 88–89; and public policy, 67–71; victim blaming, 2, 24, 31, 32, 33, 35, 89, 168; and violence in schools, 82–83
Individuals with Disabilities Act (IDEA), 241–42, 258
institutional responsibility: in construction of "at risk" label, x, 3, 18, 31, 32–34; and criticism of African American mothers, 120; and dropping out of school, 89–90; in institutional deficiency models, 3, 18, 31, 32–34; liberal view of, 63–64; and public policy, 67–71
insurance industry metaphor, 20

J

Jacobs, L., 33
Jameson, F., 8
Jencks, C., 59, 63
Jenkins, A. H., 156, 157
Jewell, K. S., 144, 156
Johnson, C., 196
Johnson, L. B., 119
Johnson, Lyndon Baines, 180n. 1
Jones, R., 60
Jordan, C., 188

K

Kagan, S., 31, 211, 231–14
Kamerman, S., 59, 70
Kamler, B., 103, 114
Kansas welfare programs, 68
Katz, M., 89
Katz, Michael, 265
Kawakami, A., 211
Kessler, S., 99
Kessler, Shirley A., 41
Khatena, J., 105
Khmer students, 212, 220, 221
Kids Count Data Book, 57, 59
King, L. M., 119
Kingsolver, B., 264
Kirton, E., 33
Kliebard, H., 31
Knapp, M. S., 266
Kolstad, Andrew J., 79, 91n. 2
Kotlowitz, A., 5, 19
Kozol, J., 5, 6, 19–20, 31

L

Labaree, D. F., 82
Ladner, J. A., 126
Ladson-Bilings, G., 201
Lakoff, R., 105
language, valuing of home/native, 175, 177, 220
Laosa, Luis, 26–27, 28, 32, 33
Lao students, 212–13, 220, 221
Lareau, Annette, 39
Lassner, P., 103
Lather, P., 6
Latino students. *See* Hispanic students
Lazerson, M., 54, 64, 67–68, 265
"Learnfare" program, 35
Learning Denied (Taylor), 23
learning disabilities: in medical model of "risk," 23; and Rainbow Room project, 227–28, 229–30, 234, 236

Leifield, Lisa: chapter by, 10–11, 238–61; other works cited, 25
LEP students. *See* non-/limited-English-proficient students
Leverage, Gene, 173
Levin, H., 18, 54
Levi-Strauss, Claude, 8
liberal view of families, 60–61, 63–67
"Life" (poem by student), 107
"Life has been like a messy room for me" (poem by student), 107
Lightfoot, D., 19
Lilly, M. S., 242
limited-English-proficient students. *See* non-/limited-English proficient students
Lincoln, Kenneth, 170
Lincoln, Yvonna S., 169
Lindblad-Goldberg, M., 147
Lipsky, D. K., 260
Lipton, M., 98–99
literacy projects, 99–101
Local School Councils (LSCs), 34, 36
Lorde, Audre, 38, 105
Lorene (study subject), 199–202
Lubeck, Sally: chapters by, 1–14, 50–75; chapters summarized, 7, 263; other works cited, 3, 17, 18, 19, 30, 31, 54–55, 70, 71nn. 3 and 5
Lugones, Maria, 164
Lykes, Brinton, 131
Lyotard, J.-F., 52

M

Maclas, A. H., 102
Madhubuti, H. R., 144
mainstreaming: vs. inclusion, 240; and Rainbow Room project, 225, 226, 233, 234, 236
Mai (study subject), 195–97
Malcolm X, 32

Mann, D., 79
Manns, W., 135, 152
Martin, Tony, 30
Marx, Karl, 170
McAdoo, H. P., 147
McCarthy, Cameron, 6
McDermott, Ray P., 168
McDill, E., 54, 82
McIntosh, P., 2
McKenney, T. L., 168
McLanahan, S., 59, 65
Mead, L. M., 3
measurement issues, and dropping out, 79–80
medical/public health model, 2, 3, 18, 22–25
meritocracy, 2
metacognitive processes cycle, 230
metanarrative, 52, 71n. 1
metaphor, in children's writing: analysis of, 106–13; methods for study of, 104, 105, 106
Michigan, definition of "at risk" in, 54
Miles, C., 230
military service, and dropping out, 87–88
Miller, F., 167
Mills, C. W., 169
minimum age of exit from compulsory education, 77–78, 83
minorities. *See* cultural compatibility; ethnic groups; racism; *specific groups*
modernism, 52
Moll, L., 199, 206
Morado, C., 54
Moraga, Cherrie, 17
moral development, of African American youth, 156–57
Morrison, Toni, 263
Moss, B., 31
mothers: conservative opinion on, 53, 61–63; effect of public policy on, 52–53; employment of, 60,

61, 66, 71n. 5, 126, 149; history
of role of, 55–56, 71n. 4; popular
depiction of, 50–52; as source of
children's problems, 54–56. *See
also* single parenting
mothers, low-income African
American: Arnold's study of,
147–59; community environment of, 123–25, 137, 150; context of Cook and Fine's study of,
121–22; criticism of, 118–20,
144; involvement in children's
education, 122, 128, 129–31,
135–37, 153–54; parenting
strategies of, 132–37, 144–45,
150–51, 152; social support for,
151–52; strengths and successes
of, 120–21, 122, 132–37, 138,
145–46; stresses on, 125–31,
138, 145, 150
motivation, Rainbow Room project for improving, 224–36
Moyer, Bill, 145–46
Moynihan, D., 119
Murray, C., 62
Murray, Charles, 264
Murray, Tina, 10–11, 238–61
Myers, H. F., 119
Myers, L., 147
"My Hands Jump" (poem by student), 110–11
"My name is lightning" (poem by
student), 108
"My Name is Like the Wind"
(poem by student), 112

N

Narayan, U., 164
Nash, Robert, 164, 178
National Center for Children in
Poverty, 57
National Coalition of Advocates
for Students, 82
National Commission on
Children, 57
National Committee for Citizens
in Education, 123
National Committee for Public
Education, 92n. 3
National Law Center on
Homelessness and Poverty, 264
Native Americans: education of,
30, 166–67, 168, 171–74,
175–76, 177; families, 176–78;
and racism, 167–68, 178–79;
socioeconomic status, 166;
stereotypical view of, 163–64,
165–66, 179; White's study of,
164, 168–80
Natriello, G., 54, 82
Neediest Cases Fund, 265
Nelson, D., 57, 66
neocolonial metaphor, 27
neo-Marxism, 191
NEP students. *See* non-/limited-
English-proficient students
New Jersey welfare programs, 68
Newman, D. L., 149
New Right, 53, 61–63. *See also*
conservatism
New Visions Schools, 86
New York City schools, 86
New York State Department of
Education, 87
New York Times Neediest Cases
Fund, 265
Nijre, B., 241
Niles, K., 4, 19, 36, 37, 38, 42
Nobles, W. W., 119, 120, 132
Noddings, N., 8
non-/limited-English-proficient
students: autonomy develop-
ment for, 217–18; collaborative
learning with, 210–11, 213–17;
communication improvement
for, 218–20; and cultural com-
patibility issues, 192–99;
description of Brand School students, 212–13

normalization principle, 241
North Carolina Department of
　Public Instruction (NCDPI), 54
Northeastern University, 57, 58–59
Northern Arizona University,
　173–74, 176

O

Oakes, J., 98–99
Ochberg, R. L., 8
Ogbu, J., 31, 132, 191, 205
"On the day I was born" (poem by
　student), 109–10
"On the day I was born the earth
　shook and the angels wept"
　(poem by student), 108–9
Ownings, Jeffrey A., 79, 91n. 2
Ozick, C., 111–12

P

Pablo (study subject), 192–93, 195
Paley, V. G., 8
Pallas, A., 54, 71n. 5, 82
Parent Empowerment Project, The
　(Baltimore), 92n. 3
parent involvement with schools:
　by African American parents,
　122, 128, 129–31, 135–37,
　153–54, 204; and dropping out of
　school, 86–87, 92n. 3; by Hmong
　parents, 198, 199, 213; by Lao and
　Cambodian parents, 212–13; by
　Native Americans parents, 176,
　177–78; and Rainbow Room pro-
　ject, 228, 234
Passmore, D. L., 92nn. 2 and 4
pathological metaphor
　(medical/public health model), 2,
　3, 18, 22–25
Pearce, D., 59
peer pressure, mothers' strategies
　with, 132–35

Pellicano, R. R., 27
Perlmutter, L., 147
personal analogy, in children's writ-
　ing, 106, 111–13
Peters, D. F., 120, 132–33
Peters, M. F., 119
Peterson, G. W., 120, 132–33
Peterson, J. M., 233
Phinney, M. Y., 106
Pinderhughes, E., 146
Placier, M. L., 19
Playing Favorites (Sapon-Shevin),
　39
Pogrow, S., 230, 231
Polakow, Valerie: chapter by, 11,
　263–70; other works cited, 2, 3, 6,
　11, 19, 20, 27, 28, 35–36, 52–53,
　71n. 1, 99, 267
political views on families, 60–67
Popkewitz, T. S., 4, 20, 167
Portes, P. R., 120
postmodernism, 52, 191
poverty: conservative view of, 62;
　and dropping out of school, 58,
　90; of ethnic minority families,
　60; individual vs. public responsi-
　bility for, 70, 264–65; liberal view
　of, 65, 66; in medical model of
　"risk," 22; in social construction
　of "risk," 3, 28; statistics on,
　57–59, 264. *See also* income;
　mothers, low-income African
　American
Poverty Indicators, 150, 153
prescriptive approach to "risk," 24
Price, Henry, 166, 168
private-public distinction, and
　dropping out, 85–86
private responsibility. See individ-
　ual responsibility
privileged class: "at risk" label and
　interests of, 5–6, 19–20, 264, 268;
　problems of children in, 37–38
progressive view of families, 60–61,
　63–67

promotion/retention, and dropping out, 81–82
proprietary schools, and dropping out, 87–88
public health/medical model, 2, 3, 18, 22–25
Public Interest, The, 77
Public Law 99/457, 1, 23
public policy on families, 67–71
public-private distinction, and dropping out, 85–86
public responsibility. <u>See</u> institutional responsibility
Puritan ideology, 29

Q

Quayle, Daniel, 143
Quintero, Elizabeth P.: chapter by, 8, 97–117; other works cited, 102

R

Racine Unified school district, 224–25, 227–36
racism: in child psychology/early education models of "risk," 30–31; in child welfare model, 27; and dropping out of school, 82, 83, 86; effect on African American families, 155; in Head Start, 70; in medical model of "risk," 24; and Native Americans, 167–68, 178–79; in social construction of "risk," 19; teaching children about, 150, 154
Rainbow Room project, 224–25, 227–36
Reading Recovery program, 201, 202, 203
reductionism, 6
Reed, Adolph, Jr., 2, 3, 6, 22, 25, 27–28, 54, 69, 70, 144, 146
Reid, P. T., 122, 138

religion: and African American families, 154–55; and Hispanic families, 192
Research and Policy Commmittee of the Committee for Economic Development, 67, 80
Reskin, B., 59
retention, and dropping out, 81–82
Reyes, M. de la Luz, 98
Reynolds, M. C., 236
Rich, Adrienne, 71
Richardson, R. A., 147
risk. *See* "at risk" label
risk factors, description of, 56–60
Ritchie, J. S., 103
Robinson, C. R., 119, 121
Rollock, P., 167
Rose, D., 169
Rosenwald, G. C., 8
Rossi, A., 63
Rubin, D., 103, 105
Rummel, Mary Kay: chapter by, 8, 97–117; other works cited, 104, 106, 108, 113, 114
Russian students, 212, 220
Ryan, W., 85, 168

S

Sadker, D. M., 166
Sadker, M. P., 166
St. Paul (Minnesota) literacy project, 99–100
Sakiestewa, Noreen, 164, 178
Salisbury, C., 241
Sanchez, Carol Lee, 165
Sapon-Shevin, Mara, 39
Scanzoni, J., 64–65, 135
Scheper-Hughes, N., 120, 133, 137
school-community relations, and dropping out, 86–87
school discipline, and dropping out, 82–83
school issues in reconstruction of "at risk" label, 32–34, 36, 39–40

school reforms, 32–34, 39–40, 54
schools, cultural discontinuities
  with home: case studies with
  African American families,
  199–204; case studies with
  Hispanic families, 192–95; case
  studies with Hmong families,
  195–99; strategies for minimiz-
  ing, 204–5; theoretical issues,
  188, 190–91, 204
schools, parent involvement with.
  See parent involvement with
  schools
Schubert, W., 213
Schulte Elementary School (Racine,
  Wis.), 224–25, 227–36
Scott, J., 138
Scott, K. Y., 151
screening, in medical model of
  "risk," 22–23
Sears, R. R., 31
self-management, metacognitive
  process for, 230
Senese, G. B., 166
Shaklee, B. D., 4
Shephard, L., 82
Sidel, R., 60
Simmons, Richard K., 29
Singer, Andrew, 164, 178
Singer, Cheryl Yazzie, 164, 177
Singer, E., 191, 204
single parenting: conservative view
  of, 62; liberal view of, 65–66; pub-
  lic policy on, 68–69, 70; statistics
  on, 59
Slavin, R., 71n. 2
Sleeter, Christine E., ix–xi
Smith, M., 82
socialization: for children with dis-
  abilities, 242, 254–55; through
  collaborative learning, 216
sociological theory, applied to chil-
  dren's writing, 103–4
Soto, L. D., 4, 8, 19
special education students, in
  Rainbow Room project, 226–36

spirituality. *See* religion
Spodek, B., 31
Stainback, S., 240
Stainback, W., 240
Stanfield, John H., 167, 170
Staples, R., 62, 145, 146, 150
Steiner, G. Y., 26, 60–61
Stewart, J. B., 147, 156
Straus, B., 147
Strickland, Bonnie, 242, 256
Strickland, Rennard, 165
Strom, R., 135
success and failure: cultural compatibility and interpretations of,
  191–92, 193, 195, 201, 204, 205;
  students' expectations of, 225
Sugrve, T., 89
suspension from school, and dropping out, 82
Swadener, Beth Blue: chapters by,
  1–14, 17–49; chapters summarized, 7, 263; other works cited, 1,
  2, 3, 4, 6, 19, 20, 21, 36, 37, 38, 42,
  99, 146, 157, 190, 202, 205
symbolic analogy, in children's
  writing, 106–9
symbolic interactionism, 103–4

T

Tabachnick, B. Robert: chapter by,
  9–10, 187–209; other works cited,
  187, 188, 190, 201, 204, 206n. 2
Taylor, Denny, 23, 39, 40, 145, 203
teachers, peer relationships of,
  220–21, 232
teaching strategies: with children's
  writing, 98, 113–15; for collaborative learning, 210–11, 213–17,
  227–28; for minimizing
  home/school cultural discontinuities, 204–5; with non-/limited-
  English-proficient students,
  213–22; for Rainbow Room pro-

ject (integrated special education/"at risk" class), 227–34
Temple, C., 106
Tharp, R., 33, 188, 190, 205
theory of compatibilities, 33. *See also* cultural compatibility
third world metaphor, 27
Thompson, Cynthia, 10, 210–23
Tiedt, I. M., 225–26
Tiedt, P. L., 225–26
Tijerina, K. H., 167
Toby, Jackson, 77–78
Touliatos, J., 147
tracking: and dropping out of school, 81–82; and poverty, 268
Trivette, C. M., 241
Troyna, B., 167
Trueba, H., 33, 190, 205
Tuba City High School, 178
Tuchman, Barbara, 163, 166
Turnbull, A., 239, 242
Turnbull, B., 266
Turnbull, R., 239, 242
Tyack, D., 19, 34
Tyrone (study subject), 202–4

U

underclass: in child welfare model, 26–28; and dropping out of school, 89; general characterization of, 2–3, 6. *See also* class stratification
unique detail, in children's writing, 104, 108, 110
United States Bureau of Labor Statistics, 58
United States Bureau of the Census, 58, 59, 60, 63, 91n. 2
United States Commission on Civil Rights, 149–50
United States Department of Labor, 90
university education, of Native Americans, 173–74, 176, 177

University of Illinois, 180
Upward Bound programs, 164, 169–70, 173, 176, 178, 180n. 1

V

Vanishing Dreams (Children's Defense Fund and Northeastern University), 57, 58–59
Vetter, B. M., 167
victim blaming, 2, 24, 31, 32, 33, 35, 89, 168. *See also* individual responsibility
Villegas, A M., 191, 205
violence in schools: and dropping out of school, 82; mothers' response to, 123–24
Vogt, L., 188
voice, in writing by children, 98, 102–3, 104, 106, 114

W

Waldoch, Joyce S., 10, 224–37
Waller, Willard, 180n. 2
Weis, L., 6, 8, 191, 206
welfare reform, 35–36, 63, 65, 68–69, 264
West Virginia programs for dropout prevention, 35, 78
Wexler, P., 52
Whatever Happened to Childhood? (film), 50–52
Wheelock, A., 82
When the Bough Breaks (Hewlett), 38
White, Carolyne J.: chapter by, 9, 163–84; other works cited, 164
Whites: and dropping out of school, 82, 90, 91n. 2; poverty among, 66
Whitnall School District, 226
WIC (Women, Infants, and Children), 18
Wiesel, Elie, 41

Wiggins, G., 229
Will, George, 264
Williams, S., 120
Willis, P., 191
Wilson, W. J., 54, 69, 126
Winborne, Duvon G., 19, 22, 33
Wisconsin welfare programs, 35, 69
Witherell, C., 8
Wolf, D., 104
Wollons, R., 19
Women, Infants, and Children
    (WIC), 18
Wong Fillmore, L., 102
writing by children: analysis of,
    106–13; "at risk" label and, 98;
    methods for research on, 104–6;
specific programs for, 99–101;
teaching strategies with, 98,
113–15; theory for analysis of, 98,
101–4

Y

Yazzie, Kee, 164, 170–77
York, J., 242

Z

Zane, N., 83
Zaretsky, E., 55
Zigler, E., 31